MW01235456

CRITICAL EXPLORATIONS IN SCIENCE FICTION AND FANTASY
(a series edited by Donald E. Palumbo and C.W. Sullivan III)

1. *Worlds Apart? Dualism and Transgression
in Contemporary Female Dystopias* (Dunja M. Mohr, 2005)

2. *Tolkien and Shakespeare: Essays on
Shared Themes and Language* (ed. Janet Brennan Croft, 2007)

3. *Culture, Identities and Technology in the* Star Wars *Films: Essays on
the Two Trilogies* (ed. Carl Silvio and Tony M. Vinci, 2007)

4. *The Influence of* Star Trek *on Television, Film and Culture* (ed. Lincoln Geraghty, 2008)

5. *Hugo Gernsback and the Century of Science Fiction* (Gary Westfahl, 2007)

6. *One Earth, One People: The Mythopoeic Fantasy Series of Ursula K. Le Guin,
Lloyd Alexander, Madeleine L'Engle and Orson Scott Card* (Marek Oziewicz, 2008)

7. *The Evolution of Tolkien's Mythology: A Study
of the History of Middle-earth* (Elizabeth A. Whittingham, 2008)

8. *H. Beam Piper: A Biography* (John F. Carr, 2008)

9. *Dreams and Nightmares: Science and Technology in Myth and Fiction* (Mordecai Roshwald, 2008)

10. *Lilith in a New Light: Essays on the
George MacDonald Fantasy Novel* (ed. Lucas H. Harriman, 2008)

11. *Feminist Narrative and the Supernatural: The Function of
Fantastic Devices in Seven Recent Novels* (Katherine J. Weese, 2008)

12. *The Science of Fiction and the Fiction of Science: Collected Essays on SF Storytelling
and the Gnostic Imagination* (Frank McConnell, ed. Gary Westfahl, 2009)

13. *Kim Stanley Robinson Maps the Unimaginable: Critical Essays* (ed. William J. Burling, 2009)

14. *The Inter-Galactic Playground: A Critical Study
of Children's and Teens' Science Fiction* (Farah Mendlesohn, 2009)

15. *Science Fiction from Québec: A Postcolonial Study* (Amy J. Ransom, 2009)

16. *Science Fiction and the Two Cultures: Essays on Bridging the Gap Between
the Sciences and the Humanities* (ed. Gary Westfahl and George Slusser, 2009)

17. *Stephen R. Donaldson and the Modern Epic Vision: A Critical Study
of the "Chronicles of Thomas Covenant" Novels* (Christine Barkley, 2009)

18. *Ursula K. Le Guin's Journey to Post-Feminism* (Amy M. Clarke, 2010)

19. *Portals of Power: Magical Agency and Transformation in Literary Fantasy* (Lori M. Campbell, 2010)

20. *The Animal Fable in Science Fiction and Fantasy* (Bruce Shaw, 2010)

21. *Illuminating Torchwood: Essays on Narrative, Character and Sexuality
in the BBC Series* (ed. Andrew Ireland, 2010)

22. *Comics as a Nexus of Cultures: Essays on the Interplay of Media, Disciplines and
International Perspectives* (ed. Mark Berninger, Jochen Ecke and Gideon Haberkorn, 2010)

23. *The Anatomy of Utopia: Narration, Estrangement and Ambiguity in
More, Wells, Huxley and Clarke* (Károly Pintér, 2010)

Portals of Power

Magical Agency and Transformation in Literary Fantasy

LORI M. CAMPBELL

CRITICAL EXPLORATIONS IN
SCIENCE FICTION AND FANTASY, 19

Donald E. Palumbo *and* C.W. Sullivan III, *series editors*

McFarland & Company, Inc., Publishers
Jefferson, North Carolina, and London

Library of Congress Cataloguing-in-Publication Data

Campbell, Lori M.
   Portals of power : magical agency and transformation in literary
fantasy / Lori M. Campbell.
      p.   cm. — (Critical explorations in science fiction and
      fantasy ; 19)
   Includes bibliographical references and index.

   ISBN 978-0-7864-4645-2
   softcover : 50# alkaline paper

   1. Fantasy fiction, English — History and criticism. 2. Fantasy
fiction, American — History and criticism. 3. Change in literature.
4. Agent (Philosophy) in literature. 5. Magic in literature.
6. Supernatural in literature. I. Title.
PR830.F3C36   2010
823'.0876608 — dc22   2009048221

British Library cataloguing data are available

Cover illustration ©2010 Shutterstock

Manufactured in the United States of America

McFarland & Company, Inc., Publishers
  Box 611, Jefferson, North Carolina 28640
   www.mcfarlandpub.com

For Mary—
my mother and my best friend

Acknowledgments

I wish to acknowledge Sam Tindall, Dan Watkins, Anne Brannen, Fred Newberry, Albert Labriola, Wallace Watson, and all of those in the Department of English at Duquesne University who made my time there so productive and enjoyable. Many thanks to my mentors, Valerie Krips and James Matthews, for their excellent advice; and to David Bartholomae, John Twyning, and all of my colleagues in the Department of English at University of Pittsburgh for their support and their respect of fantasy as serious literature.

Very special thanks go to my family (both the human and the furry). Also, a shout-out goes to the Fantasy Studies Fellowship, the student organization I started at Pitt in 2005, whose members always make me smile and always make me think.

And thanks, Dad, wherever you are in the Undying Lands, for teaching me how to read.

Table of Contents

PART IV
Haunting History:
The Portal in Modern/Postmodern Fantasy

Preface

This work began as an independent study of literary fantasy under the direction of Sam Tindall, Victorian Studies Professor (now retired) and the chair of my Ph.D. committee at Duquesne University. Many of the authors on that reading list, such as William Morris, George MacDonald, and Oscar Wilde, have found their way into this book, along with others that I have become interested in over the past several years of teaching courses in Fantasy and Romance, Myth and Folktale, Children's Literature, and the Gothic at the University of Pittsburgh. As with literary fantasy itself, the roots of this work also stretch farther back, to my childhood reading. Then and now I have always found most intriguing those stories by authors such as Edward Eager, E. Nesbit, and Susan Cooper that took place in the real world, or that showed characters moving back and forth between that world and magical places through the use of seemingly ordinary objects. Even today, every semester, I find myself only half-joking as I confide to a new group of students my hope to one day come across a magic mirror or wardrobe. From the serious, knowing looks I always receive in return, I'm sure I am not alone in this wish, though (sadly) I know the odds are not in favor of its coming true. Magical gateways to worlds of possibility can always be found in books, though, and given the popularity of film adaptations such as *The Lord of the Rings*, *Harry Potter*, and Stephenie Meyer's *Twilight* series, it seems clear that fantasy will only continue to expand its already considerable reach and power.

For that expansion to carry on chipping away at the boundaries of the literary canon requires new and insistent voices to emerge — not to defend fantasy, for that time has hopefully come and gone — but to continue the enormous task of sorting through its layers and layers of meanings to see what it has to say. Now, as an admirer and a scholar of literary fantasy, I come to the conclusion that fascination with such things does not really spring from the hope that a magic mirror might prove real, but from the awareness of the symbolic power of that mirror, or wardrobe, or Pensieve, to speak truths. As Tom Shippey says, "We do not expect to meet Ringwraiths, but 'wraithing' is a genuine danger; we do not expect to meet dragons, but the 'dragon-sickness' is perfectly common; there is no Fangorn, but Sarumans are everywhere" (328). Besides humbly contributing yet another voice to those who, like Shippey, have ardently sought to raise up fantasy to a more deserved perch in the realms of Literature, History, Psychology, Anthropology, and Cultural Studies, *Portals of Power* seeks to carve a similar place for what is so much more than a commonplace fantasy convention.

Despite the prevalence of portals in literary fantasy, few scholars have explored their use in any depth. In the 1980s Kenneth J. Zahorski and Robert H. Boyer were among the first to categorize "transitional phenomena" to include "conventional portals," "magical and supernatural conveyors," "Platonic shadow worlds," and the "scientific or pseudoscientific" (69). While helpful, these classifications simply break down the standard convention into types that more often reference the worlds these gateways open into, rather than the portals themselves or their symbolic capacity. Ann Swinfen's *In Defence of Fantasy: A Study of the Genre in English and American Literature since 1945* tangentially deals with the portal, but also without recognizing its metaphorical significance. As I do in *Portals of Power*, Swinfen accepts the passage between worlds as a manifestation of human consciousness and shows concern for what happens after the character crosses over, but she does not discuss this experience in terms of the portal concept. Depending on the presence of a "structural link" in the story, she finds the transitioning "tends to disrupt the attention and undermine belief" (71), which is the opposite of my argument here. The issue of believability lies outside the framework of my study; I am less troubled about whether events in a text are real than if they are true, and I focus on works that approach literary fantasy from this perspective. However, I do devote attention to what I see as more important considerations: belief in its correspondences to imagination, self-knowledge, and spiritual faith. Unlike Swinfen, I find any possible tendency to "disrupt the attention" to be the very thing that makes studying the portal's operations so important. By drawing our gaze to the exact places where consciousness and un-consciousness meet, the portal spotlights the intricate human processes by which we navigate the world, our selves, and the relationship between the two.

As with most studies of the fantastic since the publication of *The Morphology of the Folktale*, my work acknowledges that of Vladmir Propp, who categorizes magical agents as "donors" that provide supernatural power to the hero for use in resolving conflict and/or achieving a goal on behalf of the greater good. The conflict typically compels a physical and psychological journey during which the hero becomes transformed in some meaningful way. Although he does not say "portal" or "porter" and his donors are not synonymous with these terms, Propp's theories inform my expanded concept of the device through his identification of the forms these agents take: animals, magical objects, or objects out of which a magical donor appears (39).

To clarify, in Propp's definition, magical donors act more like guides by giving power to a hero and in so doing implying and enhancing his worthiness to succeed. In contrast, my more expansive concept of the portal/porter holds that magical agency is not guidance but ignition, a catalyst for change to occur. In other words, the portal or porter does more than help, it creates; it opens up opportunities, many times at its own expense. Also, Propp's conception of magical agency does not take into account a movement between worlds, since the folk tale traditionally operates in a sealed space similar to the real world. Propp does, however, illustrate a bond between the supernatural and the human, as well as recognizing the transformative nature of magical agency upon the hero. Thus I am indebted to Propp for helping to establish a vocabulary by which to talk about magical agency, not for insight into the operations of the portal and its symbolic implications, which do not enter into his work.

More recent studies by Colin Manlove, Richard Mathews, Lucy Armitt, and Farah Mendlesohn coincide with my own primarily in their varied delineations of fantastic tropes and of the ways in which the genre operates as "a literature of liberation and subversion" (Mathews *Liberation* xii). Of these scholars Mendlesohn deals with the portal concept most explicitly. In *Rhetorics of Fantasy*, Mendlesohn starts from the premise that the genre "succeeds when the literary techniques employed are most appropriate to the reader expectations of that category of fantasy" (xiii). Based on this foundation she identifies the "portal-quest," "immersive," "intrusion," and "liminal" story types, each of which she characterizes according to the relationship between the fantastic and the real world (xix–xxiii). As Mendelsohn admits, these categories overlap, and while her analysis is convincing, the portal itself is not her main concern and so I find her view of the "portal-quest" as "simply a fantastic world entered through a portal" (*Rhetorics* xix) too limited to cover the symbolic possibilities of the device.

In contrast to Mendlesohn, Armitt acknowledges the slipperiness of focusing too narrowly on genre, which I agree "will never do anything to legitimize the position of fantasy as a 'literary' critical discourse" (Armitt 3). Armitt's *Theorising the Fantastic* wants to situate fantasy within the realm of literary theory; a necessary task, but one that in her view does not include the portal beyond noticing that the magical tale deals with space as a psychological construct with "transformative properties" (39). Armitt comes closer to my more expansive understanding of the portal in her survey of *Fantasy Fiction*, but like Mendlesohn tends to reduce the genre and the concept of secondary space by insisting on "dream narrative ... [as] a metaphorical model for the reading of fantasy texts in general" (42). Rather, I find with Tolkien that by explaining fantasy as a dream, the writer "cheats deliberately the primal desire at the heart of Faërie" ("On Fairy-Stories" 42). Manlove's 1999 investigation of *The Fantasy Literature of England* supports the theoretical stance of *Portals of Power* in its understanding of the genre as "fiction involving the supernatural or impossible" (3). Manlove also provides helpful context for my work in terms of the genre "as a modern literary category ... [that] took shape through a dialectic with the new literature of realism" in the eighteenth and nineteenth centuries (*Liberation* 2–3). While he devotes a section to "Secondary World Fantasy," Manlove generally avoids mention of portals in favor of focusing on implications — social, political, spiritual — of the various types of fantasy for Victorian society. These implications form a major part of my work as well, but always in direct relation to the more expansive understanding of the portal.

As the title indicates, this project is concerned with the fantastic as a way of articulating and transforming real-world power dynamics. With targets that can include "politics, economics, religion, psychology, or sexuality, [literary fantasy] seeks to liberate the feminine, the unconscious, the repressed, the past, the present, and the future" (Mathews *Liberation* xii). The fantasist carries out this process indirectly, through symbolism and imagery, and more important, through the use of worlds other than our own that mirror the same challenges and experiences. Because the writer can never completely detach from the Primary world, the Secondary cannot help but absorb the questions, relationships, and troubles of that world. Distancing the commentary from the Primary space and attacking the problems of that space through symbolism endows the writer with great freedom to speak the "truth." Through the portal or porter, the concrete or metaphorical manifestation of magical agency, the Primary and Secondary spaces meaningfully collide. *Portals of Power* maps these collisions and tries to make sense of them specifically as internal responses to external change from the nineteenth century through today.

Introduction

Unsealing the Portal

When Alice followed the rabbit into his hole and passed through the looking-glass, she demonstrated a stock convention of literary fantasy: the portal between worlds. Although his approach was innovative for the time, Lewis Carroll's use of the White Rabbit's hole and Alice's drawing-room mirror to transport her and his reader into an alternate world was, of course, not new. From ancient Egyptian and Greek mythology to medieval romance and Shakespearean drama to twentieth-century high fantasy and postmodern magical realism, the notion of accessing a space beyond the everyday has captured the imagination. A variety of factors — chiefly the massive upheaval of the Industrial Age, the rise of the social sciences, and the Occultist movement — made the idea of "elsewhere" especially intriguing in the nineteenth century, elevating fantasy above mere entertainment to become a critically recognized and aesthetically valuable (not to mention commercially popular) art form. Since then writers, readers, and critics have often felt the need to defend their chosen genre against charges that it "celebrate[s] reader gratification at the expense of being literary" (Armitt *Theorising* 1). Despite this battle against canonical marginalization, however, fantasy stands as "the dominant literary mode of the twentieth century" (Shippey vii) and has only increased its scope and popularity now in the twenty-first. So I will dispense with the "apology" Lucy Armitt says usually opens any "academic study of literary fantasy" (*Theorising* 1), and get on with more important work, which is to reposition the critical conceptualization of the portal as a powerful site of meaning for understanding the relationship between the fantasy text and the world beyond it.

Since setting is one of the most identifiable traits of fantasy, an author's particular approach to creating authentic, believable worlds takes on special importance, as does the inevitable comparison between fictional and "real" environments.[1] As a "sub-creator" the fantasist provides a "glimpsing of Other-worlds," starting what J.R.R. Tolkien calls a process of "recovery, escape, and consolation" that enables the reader to gain a fresh perspective on mundane conditions, temporarily leaving them behind as a way to deal with them ("On Fairy Stories" 75–85). These "Other-worlds" are generally accessed through the use of magical passageways or conveyances that allow exploration of the complexities of the secondary space, most often implied to be externalizations of the hero's inner workings. Farah Mendlesohn rightly assesses the importance of "both protagonist and reader gaining experience. Where the stock technique of intrusion is to keep surprising the reader, portal fantasies lead us gradually to the point where the protagonist knows his or her world enough to *change* it and to enter into that world's destiny" (*Rhetorics* xix, emphasis added). Mendlesohn's key phrase here, "change it," roughly coincides with the portal's most important function as it is defined in *Portals of Power*: to initiate a process of transformation on numerous levels — social, psychological, political, and spiritual.

A portal is conventionally understood in literary fantasy as a door or gateway between worlds. However, in a larger sense that has consistently escaped critical attention, a portal signifies a nexus point and instance of magical agency, the place where one world not only physically borders but also *engages* another. Beyond this, I will argue that in marking these "in-between" spaces, the portal connotes a myriad of power associations and imbalances, centralizing and making transparent the ways in which literary fantasy attacks real-world problems. As Mendlesohn explains, "We commonly assume that the portal is from 'our' world into the fantastic, but the portal fantasy is about entry, transition, and negotiation" (*Rhetorics* xix). Given its prevalence in literary fantasy, it is surprising that up until now those critics who recognize the portal as a convention have been content not to go much further or even as far as Mendlesohn does here to examine its implications in a genre that is *by definition symbolic.*

While upholding the established definition of the concrete variety, *Portals of Power* provides that deeper examination in an effort to open up the device to more accurately express its symbolic power. Even a cursory glance reveals that portals do not solely enable a physical move from "here to there," but operate on multiple levels and in limitless shapes that reflect the conditions of the author's time and place. To position the portal as a textual element for communicating complex and often-volatile messages, this book roughly follows fantasy's evolution as a genre and the societal changes paralleling that growth from the late nineteenth century through the present.

Specifically, this study proposes a more expansive definition of the portal to include not only the concrete doorway like Alice's mirror, but *all those living beings, places, and magical objects that act as agents for a hero(ine) to travel between worlds and/or to access higher planes of consciousness.* In providing such access — by either literally or symbolically carving out the space through which the mortal enters an "Other-world"—these entities enable and influence the protagonist's *internal* quest, which results in some form of internal *and* external change. These characters model the human journey each individual takes from birth to death (and beyond). In his famous essay "The Quest Hero," W.H. Auden defines this journey as "one of the oldest, hardiest, and most popular" in literature, noting, "human 'nature' is a nature continually in quest of itself, obliged at every moment to transcend what it was a moment before." For Auden, the Quest is such a prevalent trope due "to its validity as a symbolic description of our subjective personal experience of existence as historical" (32–3). In literary fantasy this process is wholly bound to the idea of Faërie and to the magical agents, or *porters* as I refer to them when in living form, that are crucial for bringing about a transformation of the protagonist, and by extension of his or her society. Given the widely-held Romantic and Victorian view that changing the world starts with changing the self, the quest in literary fantasy easily extends to that of the author and more importantly, to the reader.

Magical Meeting Places: Ritual, Folk Belief, and J.R.R. Tolkien

In her study of *Contemporary Women's Fiction and the Fantastic*, Lucy Armitt refers to "boundaries, borders and thresholds" as "key concepts for any reading of the fantastic, linking together concepts of nation and the otherworldly, bodies and the grotesque, housing and hauntings" (1). This notion of boundaries, especially between the living and the dead or spirit world, derives not only from the interest in the complexities of the mind that drove the emergent branches of nineteenth-century psychology, but goes much further back to every folk culture around the world. As Shelley Tsivia Rabinovitch notes, the word "pagan" comes from the Latin *paganus*, referring to a "'rustic peasant,' and has historically meant one who was not a follower" of Judaism, Christianity, and Islam (75). I mention paganism to indicate the long history of one of the portal's associations with spirituality and mysticism — as well as with belief in general.

That fantasists often methodically appropriate actual nature-centered spiritual rituals and folk beliefs confirms the genre's continued anthropological significance and capacity to say something about human experience. For many scholars, pagan ritual "is itself folkloric" in the sense that it "makes extensive use of folkloric materials to recreate the lost ethos of the past ... exhibits continuity through time and space ... and reflects a community's ethos" (Magliocco 95). From the Native American shaman to the Irish peasant wise woman, pagan ritual and its purveyors provide the core of story-telling. Their operations and their tales invariably center on magical experience, which normally involves practices of meditation and visualization; in other words, moving between "worlds" with the mind as the vehicle. If we accept Siân Reid's definition of magic as "an elaborate dramatic *metaphor for the relationship between an individual and the universe* ... [that] hovers on the boundary between the figuratively and the literally true (160, emphasis added), it stands to reason that the *agents* of this relationship must be understood as both concrete manifestations and complex symbols of its myriad operations and consequences. Applying this idea to literary fantasy, the movement between worlds approximates the mystical idea of traversing states of consciousness with the mind as the portal, and the human being as the porter or vessel for filtering cosmic energy.

As with the folktale out of which it develops, literary fantasy borrows heavily from magical philosophies and techniques to universalize expression, while purposefully addressing the concrete conditions of a given time and place. Then and now, deeply-ingrained folk rituals and beliefs fuel the fantastic as a way to transcend the earthly, to help people reconcile their place within the infinite and face their fears of what may or may not lie beyond death. Sabina Magliocco sees the "importance of ritual ... [as] its power to link individuals to the natural world and to the divine as manifest through nature." These links provide "meaning, which allows [people] to spiritually transcend the routine of their daily lives" (Magliocco 98). While Magliocco's study specifies twentieth-century Neo-paganism, the idea applies across the nineteenth century when Romantic and Victorian artists and intellectuals responded to the challenges of industrialization by exploring the workings of nature and its relation to the human mind.

It is unsurprising that the portal becomes especially popular as a mode of expression at this time, which became known as the first "golden age" of literary fantasy, since people were grappling with so much upheaval on numerous fronts. A new spirit of individualism emerging out of industrial capitalism defined the entire nineteenth century. At the same time, organized belief lost its foothold in family life, paving the way for modern secularism. The quest for meaning became insistent, reaching a pinnacle in the 1880s and '90s when "a reaction to the increasing materialism of the age arose in the widespread interest in the occult — secret knowledge that had ancient and mysterious sources — which provided 'Adepts' with confirmation that the cosmos consisted of an eternal order beyond the world of the senses" (Beckson 320). An adjunct or cousin to Occultism with respected proponents such as Thomas Carlyle, Alfred Tennyson, and Charles Dickens, literary fantasy became a powerful vehicle in the nineteenth century for confronting real-world problems and expressing "a sense of dislocation and the search for order in the midst of rapid change" (Weinstock 6). The rise of occultism also confirms "in-betweenness" as a characteristic trait of the *fin de siècle*. What literary genre could be more apt than the fantastic for articulating a search for truth and a hope for communication with Other-worlds than that which relies upon belief and the existence of magical spaces, where anything is possible?

As I mentioned above, the portal was already a longtime fixture in folk culture and in literature by the nineteenth century, yet it was not until 1938 that Tolkien coined the terms "Primary" and "Secondary world(s)" in his Andrew Lang lecture presented at St. Andrews University. These terms remain in use today to distinguish the mundane — as approximated in realist fiction — from a world "sub-created" in what Tolkien and other fantasists see as "the most potent" ("On Fairy-Stories" 69) art form for addressing the "primordial human desires" (Tolkien "On Fairy-Stories" 41). Thus the fairy-story itself equates a portal by which both the writer and reader can enter a Secondary space (Tolkien "On Fairy-Stories" 73). Rather than being an Other-world alien from the Primary, particularly in nineteenth-century fantasy, Faërie exists as a parallel place in which the "impossible" is "codified" and from which the author can "send messages ... about the boundary between the fictional and the real" (Attebery 55). As a crucial component of this code, the portal provides a unique and powerful way of navigating the correspondences and disruptions between the text and the culture in which it is produced and read.

"Wandering Between Two Worlds": Social, Psychological, and Literary In-Betweens

By the late nineteenth century, the real world had been dealing with the side effects of industrialization for decades. Writers increasingly turned to fantasy to ponder how these problems might be corrected and to imagine what the next 100 years could bring. Historians and cultural anthropologists agree that the ends and beginnings of centuries evoke mixed feelings of dread and anticipation, as our own move into the new millennium a decade ago obviously showed. At such times "[t]he collision between the old and the new" typically manifests as "an excitingly volatile and transitional period ... fraught with anxiety and with an exhilarating sense of possibility" (Ledger and Luckhurst xiii). Matthew Arnold already anticipates these sensations around the middle of the nineteenth century in "Stanzas from the Grande Chartreuse" with his famous lines, "Wandering between two worlds, one dead, / The other powerless to be born / With nowhere yet to rest my head" (85–6). Dramatizing a sense of being "in-between" two equally unreachable worlds, Arnold envisions a new society to come, one perhaps now realized as the twenty-first century. The phrase "nowhere to rest my head" poignantly conveys the confusion and displacement defining the Victorian period, particularly the later part, for many who lived through it.

By primarily focusing on a time period that not only establishes the foundation of the modern era, but which in itself marks a historical/cultural transition point, *Portals of Power* shows how fantasists symbolically employ the device to define power dynamics during moments of extreme change. Indeed the concept of the in-between applies particularly well to a genre known for celebrating the power of the imagination to create Other-worlds whose systems improve upon or run counter to those of real life. By the end of the nineteenth century, "the relationships between 'imagination' and 'action' and between 'fantasy' and 'reality' were becoming more complex ... as the religious props which had sustained traditional societies began to be knocked down and as the scale of economic enterprise was enhanced" (Briggs 173). If, as Tolkien says, fantasy provides recovery, escape, and consolation for dealing with painful Primary world conditions, then the Victorian age shows a special need for such literature (as does the twenty-first).

It is commonplace to accept an alternate realm in literary fantasy as a state of consciousness seen as a physical place that is palpable for the protagonist and for those with whom he or she interacts. As a magical agent of transformation, the portal creates a way out, or a removal from the mundane, but its *main function* is as a way in, or inward. Indeed, most fantasies that use movement between worlds construct and populate Faërie so as to externalize the protagonist's most intimate and usually unacknowledged needs. For example, as I discuss in chapter five, George MacDonald's *Phantastes* and *Lilith* design Faërie as a place where the young male protagonist faces tests that help him to understand himself. In the end he (seemingly) leaves Faërie and starts to apply this experience and knowledge in his primary world.

Armitt explains, "Fantasy fiction enables not only the self-not-self boundary, but also the boundaries between 'inner and outer' and 'past, present, and future' to be placed under scrutiny in this manner" (*Theorizing* 53). Lance Olsen puts this notion into broader terms, saying, "the fantastic reveals that which must be concealed so that one's internal and external experience may be comfortably known, so that one may get along day to day in the communal world" (290). If in literary fantasy a mirror or the back wall of a wardrobe can be a passage into an Other-world, then a being, place, or object can also allow a mortal character to venture into the ultimate undiscovered country of the self. As Olsen reminds us, though, "the psychology of the fantastic need not be limited to the individual. It exists on the cultural level as well" (290). A *fin de siècle* is certainly not the only time when such exploration is likely to occur, but people living in such times are especially conscious of their position in history and susceptible to the conditions surrounding them. In literary fantasy, "internal and external experience" meet, overlap, and interrogate each other at magical nexus points called portals.

While the traditional understanding of the portal as a simple instrument of mobility holds true, unburdening the concept from the restrictions of physical "door-ness" allows for its concrete *and* metaphorical qualities. Even in fantasy that takes place in an approximation of our world, or wholly in a Secondary world where movement between does not occur (*The Lord of the Rings,* for example), it remains useful to identify in portal terms those characters or other magical agents who influence a hero(ine)'s path toward knowledge and/or growth. Virtually without exception, regardless of the exact nature of the magical space or spaces involved, the living portal — the *porter—* brims with significance since the idea of being "used" to further or solidify another person's experience in the world always brings complications. Such portrayals encourage and even demand that the reader make connections to parallel power dynamics outside the text. This is especially true for women and children, who in literary fantasy often serve as porters or are in some way affected by portals, both of which are exemplified in the representative texts forming the focus for this book.

As most fantasists and scholars agree, magic equals power. In Neopaganist terms, as Rabinovitch explains,

> When power is viewed as coercive and internally vested in the individual, powerful individuals can use force, violence, and what Starhawk (1987) calls "power-over" to gain control. When power is viewed as external to the individual, however, a different understanding of human nature is in evidence. Because every person (and in some worldviews, every *thing*) is so imbued, there can be no threats of violence to gain power-over [78, emphasis in original].

In keeping with the folk culture connection to literary fantasy, it is important to note that social scientists and religious scholars have found that many of those professing paganism or practicing magical beliefs in modern times have experienced some form of "trauma" in childhood (Reid 148). In the twentieth and twenty-first centuries, "it is recognized ... that the techniques considered to be central in magical training are also ... valuable therapeutic tools in the context of healing from abuse" (Reid 154). Primarily, this is thought to be the case because magical training "explicitly legitimizes a group of experiences that are minimized in the wider society, and acknowledges that, although they are not justified and cannot be condoned, they nonetheless contribute to an individual's growth, to their personal strength and their magical power" (Reid 156).

Abuse and domestic dysfunction stand outside the parameters of *Portals of Power*, but Reid's research on magical experience applies here since each of the texts in my study depict magic being either performed by or provided to (via a magical helper) an entity typically lacking, or perceiving an absence of control and knowledge in real-world terms. As such, these texts — and literary fantasy in general — are valuable for understanding social marginalization, and may be therapeutic in their own right. Again, the fantastic text finds its most comfortable place in-between, by bridging the gap from lived experience to psychology, from the real to the imagined, and from the concrete to the elusive (and back again, as Bilbo Baggins might say).

In the case of Victorian/Edwardian women and children, who shared essentially the same social status, "trauma" becomes somewhat easier to recognize, but no less painful than the experiences for which some Neo-pagans may be seeking a magical balm today. Personifying the in-between-ness that defines the portal, *fin de siècle* women voiced their increasing opposition to that position. In their groundbreaking study, *The Madwoman in the Attic*, Sandra M. Gilbert and Susan Gubar place the literary Victorian woman in a state of societal limbo: "Precisely because a woman is denied the autonomy ... that the pen represents, she is not only excluded from culture ... but she also becomes herself an embodiment of just those extremes of mysterious and intransigent Otherness which culture confronts with worship or fear, love or loathing" (19). Thus the female writer "*mediates* between the male artist and the Unknown, simultaneously teaching him purity and instructing him in degradation" (Gilbert and Gubar 20, emphasis added).

In fiction such a figure most often takes the shape of a ghost, a fairy, or a witch — all marginalized and ethereal beings. These entities share the position of having one foot in the Primary (living) and one in the Secondary (dead or Faërie) space; in other words, occupying a space in-between concrete and imaginative experience (Gilbert and Gubar 20). On her travels she carries with her the suffering of the real place, which becomes dramatized and dealt with in the magical landscape. Gilbert and Gubar's concept of the Faërie woman applies to the real-world Victorian/Edwardian female, who even as an adult maintains an unbreakable connection to childhood due to her biology and her status as the property of her male relatives. By the early twentieth century, of course, women had become "competitors in the more privileged sections of the economic marketplace to an extent that had never before been apparent" (Ledger 19). At the same time, though, power for such a female — for whom writing for and about children was a somewhat socially acceptable occupation — continued to necessitate her opposition to the status quo. More importantly, her endeavors to transcend or even shatter the frame of her existence contribute to and in many ways exemplify the overall uneasiness with which the British (male) approached the dawn of a new era.

Sharing a similar yet slightly lower position to women on the social scale, children were generally idealized during the period by writers such as Carroll, Dickens, and J.M. Barrie, but had no real control over their lives. The modern concept of childhood as we know it — as a phase with distinctive traits and requirements — emerged in the late eighteenth century, along with a literary genre dedicated to representing and exploring the phases of youth. As Beverly Lyon Clark indicates, by the late nineteenth century children's reading "increasingly separated from that for adults" (52). Yet while the association remains contentious even today, when Childhood Studies stands on its own as a respected discipline and juvenile books regularly enjoy adult readership, children's literature remains at least loosely linked to literary fantasy. Perhaps this is partly because children and adolescents frequently make fantasy protagonists, with the quest for maturity being a familiar trope that also equates a lack of power. More or less starting with Bruno Bettelheim, numerous critics have argued as Nina Mikkelsen more recently does, that "[c]hildren have a *need* for fantasy ... and to ignore that need to is to lose contact with child worlds and the secrets of those worlds" (3). At the same time, Tolkien is quick to defend fantasy from being "relegated to the 'nursery'" (58), famously arguing "if fairy-story as a kind is worth reading at all it is worthy to be written for and read by adults" ("On Fairy-Stories" 67).[2]

The tug-of-war between these ideologies illustrates that, like the Victorian and Edwardian woman, literary fantasy occupied a place *in between* the adult world of realist fiction so popular at the time and the realm of imagination represented by children's literature. Indeed the notion of an in-between existence applies particularly well to a genre most significantly defined by its belief in the power of imagination to create Other-worlds whose social and political systems improve upon or run counter to those of real life. While referring to Barrie's *Peter Pan* and "the adult/child binary" as represented in real and imagined spaces, Martha Stoddard Holmes' comment also extends to fantasy: "The question of how adults and children are different is at the heart of children's literature partly because it is so often at the heart of contemporary culture in regard to relations of power and (even more) desire" (144). As has been widely observed, children do not write nor purchase their own books, but "in times of great change some of the radical ideas about what the future ought to be like will be located in books which are written for the new generation" (Dusinberre 33–4). Put another way, children have power in their status as audience as well as for their position *between* their world of make-believe and that of adult reality.

While she does not use the term "porter" and the forms and operations of the portal lie outside her concern, in *Elusive Childhood* Susan Honeyman similarly envisions the child reader as a conduit for adult experience. Looking at the idea of "dual audience" Honeyman points to "the pervasive silencing of those we call children" in their books. "Just as fantasy spaces are often accessible to child-characters through special means," she says, "the child-character *becomes the vicarious means* to accessing such spaces for adult writers, consumers, and (dual) readers" (53, emphasis added). What Honeyman describes is very much akin to my view of the way a real-world child acts as a porter through which the fantasist can use art and imagination to impact adult society. This also becomes important in the later twentieth century and today as increasing numbers of adults read and enjoy supposed "children's books," J.K. Rowling's *Harry Potter* series being the most prominent example.

While sometimes (wrongly) identified as specifically writing children's literature, the majority of the authors in this study, both from the nineteenth century and more recently, have sought an adult or dual child/adult readership, based on their interest to provoke mature attention to contemporary problems and instruct the next generation. Kath Filmer sees fantasy as a way for a writer to "confront readers with inescapable, perhaps unpalatable, truths about the human condition ... and then to posit alternatives which address the particular injustices, inequalities and oppressions with which the writer takes issue" (3). Within children's literature, Alison Lurie defines as "subversive" those stories that "mock assumptions and express an imaginative, unconventional, noncommercial view of the world in its simplest and purest form." Such books "appeal to the imaginative, questioning, rebellious child within all of us ... and act as force for change" (Lurie xi), making the text itself into a portal whereby the reader of any age (or time) can derive meaning. Although literary fantasy is a category of its own separate from children's literature, the inherent metaphorical nature of it enables it to act subversively in precisely the way Lurie describes. As a defining convention of literary fantasy, the portal is the best place to look when analyzing exactly how and to what effect an author is using it to influence change.

The Scope of Portals of Power

Obviously no study can cover every writer and text that meets the criteria, so I have gathered examples that centralize women and children, and that uniquely exemplify the portal as a symbolic magical agent with social, political, psychological, and spiritual implications. Although some do, most of these texts do not use the portal in a traditional way at all, meaning no literal gateway takes a character from the Primary to a Secondary space, but rather he or she finds, personally or in another character, object, or place, a means of transformation. For example, Frances Hodgson Burnett's *The Secret Garden* is not in the truest sense literary fantasy, but is often viewed as such for including magical or uncanny elements. More significantly, Burnett's work, which I contrast with Barrie's *Peter Pan*, centers on a girl who becomes a porter for the men around her to mature and take their "rightful" places in the real world.

As with most genres, fantasy works within a "supportive continuum," that includes related sub-categories (Mathews *Liberation* 5). Together these branches form "allied modes [which are] fed like fantasy from many ancient sources in myth and folklore" (Mathews *Liberation* 5). Toward proving the vast expansiveness and flexibility of the portal, this study covers the major subcategories of romance, fairy tale, children's fiction, the Gothic/ghost story, high and low fantasy, and science fiction. While Victorian and Edwardian writers provide a case-in-point here, to speak of literary fantasy as a tradition means acknowledging its ancient past in the form of the medieval, folkloric, and romantic sources that inform their work, both historically/culturally and in literary terms. I address these connections throughout the book. I also devote a final section to more recent writers who appropriate the past to further evolve the portal concept in modern and postmodern texts.

Not unexpectedly most of the Victorian and Edwardian writers here share at least a nodding association with socialism. Since I am particularly concerned with literary fantasy as a way of challenging established or conservative social and political conditions, William Morris, Ford Madox Ford, E. Nesbit, and Oscar Wilde are dealt with partly in terms of their sometimes-paradoxical visions of equality. The text unfolds in four parts, the first three of which focus on specific symbolic portal and generic categories, starting with "Women and Other Magical Creatures: Portals in Romance and Fairy Tale." Here I pair chapters on Morris and Ford, whose conflicted portrayals of women juxtapose medieval ideals with Victorian realities. Chapter One, "Who 'Wears the Pants' in Faërie: The Woman Question in William Morris's *The Wood Beyond the World*," attempts to unravel the contrast between the author's egalitarian philosophy, and his uneven depictions of female power in his take on the prose romance. In *Wood*, females appear as porters enabling the hero to navigate and achieve power in Faërie, which demands that both magical women give up their power and that one give up her life. Equally complex is Ford's characterization of the Princess Ismara in *The Brown Owl,* the main topic of Chapter Two, "'For I am but a girl': The Problem of Female Power in Ford Madox Ford's *The Brown Owl.*" Similar to Morris, Ford bestows then undermines female power. Creating a brave, assertive variation on the fairy-tale Princess archetype, Ford repeatedly defines her reliance on the Brown Owl (her supposedly dead father, the king in disguise) as the source of her power. In Morris' *Wood,* the Maid and Mistress exist as porters for the male hero. Ford seems to reverse these positions as the male Brown Owl becomes the porter for the princess. In both cases, though, the female's social and political autonomy remain at stake and sex is the common denominator for the way power is gained, wielded, or lost.

Part II of the book considers "Charms, Places, and Little Girls: Portals in Children's Literature." The writer most often credited with developing the passage between worlds as a fantastic convention, E. Nesbit follows Morris and Ford in her contradictory approach to gender roles. Married to a notoriously sexist founding member of the Fabian Society, Nesbit is known for her public conservatism on women's rights, while personally living in very unorthodox fashion for the time, sharing a household with her husband's mistress and raising their illegitimate child as her own. Chapter Three, "E. Nesbit and the Magic Word: Empowering Child and Woman in Real-World Fantasy," argues that in her children's fantasies, most notably *The Story of the Amulet* and *The Enchanted Castle,* Nesbit uses both traditional and metaphorical portals to filter the beliefs she may not have felt comfortable voicing more directly. Here also a brief discussion of American Edward Eager, a keen Nesbit follower, shows how in the 1950s he acknowledges her influence and uses the portal device to address the issue of racism. Although both Nesbit and Eager remain limited in their visions of equality and their portrayals verge on racist by our standards, their efforts remain intriguing and must be taken in the contexts of their respective eras. More importantly for my purposes, both use interactions between worlds to meaningfully contribute to the development of children's literature as a genre and as a portal of power for its writer and reader.

Child characters — specifically little girls — also wield the power in Burnett's *Secret Garden* and Barrie's *Peter Pan.* Chapter Four, "Lost Boys to Men: Romanticism and the Magic of the Female Imagination in J.M. Barrie's *Peter Pan* and Frances Hodgson Burnett's *The Secret Garden,*" shows that even though neither is magical per se, both Mary Lennox and Wendy Darling exhibit imagination that parallels their biological ability to "create" in their development from girl into mother. This chapter also acknowledges Neverland and the secret garden as place portals, but as manifestations of female agency. While the nursery window and the garden gate equal traditional portals to alternate worlds, they only operate because Mary and Wendy imaginatively create the secret garden and the Never-land respectively. While Morris and Ford look to the Middle Ages for inspiration in their magical tales, Burnett and Barrie stay much closer to home, grounding *The Secret Garden* and *Peter Pan* in the real world and using Romantic philosophy to explore the relationship between maturation and imagination, child and adult. Thus Mary and Wendy personify the "doors" by which the men and boys around them journey from immaturity to experience in Wordsworthian terms. Reading these classic stories this way reveals the problematic nature of gender relations at the time, while also showing how Burnett and Barrie pave the way for the more empowered girl characters that emerge later in the twentieth century.

Darker portrayals provide the focus for discussion in Part III, "Haunted Houses and the Hidden Self: Portals in the Gothic, Low Fantasy, and Science Fiction." This section starts with a look at the work in this study that has up until now, quite undeservedly, received the least amount of critical attention. Chapter Five, "Confronting Chaos at the In-Between: William Hope Hodgson's *The House on the Borderland*," offers contextual reading of the 1908 novel, arguing striking similarities to works by his more successful near-contemporaries, Alfred Tennyson and George MacDonald. This chapter places Hodgson's least obscure work into historical and literary perspective by showing how the portal operates to reveal the effects of increasing female pressure on a threatened masculine status quo. While recognizing the obvious place/object portals of the house itself, this chapter sees the main character's dead beloved as a porter through which he confronts his feelings about her loss. Also, this chapter does not limit itself to the issue of gender power relations, arguing that Hodgson engages *all* of the major concerns of his age, but especially "The Woman Question." As a result *The House on the Borderland* becomes an extremely useful example for defining the expansiveness of the portal as a symbolic device, and also for understanding the power of literary fantasy to engage contemporary as well as universal conflicts.

In addition to the darker self, Chapter Six, "The Society Insider/Outsider and the Sympathetic Supernatural in Fantastic Tales by Edith Wharton and Oscar Wilde," explores the ways in which Wilde and Wharton use magical beings, spirits, and inanimate objects to expose frightening aspects of Society life during the Decadent/Gilded age in Britain and America. Although for different reasons, Wilde and Wharton each represent an "Other" as well as a participant in their respective societies. The porters in Wharton's ghost stories as well as in Wilde's gothic tales and *The Picture of Dorian Gray* are nearly all female magical entities. Yet it is not the ghost or goblin that causes anxiety in these stories but Society itself, and the stereotypical, unimaginative woman and man who blindly accept and cultivate behavioral patterns Wilde and Wharton codify as flawed and impossible. In these terms I argue that both writers employ the special symbolic nature of the portal to define Society as a corruptor of the human soul.

Finally, as I noted above, more recent uses of the portal form the basis for Part IV, "Haunting History: The Portal in Modern/Postmodern Fantasy," which shows how the contributions of the previous authors — whom I consider to be major architects of the portal — inform present approaches to literary fantasy. Emphasizing the overwhelming tendency of modern fantasy to acknowledge and/or appropriate the past in various ways, Part IV begins with a new look at J.R.R. Tolkien's epic, *The Lord of the Rings*. Middle-earth is the epitome of the "one-world" fantasy landscape, meaning that the space exists independently and Tolkien does not show any movement from it to alternate spaces. Therefore, his use of the portal is subtle and offers convincing evidence for the diversity and symbolic power of the device in modern and high fantasy. To clarify, Tolkien's doorways most often occur as complex psychological agents in living form, such as in the case of Frodo, Gollum, and their ironclad pacts with the One Ring. Portals in the shape of magical or meaningful objects — Galadriel's Mirror, the Sword that Was Broken, and the One Ring — further illustrate Tolkien's expansion of the device to convey messages about fate, identity, and power with particular resonance in the world outside the text. Since women and children are a major concern throughout *Portals of Power*, Chapter Seven, "One World to Rule Them All: The Un-Making and Re-Making of the Symbolic Portal in J.R.R. Tolkien's *The Lord of the Rings*," also responds to the frequent criticism of Tolkien's lack of female presence by analyzing Galadriel, Arwen, and Éowyn in the context of magical agency.

Chapter Eight focuses on what is clearly the most popular and at least one of the most important examples of modern "children's" fantasy, J.K. Rowling's *Harry Potter* series. "Harry Potter and the Ultimate In-Between: J.K. Rowling's Portals of Power" argues that his quest for identity implicates that of twentieth-century Great Britain coming to terms with its heroic past. Rowling responds to challenges not dissimilar in scope and type to those the Victorians and Edwardians confronted more than a century ago. Like E. Nesbit, to whom she is sometimes compared, Rowling is a master of the concrete portal while also significantly evolving the metaphorical variety. The Patronus charm, Marauder's Map, Invisibility Cloak, Pensieve, and Tom Riddle's Diary operate as evocative magical agents linking Harry's personal journey to the history and culture of the wizarding world and of his (and Rowling's) home nation of Great Britain. As with *The Lord of the Rings*,

Rowling's series takes place in the primary world, but a much more recognizable, contemporary version of it. Unlike Tolkien, she partitions her version of enchanted Britain into regions only accessible by magic. Arguably Rowling's most interesting porter is Harry himself, as he overlaps two cultures (Muggle/Wizarding) as well as bridging past and present, good and evil. Harry's porter status also has important darker implications: reading the series as a whole reveals that he is used not only by Voldemort but also by his most trusted guide and Hogwarts Headmaster, Albus Dumbledore. Ultimately, reconciling Harry's porter status in the context of Rowling's appropriation of British cultural identity and mythology provides fresh insight into the quality of her contribution to the evolution of the portal and to modern literary fantasy.

Finally, Chapter Nine considers some of the most innovative of Rowling's contemporaries or near-contemporaries: Susan Cooper, Alan Garner, Diana Wynne Jones, Neil Gaiman, and Jonathan Stroud. Like Tolkien and Rowling each of these writers uses a one-world approach. This last section shows how these writers follow Tolkien and Rowling to stretch and reinvent the portal based on present concerns and the genre's evolution. All of these fantasists also channel the past in one way or another, so *Portals of Power* concludes by considering how and to what effect they do this. Closing the volume this way furnishes another, more proximate way to assess the link between folk culture and literary fantasy, real-world society and the text, which opens a space for further study while confirming the remarkable influence of Victorian and Edwardian writers on their successors.

The concept of a passage between worlds does not, of course, originate with the Victorians and Edwardians (nor indeed end with Rowling, Gaiman, and Stroud), but the sub-genres of literary fantasy "grew up" during that rich and intricate historical moment. Since the portal is by definition a place where two entities meet, the use of this multi-faceted literary device takes on so much added meaning when one thinks about how the book itself and the act of storytelling participate in the extra-textual world. By unsealing the portal to more accurately represent its innumerable shapes and subtleties, I also hope to offer a door between "here" and "there," between the Victorian *fin de siècle* and our own recent millennial shift. As the texts in this study illustrate, fantasy provides the freedom to dream up solutions to contemporary problems, in a place where the real and the ideal invariably meet and comfortably co-exist: in the Other-world of the printed page.

PART I

Women and
Other Magical Creatures:
Portals in Romance
and Fairy Tale

CHAPTER ONE

Who "Wears the Pants" in Faërie?
The Woman Question in William Morris' The Wood Beyond the World*

Man as a social animal tends to the acquirement of power over nature, and to the beneficent use of that power, which again implies a condition of society in which everyone is able to satisfy his needs in return for the due exercise of his capacities for the benefit of the race.

William Morris, "A Theory of Life" [151]

A true Renaissance man, William Morris (1834–1896) made contributions to art, politics, and social discourse that make him an indispensable study for anyone interested in nineteenth-century culture. Specifically, Morris focused his business and creative endeavors toward realizing a more humane, graceful approach to living than he witnessed in his society. In the process he founded the Arts and Crafts movement, significantly evolved Utopian fiction into a staple sub-genre of late Victorian fantasy, and re-imagined the medieval romance for the Industrial Age. Around the same time that he began this work, in the 1850s, Morris became friendly with Dante Gabriel Rossetti and the Pre-Raphaelite Brotherhood, a coterie of artists and intellectuals that included, at various times, William Holman Hunt, Morris, Algernon Swinburne, and Rossetti's sister Christina, whose *Goblin Market* (1862) remains an important example of Victorian fantasy. The primary goal of the Brotherhood was to restore beauty to the arts, with their notion of "beauty" being primarily drawn from their perceptions of the paintings of Raphael and the culture of the Middle Ages.

Lionel Stevenson sees the Brotherhood as having "glorified medieval honesty at the expense of Victorian hypocrisy ... artists revolting against the established school of painting but [who] believed the new principles could

---

*An earlier version of this chapter appeared as "Where Medieval Romance Meets Victorian Reality" in Loretta M. Holloway and Jennifer A. Palmgren (eds.), *Beyond Arthurian Romances and Gothic Thrillers* (New York: Palgrave Macmillan, 2005).

be applied to writing" (7, 14). As much of Morris' poetry and all of his prose romances illustrate, he avidly supported the Brotherhood's philosophy in this regard, perhaps because it overlapped to an extent with his own socialist beliefs. More problematically, Morris also seemed to espouse the conflicted Pre-Raphaelite attitude toward gender roles, which alternated between "a yearning for a fully-equal relationship of love and companionship between the sexes" and an "extreme idealization of Love itself" whereby "the woman was the 'soul' of the man, to be isolated and sheltered from the cares and realities of life" (Thompson 93). In medieval romance, the performance or possession of magic often occurs as a similar kind of tug-of-war, a symbolic expression of "the anxiety ... concerning who has power in society" (Sweeney 28). This struggle underpins much of Morris' writing, but especially the romances, where he uses medieval romantic tropes to confront contemporary problems that do not have easy answers. Still, despite the large body of work Morris left behind upon his death in October 1896, the romances have been left largely unexplored, and his true opinions on equality remain clouded by avoidance and contradiction, particularly given his troubled marriage to Jane Burden and apparent toleration for her affair with his friend, Rossetti.

In this chapter I apply the portal/porter concept to show how Morris uses the prose romance mode to work through his opinions about power, identity, and equality for and between man and woman. The tale of a merchant's son who journeys in a Faërie realm ruled by two women, *The Wood Beyond the World* (1894) is obviously medieval in its language and setting, but Walter's real world mirrors the author's Victorian society. In the novel Morris uses one conventional portal, the shard in the cliff wall through which Walter enters Faërie. More importantly, though, Morris presents two striking examples of the portal personified — the porter in the terms established in my introduction. The Maid and Mistress embody the crux of the problem in *Wood:* Morris provides extraordinary power to both, yet insists they help Walter at great personal sacrifice. Reading Walter's journey in this way, informed by examples from Morris' other prose romances and *News from Nowhere,* provides a valuable way to begin unraveling his intricate social and political vision for real men and women.

The Woman Question and William Morris

Donald Hall's 1996 study *Fixing Patriarchy* focuses on the mid–nineteenth century, but his point that the "dialogue on the 'woman question' is not reducible to a simple paradigm of feminist demands and anti-feminist rejection of demands" also applies to the whole 1800s and even into our own time. Hall also finds "men were both threatened and fascinated by women" at the time, and sees the real issue as "a fractured sense of self" in the Victorian male (3–6). Along these lines, Florence Boos remarks how some Victorian writers, including Morris' major influences, Thomas Carlyle, John Ruskin, and Dante Gabriel Rossetti, "may have noticed with tacit approval the degree to which [medieval] ... sources marginalized and romanticized the lives and social roles of women ... [since] portrayals of knighthood and chivalric paternalism tended rather obviously to ratify and encourage a patriarchal model of the ideal Victorian family" (Boos *History* 9–10). Indeed the temporal gap between the medieval and the "modern" (here as the Victorian) seems inordinately wide, but in creating a version of the medieval place and time through imagination, Morris envisioned "an organic pre-capitalist community with values and an art of its own, sharply contrasted with those of Victorian England" (Thompson 59). According to E.P. Thompson, "[I]n this reconstructed world Morris found a place, not to which he could retreat, but in which he could stand and look upon his own age with the eyes of a stranger or visitor, judging his own time by standards other than its own" (59). For Morris' time the Middle Ages were almost always an inspiration — in many cases a highly conservative one, particularly in regard to female power.

In assessing "The Problematic Self of William Morris," Frederick Kirchoff finds "a collection of parts too various to organize as a coherent idea of a coherent human being" (4). A major part of this difficulty has to do with Morris' attitudes toward male-female equality, which become both complicated and illuminated by his appropriation of medieval romance. As my epigraph shows, Morris advocates in "A Theory of Life" — and in much of his nonfiction — a world where *man* has the potential to use *his* talents for the common good. Using "man" to denote "human" was of course standard in Morris's day, although often in his essays he does refer to "ladies" as a discreet group. An ardent socialist, Morris endorses in his nonfiction an equality that, if applied to sex, suggests a progressiveness opposing the "Angel of the House" model for middle- and upper-class Victorian ladies. Nevertheless, as Boos notes in one of her insightful readings of Morris's "socialist-feminism," he resists definitive statements on equality for women beyond "his preoccupation with male sexual responsibility toward female partners" and an openness to the idea of woman as a sexual being in her own right ("Egalitarian" 187).

For any late–Victorian man, recognition of such a possibility would have been seen as progressive, suggesting that his notion of equality may have indeed extended to include both sexes. Yet, "there are depressingly few direct references to women" in Morris' nonfiction until late in his career (Boos "Egalitarian" 189). The reticence may be due to the fact that while rarely being shy about voicing opinions, Morris would have been aware that men composed the majority of his audience for his socialist papers. The Victorian age was fraught with questions and contradictions, especially in regard to gender roles, being a time when "British law required men to pay obeisance to a queen regnant while it figured women in general as subordinate to male subjects" (Houston 10). None of his published essays explicitly define woman as "inferior" (Boos "Egalitarian" 193), but to "organize" Morris's socialism into a "coherent idea" requires looking at his fiction, particularly the prose romances whose inherently symbolic nature offers the writer great freedom to express potentially volatile opinions.

Morris wrote the prose romances near the end of his life out of his interest in Icelandic legends and medieval tales. Many contemporary reviewers pinpointed this work as the core of his criticism of Victorian society, so that his characterization of the "female hero ... [made him] an enemy of his age in its patriarchal as well as its economic, aesthetic, and ethical assumptions" (Talbot *Water* ix). Some of these tales show female characters displaying courage, strength, and power that would assure them social and even political status far above that of the Victorian lady. Again, this suggests progressiveness, but Morris's fantasies also show the female as a porter using her power to help the male hero achieve *his* goals. Such portrayals complicate our understanding of the author's vision of a society in which "laws of oppression would be minimized ...[and] domination over persons would cease to exist" (Morris "Theory" 152). Not unexpectedly, Morris's fiction sometimes evokes as many or more questions than his nonfiction. Yet in the tensions caused by these questions and expressed through his signature approach to the portal, one can begin to trace the effort of Morris — and of his society — to come to terms with the myriad emotions evoked by feminist challenges to masculine dominance at the *fin de siècle*.

The Power

In *The Wood Beyond the World*, Walter and his men reach an island after his ship is blown off course by a storm. He meets the Carle, an older double for Walter who tells of his own experience in the land beyond the cliff wall (33–6). Against the Carle's advice Walter takes an opportunity to pass through the cleft in the wall. Although he interacts first with the Dwarf, who personifies Walter's lustfulness, throughout the tale, his progress occurs under the direction of the two women of the Wood, the Maid and Mistress. He meets the Maid first and her control of the situation is obvious as she tells Walter, "whereas thou speakest of delivering me, it is more like that I shall deliver thee" (70). Her power over him most vividly emerges after he has been a houseguest/prisoner at the Mistress' house for some time. Here he meets the Maid in the forest after she engages in an unwelcome tryst with the King's son, once the Mistress' partner. Giving Walter a series of orders, the Maid concludes, "When we are free, and thou knowest all that I have done, I pray thee deem me not evil and wicked ... whereas thou wottest well that I am not in like plight with other women" (125). From the beginning Morris makes the Maid appear as Walter's superior, but she admits her ability to make him bow to her will is not usual or even acceptable. Since the Maid tells Walter just previous to this scene that she can magically "change the aspect of folk so utterly that they seem other than they verily are" (124–5), the reader already accepts her as extraordinary. Fulfilling the definition of the porter, her words also characterize Faërie as a place where things are usually not what they seem and magic — here specifically that being used by the Maid — as the catalyst for transformation.

The Maid's early control over Walter is even more intriguing since she wears an iron ring around her ankle, the mark of thralldom to the Mistress. His first meeting with this ruler of the Wood happens as she sits beside her consort, the King's Son, in the Golden House. Here sex-based authority is clearly an issue when the Mistress tells Walter, "I have not bidden thee hither; but here mayst thou abide a while ... take heed that here is no King's Court" (79–80). In other words, in this *queen's* court a man should be especially careful about his conduct and aware of his place. Even though the Mistress indicates Walter is free, both he and the reader understand this to be false, for the Maid explains in their first encounter that Walter is the "latest catch" of the Mistress and implies his urge to enter the Wood is the result of her magic (71).

It is important to keep in mind that Walter's journey occurs in the first place because of a woman: he leaves home to avoid the emotional strain and responsibility of confronting his wife about her likely infidelity. He leaves his father to deal with his wife's family, who take it amiss when Walter takes his leave (Morris *Wood* 2–4). His father's death in a feud between the two families motivates Walter's turn homeward, which is interrupted by the storm and his talk with the Carle (Morris *Wood* 24–6). Thus even without once speaking in the story, Walter's wife plays a powerful role in his decision-making, and he seems incapable of finding the courage to face her. In the Wood the untrustworthy Mistress makes a more formidable double for the real-world wife, similarly instigating Walter's actions. Since the ruler of the Wood appears in the flesh and interacts with Walter on her own rather than on his terms, she signifies a real force in the story. Obvious from their first meeting, and even before this in the visions we find out later are her doing, the Mistress's control over Walter makes him appear as even less the master of his fate in the Wood than he was in his own world. Thus Morris confirms Walter's immaturity and marks the females in the story (wife, Maid, Mistress), as porters through which he eventually achieves adulthood.

In keeping with the problematic nature of Morris' approach to gender, his first and arguably least feminist prose romance, *The Story of the Glittering Plain*, published a few years before *Wood* in 1891, contrasts the later novel's portrayal of male-female power. Like *Wood*, *Glittering Plain* presents a maiden as a tool for the hero's maturation quest, but in a decidedly less progressive way. For example, while the Maid and Mistress provide authoritative, palpable presences for Walter in *Wood*, *Glittering Plain* downplays the female role. As the title that serves as her name suggests, The Hostage carries weight in the story only as far as her *absence* compels Hallblithe to leave home in search of her. The Hostage equals the "lack," or the "initial situation in a tale," that makes the hero leave home, as coined by Vladmir Propp in *Morphology of the Folktale* (35). Villainy most often instigates the quest, as it does with The Hostage's abduction in *Plain*; however, Propp says the "lack" can occur "within or without" the hero, and the "object which is lacking does not determine the tale's structure — it's the 'lack' itself that's important, not the object" (36).

Given Propp's qualifications and my expanded definition, The Hostage is not a porter in the same way the Wood women are for Walter. As we will see, the Maid is an assertive, guiding presence almost until *Wood*'s end. However, a porter differs from a magical guide in that the hero's transformation occurs through the agency of the porter while the guide merely offers occasional advice and inspiration. More different still, Hallblithe's beloved serves as more of a plot contrivance in the way that Propp describes. In contrast to the Maid and Mistress, The Hostage remains physically absent until his journey is nearly complete. *Glittering Plain* employs The Hostage almost as an object rather than a living agent: her loss opens the "doorway" of the sea, which has up until now only represented a source of mystery, and more practically, of harvesting food to Hallblithe. After his beloved's abduction by boat, the hero sets out to retrieve her, initiating a maturation quest sparked by the woman's absence rather than one continually aided by her presence the way Walter's journey appears in *Wood*. Seen in this way, The Hostage becomes a pawn rather than a magical agent, a fairy-tale damsel in distress. Such a reading supports Morris's nonfiction tendency to exclude the female from his map of social equality, but contradicts the power he provides to the Maid and Mistress later in *Wood*. Also Hallblithe conducts his journey alone with the minor aid of only a few helpers he meets along the way, all of which are male. Compared to *Wood*'s Walter, who spends most his time doing what he is told by the Maid and Mistress, Hallblithe makes mistakes and relies upon his own devices. His heroism is consequently more clearly defined and his maturation better earned in traditional medieval romantic terms.

Morris's use of dialogue in *Glittering Plain* reinforces the difference in his portrayal of gender between the earlier romance and *Wood*. Once The Hostage does appear, her very being is questioned and her character qualified. In contrast to the Maid who spends the majority of *Wood* giving Walter instructions and telling him to "refrain thee" so she can speak, The Hostage is silent until the reunion. Hallblithe's experiences up until that point prompt him to ask, "Art thou woman and my speech-friend?" After affirming this, The Hostage inquires, "Art thou verily Hallblithe?" (325–26); she does not question the hero's manhood or his relationship to her, only his identity. Here of course Morris partly bows to medieval romantic convention and it is important to consider his particular appropriation of it. The King Arthur legend abounds with powerful females, but as Sweeney acknowledges, "For a woman in the romance world there are only two tried and true avenues to power: God and men" (158). For example, Morgan LeFay destroys Arthur, but she does so through Mordred and as an outsider of the court. Similar to those in Morris's time, medieval women who challenged male authority were usually ostracized, labeled as witches living on society's fringes, or banished to the nunnery.

Morris's blending of medieval and Victorian social standards is apparent in his characterization of The Hostage. To believe she is looking upon Hallblithe, she need only be told that the name and physical being match, but to accept her, Hallblithe must first assure himself she is "woman" and "speech-friend." Her name alone does not suffice, and she does not even have a name in any real sense. Sheila Fisher addresses the use of naming in her study of *Sir Gawain and the Green Knight*, explaining, "The Lady is simply the Lady because she comes to represent essentialized womanhood ... she is so private that she needs no public token by which to identify herself" (79). The Mistress in *Wood* is also alternately called "the Lady," and while using personal names sparingly to suggest universality is standard in folktale and medieval romance, in Morris's reinventions *heroes* are usually named: Walter (*Wood*); Hallblithe (*Plain*); Ralph (*The Well at the World's End*). The major exception remains *News from Nowhere*'s Guest, whose status as a visitor from the Victorian to the medieval era is central to the plot.

In *Wood*, the Maid and Mistress carry on Morris's penchant for keeping his female characters nameless. Again unlike The Hostage, though, the *Wood* women are important characters distinct from Walter. Indeed they share a rivalry, already long established by the time Walter arrives, as the Maid explains when she tells how, for as long as she can remember, she has "been the thrall of the Lady" (173). Coming after *Glittering Plain, Wood* shows the hero's journey being directed by the female element rather than defining her as a shadowy catalyst (i.e., The Hostage) for masculine development. The chronology begs consideration about the direction in which Morris's thinking was heading at the time. I do not mean to suggest Morris purposely sets up *Glittering Plain* as an alternative or correction of the gender dynamic in *Wood.* Rather I see the difference in the portrayals indicating the fluidity of Morris's thinking on an issue he continues to explore in his quest to map a "better" society. Supporting this, Boos reminds us that in his earlier non-fiction, Morris "uses the word 'man' and its derivatives more often than any other major Victorian essayist," yet the writings composed in his later life exhibit more frequent and direct allusions to women ("Egalitarian" 189–90). Another of Morris's prose romances, *The Water of the Wondrous Isles* (1896), comes after *Wood*—near the end of Morris's life — and provides a rare example of his fiction that does name its women. In fact *Wondrous Isles* has a heroine and is saturated with female presence, as I discuss later.

One of the most obvious instances of female magical agency in *Wood* occurs early on, in a more traditional portal through which Walter enters Faërie (38). Walter questions the Old Carle about the place "where yonder slopes run together up towards that sinking in the cliff-wall" as a possible location for "a pass into the country beyond" (38). Directly aligning the gateway to the other world with the female body, here Morris foreshadows the crucial roles Maid and Mistress will play in Walter's progression through Faërie. The narrator confirms the connection later, explaining how the possibility of entering the "far land" (Faërie land?) sparks Walter's memory of the "wondrous three" (Mistress, Maid, and Dwarf) whom he had seen in "visions" prior to arriving on the island (39). As a conventional portal, the cleft in the cliff wall not only suggests the strength and formidability of the Wood women, but also hints at an underlying vulnerability that will allow the hero to achieve success at their expense. In passing through the "rough road betwixt two great stony slopes" (38) Walter both literally and figuratively penetrates female-dominated Faërie, where his presence will ultimately destroy or at least diminish the women there who serve as the catalysts for his maturation.

Morris's treatment of gendered power dynamics in *Wood* occurs most explicitly through his reversals of stereotypical positions each would hold, both in medieval romance and Victorian reality. Perhaps the best example occurs in the scene where the Maid tells Walter she hopes he will forgive her for what she might be forced to do in an effort to gain their freedom: "when the knight goeth to the war, and hath overcome his foes by the shearing of swords and guileful tricks and hath come back home to his own folk, they praise him and bless him" (125–6). In casting herself as the knight entering combat, the Maid elevates her status and lowers Walter's: she is the valiant warrior, he the submissive lover. Her aggressive, deceitful efforts, which she likens to the strategies a man would legitimately use in battle, will enable her to "save" them both. John R. Wilson sees the gender reversal as a function of Morris's choice of form and setting: "If physical courage and leadership are norms in this romantic medieval world, Walter must clearly be seen as subordinate to the Maiden" (53). The above passage from *Wood* confirms Wilson's belief in its use of the trope of the knight's quest in the name of a lady's honor, but with the Maid rather than the hero in the knight's position. On the other hand, we must keep in mind that Morris means to uphold the tenets of courtly love, which teaches "young men to desire, but not to act upon that desire ... [and thus] privileges the knight who can best submit himself to the desires of others" (Sweeney 15). Viewed this way the Maid's elevation would be read as a function of medieval custom, but given Morris's politics and Wilson's claim, the scene demands a deeper look.

Rather than emphasizing stereotypically feminine magic, the Maid reinforces her power by choosing an analogy to the masculine idea of war, one Morris repeats later in Walter's test for kingship. Yet, Morris's Victorianism complicates matters. His *News from Nowhere* (1890), a fantasy without the explicit use of magic, helps to illustrate the point, being set in a Utopian society with medieval customs and costumes. Similar to the Wood, Nowhere is populated by women free to "do what they can do best, and what they like best" (56). This picture supports Boos's belief that Morris "remained strikingly distinctive among end-of-century socialists in the ... sincerity of his insistence that no legal or social coercion should constrain a woman's choices" ("Egalitarian" 203). Despite the extent of her freedom, though, the Nowhereian female still exercises it in a milieu where a "clever woman" accepts housekeeping as "a great pleasure" and an important vocation (*News* 234). Obviously, maintaining a household continues to be a hefty responsibility as well as a noble occupation in the twenty-first century. A Victorian woman, though, would rarely have the ability that most modern women have to *choose* this occupation. Sally Ledger acknowledges *News* has some "feminist credentials" but reminds us that "[w]hilst the division of labor along class lines has been abolished, the same is not true along gender lines" (*New Woman* 51). Nowhereian society emancipates woman from her Victorian legal ties to men; but the freedom is illusory. Morris's Utopian England maintains the Victorian status quo by promoting the female's ability to choose the positions of wife and mother that had previously been prescribed to her.

In contrast to *News from Nowhere*, which approximates a futuristic version of Morris' real world, *Wood* presents a Faërie realm "*beyond* the world," where the Mistress wields the political power, and where both she and the Maid show cunning and strength. One must keep in mind, though, that the Wood is a land of "trickery and guile." The power its women exert does not extend to their counterparts in Victorian society. Further, Langton-on-Holm, where Walter's father is a "great merchant" (1), seems more like nineteenth-century capitalist Britain than the feudal Middle Ages. In Morris' later romances "historical fact ... merely colours the inventions of a freely roving imagination" as he continued to view the genre as "a powerful and valuable vehicle for serious ideas" about his own time and place (Hodgson *Romances* 158). Read this way the reversal of traditional gender roles between the Maid and Walter becomes a function of Faërie's altered logic. More significantly, the reversal defines the Wood women as porters, not only for Walter but also for Morris, as he tries to reconcile the disorder he finds around him.

Morris upholds medieval romantic convention more closely in *The Water of the Wondrous Isles* (1897), where Birdalone provides the information and the Sending Boat that enable the knights from the Castle of the Quest to seek and locate their lost loves (127–36). In fact the Questers' mission becomes an issue in the story long after Birdalone figures out how to operate the boat and conducts the first part of her own quest. Like *Wood*'s Maid and Mistress, Birdalone diverges from the damsel-in-distress role ala *Glittering Plain*'s The Hostage. In contrast even to *Wood*, which begins and ends with Walter, nearly one hundred pages pass in *Wondrous Isles* before a male character enters. Additionally, *Wood*'s Maid and Mistress both possess great magic, while Birdalone is a sorceress-in-training, learning through her interactions with her "Wood-mother" Habundia, and by spying on the witch who raised her. She relies on intellect and courage to resolve the tests of her *own* quest, while the Maid and Mistress use magic and are virtually created in aid of the male hero.

Birdalone behaves more like a hero than a heroine, leaving home on a quest and facing daunting tests along the way. Like Walter she receives the most useful help from wise women: the three sisters and (unknowingly) the witch. In keeping with folkloric and medieval romantic conventions of the damsel, Birdalone does also enjoy male support from the priest, the Champions of the Quest, Sir Thomas, and later Gerard and his sons. Unlike Walter, though, whose female helpers undermine his masculinity, Birdalone does not look weak for accepting aid. She still shows courage and ingenuity; and, for most of her adventures, operates alone, as her name emphasizes. In this way, Birdalone is more like *Glittering Plain*'s Hallblithe, who also travels by boat for much of his journey. These connections among Morris's romances suggest his attitudes toward real-world male-female power dynamics develop as a line of inquiry carried out through fiction, with each story revealing new turns in his thinking.

Invented later, Birdalone proves to be much more adventurous than *Wood*'s hero. She even seeks adventure by going into the Black Valley against her hosts' instructions. In contrast, from his entry into Faërie until he seemingly kills the lion during a hunting expedition with the Mistress, Walter remains curiously passive, not unlike the hero of a well-known authentic romance, *Sir Gawain and the Green Knight*. While his host (the Green Knight in disguise) pursues the traditionally masculine sport of hunting, Gawain spends much of his time sleeping late and playing games indoors with the women. Of course, Gawain has earned some rest; his journey provided such difficult conditions that he prayed for "shelter" more than once, and his final test could prove fatal. While perhaps less physically demanding, his most significant tests occur indoors, and as with those of Walter in *Wood*, they are administered by women. In the end, each man's ineffectuality amounts to a choice between earthly desire and upholding the honor of the knightly quest.

The difference between the two options is one of emotion over physicality; in other words, a stereotypically female trait versus a stereotypically masculine one. For Gawain this impulse takes a logical and forgivable form: he resists the advances of the Green Knight's lady, but flinches when his host wields the ax in fulfillment of their bargain (62–3). Gawain reveals his humanity and goes away bearing the mark of it on his neck, a wiser man. While similarly earthly, Walter's desire for the Mistress — which parallels the lustfulness that leads him to marry in the text's real world — makes his choice more difficult to reconcile. Gawain's choice places him in danger, as does Walter's decision to put aside his belief that the Mistress is "hateful and not love-worthy" and instead give in to his lust for her body (Morris *Wood* 81). In each example, the woman becomes a feature of the quest, another test on the hero's path toward achieving a higher self. At the same time, the woman becomes elevated in her manipulation of the hero and in the fact that it is she who devises and carries out these tests.

Revealing his identity as the Green Knight, Bertilak credits Morgan Le Fay with putting him up to the game as part of an effort to frighten Guenevere to death and to challenge "the great renown of the Round Table" (118) for its chivalry. Bertilak's wife is an accessory to Morgan's plot, and although this makes her an object to some extent, it also empowers her. Like Morgan, she retains the knowledge of and control over the exercise while in keeping with the very definition of the quest he must conquer the challenge himself. Bertilak and Gawain are tools in the testing, yet in both *Gawain* and *Wood*, female power remains problematic. As Fisher points out, Morgan is not even mentioned until after the hero fulfills his promise to the Green Knight. For Fisher, the poem ultimately transforms the Lady and Morgan "from the generators of exchange into tokens that men can use in their own literary and political exchanges" (72). In this way, focusing on "Morgan's agency ... alerts us not only to the nature and function of the power assigned to female characters, but also to the process by which that power is denied so that women can be converted into the tokens of men" (Fisher 72). Similarly, in *Wood*, by the end of the story both Maid and Mistress relinquish power so Walter can become a king in Faerie.

One especially key difference between Gawain and Walter also illustrates the female porter at work in *Wood*. As with *Glittering Plain*'s Hallblithe, Gawain acts with only minor, shadowy aid while Walter has substantial help from the Maid, and to some extent, the Mistress. In fact, Walter almost never acts out of his own motivation after the time when he ignores the Carle and passes through the cliff wall. Morris repeatedly highlights Walter's subordinate status to the women; for example, by letting the reader into the hero's thoughts after he receives orders from the Maid regarding escape and walks away "thinking ... at the present moment there was nought for it but to refrain him from doing, and to let others do; yet deemed he that it was little manly to be as the pawn upon the board pushed about by the will of others" (142). Here Walter not only admits his "pawn" status but also sees that, while his behavior may be "unmanly," he feels he has no choice in the matter.

Once again, compared to *Wondrous Isles'* Birdalone, or even to *Glittering Plain*'s Hallblithe, who shows courage in rejecting the Land to pursue his stolen love, Walter presents a decidedly un-heroic figure. His inaction may be read as a function of his recognition, whether conscious or no, that the time has not yet arrived for him to assert himself, but this does not match the narrator's description of Walter's thoughts above. Being "pushed about by the will of others" suggests the place of a child, and in nineteenth-century terms, a woman in society. In expressing a sense of being "unmanly" in letting "others do" for him, Walter shows the immaturity that initiates his quest. Going back to Gawain, who also privately acknowledges himself as a pawn to the Green Knight's Lady, one can see Walter is much less in control of his decision-making, at least in his journey's early stages. While Gawain plays along with the gifting game into which he enters at the Knight's insistence, he does so without sacrificing his knightly courtesy and virtue, right up until the end when his life hangs in the balance. In this way he displays masculine courage in medieval romantic terms, whereas Walter, as a knight facsimile born out of Morris's Victorian imagination, only *approximates* such a persona as the prize in a game between the Maid and Mistress. Thus Walter personifies the Victorian man's confusion at a time when women are increasingly vocal about gaining equality, again in keeping with Hall's notion of the "fractured sense of self."

Also, while the Green Knight's Lady questions Gawain's reputation and courtesy, she does not challenge his manhood as the Mistress does with Walter. The best example of this occurs during the lion episodes, starting with the hunting trip upon which Walter goes as the Mistress' Squire. Once in the forest, she becomes the hunter, recalling the reversal when the Maid casts herself as a knight. Here again, Morris makes Walter the passive damsel; but the outcome of this scene is more important for characterizing the hero's display of stereotypically feminine weakness. After Walter bolts to the rescue and kills the lion, the Mistress reminds him to choose his reward, causing "his heart [to be] clouded with manlike desire of her" while thinking he should rightly request the Maid's freedom rather than a sexual encounter with the Mistress (116–17). Noticing his discomfort, the Mistress accuses Walter of being afraid (117), suggesting an "unmanly" weakness that echoes his own earlier thought and contradicts the "manlike desire" her presence inspires. Indeed Morris's use here of "man*like*" (my emphasis), while a replication of medieval speech, also suggests Walter is more like a man than he is masculine, which the Mistress confirms in accusing him of fearfulness. She says, "It is growing in my mind that thou deemest the gift of me unworthy! Thou, an alien, an outcast; one endowed with the little wisdom of the World without the Wood!" (129). Her comment expresses Walter's subjectivity as a stranger in a strange land ruled by women. Also, the Mistress' charge that Walter is "endowed with the *little* wisdom of the World without the Wood" (my emphasis), carries dual meaning: not only that the real world is substandard to Faërie, but also that Walter is ignorant about life in any realm.

The tension between Walter's subjectivity and his female helpers' dominance easily reads as a statement on the disparity between the *Wood* women and those of Morris's day. Rather than being an "angel" in someone else's "house," the Mistress runs her own establishment. She represents the kind of life the suffragette aspired to in displaying an implicitly masculine stance to forward her cause. With the New Woman being "a challenge to the apparently homogenous culture of Victorianism which could not find a consistent language by which she could be categorized and dealt with," she became increasingly "dangerous, a threat to the status quo" (Ledger *New Woman* 11). Such a figure abounds in fantasy, particularly in the gothic fiction of the time, usually taking "monster" shape: for example the character of Lucy in

Bram Stoker's *Dracula*. That construction of late nineteenth-century journalism, the New Woman was "concerned to reject many of the conventions of femininity and to live and work on free and equal terms with the opposite sex" (Bland 144). Morris composed the prose romances at a time when the New Woman was especially prominent, and given his social and political interests, *Wood's* Mistress clearly reads as her magical counterpart.

The Mistress politically and personally dominates her male subjects, the King's son, the Dwarf, and most importantly, Walter. Here it is important to recognize, too, that a Queen ruled Great Britain when Morris was writing, especially since the animal Walter supposedly slays in the forest is a lion, an icon of the Empire. Still Victoria's husband played a key role in her governance and, having a large family, she was looked upon as a mother to the Nation. Victoria (and Albert) personified the confusion of the age in regard to male-female power, as Gail Turley Houston details in *Royalties: The Queen and Victorian Writers*. Morris creates the Mistress in *Wood* as a different sort of queen; *through* the Mistress and her relationship with Walter, he dramatizes the issue of female power itself, exaggerating the contradictions and fears he witnesses in the politics of his own world.

As porters for Walter's maturation quest, the Maid and Mistress resist the pawn status presented by The Hostage in *Glittering Plain*. It is the Wood women's *presence* that makes them powerful agents for moving the hero forward. Interestingly, through its absence the lion also marks an important symbol for measuring the extent of Walter's subjectivity in the climax of the hunting episodes. He follows the Mistress's order and, venturing to the spot where the lion's body should have lain, finds the beast has disappeared (*Wood* 138–9). The lion's body is crucial, representing Walter's only definitive act since entering the Wood. Without this evidence, the beast's slaying never occurred and Walter has yet to exhibit any noteworthy strength, either in character or physicality. Since the Maid indicates the conjuring of "the lion that never was" (183) is part of the Mistress's plan to instigate a sexual liaison, Walter's only act of bravery leaves him looking weak and foolish. Confirming this, Walter appears "all abashed" and says, "Forsooth I deemed I had done manly; but now forsooth I shot nought, and nought there was before the sword of my father's son" (140). Walter's identification of himself as his "father's son" further links him to his patriarchal world beyond the Wood and into Morris's Britain.

The Problem

Given the dominance of the Maid and Mistress in *Wood*, one can accept that Morris's socialism does allow for some equality of the sexes. Only by raising the *Wood* women so far above Walter can the author fully express the divergence between Faërie and his own reality. Further, the contrasts with *Glittering Plain* published before and *Wondrous Isles* coming after *Wood* show marked shifts in the author's thinking toward more equitable gender roles. If this is the case, however, why does Morris go to such lengths to tear down what he so carefully constructs in *Wood* by ensuring Walter's maturation comes at the expense of both Maid and Mistress? Given the literal definition of a porter as one who carries someone else's baggage, we can see how the Wood women begin to metaphorically absorb the consequences of Walter's weakness. In turn, he grows strong.

The shift first occurs when the Maid tricks the Mistress into suspecting a tryst between Walter and the Maid. Explaining how she used magic to make the King's Son look like Walter, the Maid tells him, "I cast over him thy shape, so that none might have known, but that thou wert lying by my side" (184). In describing her literal conjuring of Walter's facsimile, the Maid implies a metaphorical transformation. Instead of the ineffectual youth afraid of the *Wood*'s powerful ruler, with the help of the Maid, Walter becomes the man capable of inspiring such passionate jealousy that the Mistress is moved to slay his image and then herself (184–6). Although Walter's figure in this scene is an illusion, the effect equates a divine act of Creation whereby the hero's chief female helper literally shapes him into a man.

Despite this great step forward, however, Walter only makes a degree of progress toward maturity that will be realized later when he becomes king of Stark-wall. Morris's juxtapositions of the Maid's power against Walter's submission furnish the means by which to gauge his growth. For example, when the couple stops in Bear-Country, a region of Faërie outside the Wood, the Maid confirms her Creator role by replacing the Mistress, the Children of the Bear's former leader. Offering a message of "resurrection and renewal" (Mathews *Worlds* 46), she says, "The old body is dead, and I am the new body of your God" (Morris *Wood* 212). More significantly, the Maid casts Walter in her shadow, telling him to "abide a while" so as not to undermine her status as "God" by appearing "over lover-like" (206). Her parting words to the Bear-folk also connote Walter's inferiority: "leave me to go my ways; and my man [Walter] with the iron sword shall follow me" (218–19).

Walter's response to all of this suggests a Victorian male reaction to threatening female power. For the first time in the story, Walter shows doubt about the Maid's intentions: "Is it so, that she will ... live without me?" (205). With her help, he overcomes this insecurity, but that he indulges it at all dramatizes what Leonore Davidoff calls "the danger lurking below the surface" in the Victorian household (30). Also, Morris underscores the Maid's superiority in the above scene by having Walter walk behind her. The iron sword echoes the iron ankle ring the Maid once wore to mark her thralldom to the Mistress. Davidoff's study of "Servant and Wife in Victorian and Edwardian England" describes the "disruptive forces" acting upon the nineteenth-century master-servant relationship and thereby making the husband vulnerable (30). Just as seeing the Maid, formerly a thrall, as a "god" causes Walter to doubt her love for him, the Victorian man of the household felt the pressure of the New Woman's influence just outside his door. In both instances the female appears as a subversive force, though in the latter case, an often-unknowing one. In the Wood, however, the Maid controls Walter almost until the end. This overturns Mathews's argument that "the main thrust [of the tale] is toward liberation of the repressed feminine principle" (*Worlds* 106), which overlooks the fact that the Maid's independence comes about through her own agency. She conjures Walter's likeness, which leads to the destruction of her oppressor, the Mistress. From that point onward, Walter's status elevates, but does not reach that of the Maid until hers begins to diminish. So, while Walter does eventually exhibit a heroic self, at no time do the Maid and Walter share equal footing. The Maid moves from thralldom to the Mistress, then to freedom, and finally to another kind of oppression in the end.

Coinciding with the initial stages of Walter's transformation, the Mistress' death further illustrates a problem in Morris's treatment of *Wood*'s female characters. The narrator explains how after slaying the fake Walter the Mistress "caught up the knife from the bed and thrust it into her breast, and fell down a dead heap over the bed and on to the man whom she had slain" (186). Immediately following the Mistress's death, of which he remains unaware at this point, Walter leaves with the Maid, signifying a first step toward maturity: he chooses her pure love over the Mistress's guileful beauty. Walter begins a new journey with the Maid just after the lady in charge of the Wood kills herself. The proximity of these two events connects the Mistress' destruction/loss of power with Walter's newly gained freedom. He can only leave the Golden House after its owner relinquishes her power; before this Walter is compelled to "refrain him from doing, and to let others do" (142). Since this relinquishing happens via the Maid's magic, Walter's maturation is thus far incomplete, especially given that he leaves the Golden House being "led" by the Maid (155). Her porter role accomplished, the Mistress is no longer needed and Walter completes the rest of his journey toward adulthood under the supervision of her seemingly gentler counterpart.

Immediately following the couple's flight, Walter effects "his first independent action" by killing the Dwarf (Hodgson 178). As the first male Walter encounters in the Wood, the Dwarf reappears at various points, at which times Morris emphasizes his hideous aspect. While possessing some magic and serving as "rulers of metal and mines," in folkloric terms dwarfs are traditionally "threatening ... primitively sexual" creatures (Silver *Strange* 120, 128). The Dwarf slaying symbolizes Walter's growth in the clearest possible way. Coming on the heels of the Mistress's destruction, the killing shows bravery, a trait Walter keeps hidden throughout most of his stay in the Wood. Once again, though, the Dwarf-slaying remains bound by Walter's relationship with the Maid since it is in her defense that he acts and at her command that he beheads the creature (*Wood* 158–64). Earlier, Morris contested Walter's slaying of the lion, so his killing of the Dwarf corrects the hero's previous failure.

Whereas the lion's carcass disappears, making Walter "unmanly," the Dwarf remains, allowing Walter to smite off "the hideous head ... with his own weapon" and bury the body (*Wood* 165). Because the Maid is also referred to as the "Enemy" by both the Mistress and the Dwarf, her identification with the creature supports Walter's maturation as being bound by female agency. Walter repeatedly feels revulsion at seeing the Dwarf, but it never actually harms him; in fact the Dwarf provides Walter with bread when they first meet in the Wood (55–6). With its undeniable connection to the Mistress, the conjured lion appears only once, while the presumably real Dwarf crosses Walter's path numerous times. Yet he makes no move against it until after fleeing with the Maid upon the Mistress's death. Walter's aggressive action against the Dwarf suggests his emerging masculinity is possible only due to the annihilation of the Mistress, the most powerful female of the Wood.

Although in Christian terms the Mistress's action might represent a supernatural being's sacrifice for humankind as represented by Walter, this logic does not bear scrutiny because the Mistress only kills herself as a result of the Maid's spell, not due to any noble desire to aid the hero. Indeed the Mistress spends the majority of her time trying to trick Walter and her treatment of the Maid hardly suggests a virtuous nature. By the same token, the Maid's deception in transforming the King's Son is meant to aid *her own* escape from thralldom to the Mistress as much as it is to benefit Walter. Anne Mellor's assessment of the male Romantic poets, whom Morris and other Victorians follow in the use of medieval modes, extends to help unravel Morris's tricky approach to gender in the prose romances, especially in *Wood*. Mellor explains,

> Since the object of romantic or erotic love is not recognition and appreciation of the beloved woman as an independent other but rather assimilation of female into male (or annihilation of any Other that threatens masculine selfhood), the woman must finally be enslaved or destroyed, must disappear or die [26].

Viewed this way, Walter's inability to absolutely possess the Mistress becomes the true deciding factor in his choice of the Maid. The Wood ruler's death occurring in conjunction with Walter and the Maid's escape also fits with Mellor's estimation of the male romantic portrayal of the feminine.

Such an idea opposes the common critical assumption that Walter's path through the Wood is purely a function of his need to learn how to reject the kind of love that ensnared him in the real world, as Amanda Hodgson asserts: "[Walter] knows that he is deceived and tormented by [the Mistress].... Yet he is not proof against her voluptuous beauty, any more than he was against his wife" (179). This view remains valid, yet I see this as a symptom of a larger issue. Admittedly, Walter's journey starts as a response to "the negative feminine instinct of pure desire without the virtues of faithfulness love, or idealism" represented by the Mistress, and before his entrance into the Wood, by his wife's supposed infidelity (Mathews *Worlds* 44). So one might say the Mistress dies in place of the wife, accepting the feelings of loss and betrayal Walter could not express or deal with in his own world. While Walter actually chooses to follow the Maid, in keeping with Mellor's comments, I would argue this is not only because her love is pure, but because she may seem to be more *controllable*. After all, when Walter meets the Maid she is already a thrall to the Mistress. Regardless of her saying she can do magic, the iron ankle bracelet acts as a constant reminder to Walter that the Maid is at least superficially the less powerful of the *Wood* women.

Coinciding with folk and chivalric tradition, emotional maturity is often the primary component of a hero's quest. Walter's words to his father expressing his desire to "see other lands" from which he will return "a new man" confirm the hero's domestic situation as a symptom rather than an embodiment of the broader issue of immaturity (Morris *Wood* 3–4). Given Walter's status as the victim of supposed infidelity in his real world, his interest in choosing a new partner in keeping with the standard of Victorian femininity is unsurprising. Walter's choice, however, complicates the story's earlier tendency to oppose the status quo in Morris's own society. Turning again to Mellor, we can understand this in relation to *Wood*'s portrayal of evil and the feminine. The Romantic poet appropriated "whatever of the feminine he deemed valuable then consigned the rest either to silence or to the category of evil. The female ... always an inevitable Other, becomes whatever the male poet does not wish to be" (Mellor 27). The Mistress approximates this "Other," not only in her status as ruler of an *Other*-world, but because even though she tricks Walter and treats him roughly, she does not enact any truly harmful acts. That she makes the Maid wear an iron ring of thralldom *is* villainous and disturbing — representing one woman enslaving rather than helping another — but in medieval terms, not unexpected. Again, appearances in Faërie are often deceiving.

The reader's understanding of the Mistress as evil comes solely from the Maid. I am not suggesting the Mistress is good and the Maid evil; only that these labels must be qualified as a function of the women's status as porters for Walter. They act to enable him to understand himself and his place in the world, even if, as in the Mistress' case, they do so unwittingly. As Bruno Bettleheim asserts, by contrasting "evil" and "good" in concrete terms, folk and fairy tales help a child's developing mind to understand immorality and its consequences (9). Similarly, the immature Walter who first enters the Wood sees two versions of femininity and chooses the more acceptable, showing the extent to which he has grown since leaving home. He learns about the Mistress from the Maid, but also interacts with her and therefore has the ability to form his own opinion, a key aspect of his maturation process. In keeping with Mellor's view, Walter, in the place of the male hero/Romantic poet, assigns the "evil" identity to the threatening, authoritative female. Because Walter's maturation wholly depends upon his interactions with both Maid and Mistress and climaxes with his decision to go with one instead of the other, his perspective defines the reader's view of each woman's character.

As Walter moves on toward maturity, the Maid appears more and more like the Victorian Angel of the House. She conveys this in her speech to Walter just after she regenerates the flowers she wears to convince the Bear people she is their new queen: "[D]id I not tell thee that I am wise in hidden lore? But in my wisdom shall be no longer any scathe to any man ... this my wisdom, as I told thee erst, shall end on the day whereon I am made all happy. And it is thou that shall wield it all, my *Master*" (195, emphasis added). In other words, the Maid will relinquish her magical powers on her wedding day, when he will "wield it all" as "master" of the household. This is just what occurs, as the narrator describes: "All wizardry left her since the day of her wedding; yet of wit and wisdom she had enough left, and to spare; for she needed no going about, and no guile, anymore than hard commands to have her will done" (257). Now that the Maid has her man, she no longer needs the "wizardry" or guile she used to vanquish her competition (the Mistress), or to help her husband to the crown and herself to a place beside him. She only requires "wit and wisdom" enough to manage the domestic space. Here Morris challenges his own earlier portrayal of nontraditional female power by forcing the Maid to give up her magic and making such appear as the natural order of things, casting her as the "servant," to use Davidoff's term.

The explanation for such an ending again involves the intrusion of the real world on Faërie. By passing through the cleft in the wall Walter infuses the other realm with his patriarchal values so that the only way for him to achieve maturity is through the subordination or destruction of his female helpers. Davidoff notes that in "a capitalist society at the high tide of liberal economic doctrine, there was no place for those whose social identity was defined primarily in terms of personal relationships, neither servants nor wives.... In theory they did not exist or at most were residual categories" (34). In *Wood* the Mistress rules Faërie until her demise, and the Maid has power via her magic and influence over Walter. He can only become a man, an accomplishment Morris expresses in true folkloric and medieval romantic tradition through kingship, by *dethroning* the women who place him there. Since *Wood* marks "the first time a hero does not return to his tribe or people at the end of a Morris novel," Richard Mathews argues that Morris means to say that Walter, with the Maid as his guide, will "establish a new order within a larger human family where the insights of the hero and heroine can be promulgated" (*Worlds* 44–5). This is reasonable given that Walter and the Maid make their kingdom in Faërie instead of in the world beyond the wood, but Mathews sees the couple's relationship as much more equal than the text allows.

Morris further upholds the status quo by seeing to it that Walter's final test to gain maturity is administered by men. Finally arriving in Stark-wall, Walter and his love are separated. He is bathed and asked to choose between "robes of peace ... [or] war-weed." When his choice makes him "the King of battle" (239–40), the Maid kneels before him, saying, "I will beseech thee not to cast me out utterly but suffer me to be thy servant and handmaid for a while" (246). As the Maid makes clear, Walter's kingship completes his maturation journey by reversing his relationship with her. When he achieves kingship, the Maid's power is so completely extinguished that she asks if he might take pity on her by keeping her on as a "servant." Intensifying the role reversal, Morris's narrator describes how, in response to her humble speech, Walter "stoop[s] down ... and raise[s] her up," introducing her to the people as his "beloved and spouse" before saying she is also "Queen and Lady" (246). Essentially the Maid trades in her iron ring of thralldom to the Mistress for a golden wedding band. Marriage obviously need not imply loss of identity or agency for a female, but for the nineteenth-century New Woman, and for those who would oppose her, the institution contains within it certain assumptions about power. In *Wood*, the new king does not forsake the woman who precipitates his success, but the words Morris puts into Walter's mouth do show that her previous sway over him is ended so she can become "beloved and spouse." Only as a consequence of being such to a king does she merit the secondary titles of "Queen and Lady."

In folktale and medieval romance, a marriage results from the tests the hero (or heroine in rare cases) overcomes, signifying success and maturity. Such a resolution also typically ended the Victorian novel, which Morris "professed to despise" for being "too focused on the character's psychological problems" (Hodgson 179). With the marriage ending of *Wood,* Morris conveys his "handling of the externalizing power of romance, using the events of the story to reveal psychological truths ... at the service of an assertion of the need for, and possibility of, integration ... [of] man's own warring propensities and desires (Hodgson *Romances* 179). This integration can occur in the concrete form of a social contract (marriage) or symbolically as a fusion of the masculine and feminine components of a self. Before his entry into the Wood, Walter exists as an undeveloped masculine self, interested in proving himself by seeking adventure and viewing woman as an object of desire, not as a human being. Through his interactions with both Maid and Mistress, Walter reconciles his earthly passion and accesses a deeper side. It is the development of this ability that enables him to find balance and achieve the true maturity that will make him a good king and man.

This balance is the key to understanding Morris' vision of gender politics. By accepting the ultimate power position in the end, Walter embodies real-world patriarchy. At the same time, however, taking Walter's kingship as an uncomplicated endorsement of such a system does not fit with what we know of Morris from his essays and especially from his fiction. Walter's journey is fraught with problems, possibly as a warning to Victorian society that conforming to rigid behavioral codes based on sex often demands great sacrifice. The frustration and loss is particularly intense for the women who, like the Maid, must feign inferiority to survive. Others, like the Mistress, are viewed as "masculine" and destroyed in one way or another by the pressure to conform. Significantly Walter achieves kingship and lives out his days with the Maid *in Faërie,* not in his own world. Morris implies that despite being king, the hero remains immature — or more accurately — unevolved. Walter's kingship leaves one powerful woman dead and another at his mercy. Through the destruction of the female porters through which Walter gains power, the story argues that a system founded on a lack of equality for all, regardless of sex, offers no hope for any real social or political progress. *The Wood Beyond the World* provides keen insight, both into the subtleties of Morris's egalitarian vision and into the ways in which he colors his medievalism with an understanding of Victorian male-female power dynamics.

CHAPTER TWO

"For I am but a girl":
The Problem of Female Power in
Ford Madox Ford's *The Brown Owl*[1]

*"And is it not grand to think of the power thou hast, my daughter? If
thou but raise thy little finger armies will move from world's end to
world's end.... Think of the power, the grand power of swaying the
world,"* ... *But long before he had got thus far, the Princess was weeping
bitterly...*

—King Intafernes [Ford *Owl* 263]

Despite an almost forty-year age difference, William Morris and Ford
Madox Ford (1873–1939) had much in common. Most notably, Ford shared
Morris's affiliation with the Pre-Raphaelite Brotherhood, being the grand-
son of painter Ford Madox Brown and nephew of William Rossetti. Led by
Brown's pupil Dante Gabriel Rossetti, this "self-consciously archaic group
of artists, poets, and critics" are widely credited with making "the greatest
contribution to Victorian fairy literature" (Hearn xxiii). While Ford is best
known as one of the architects of English Modernism, his earliest literary
endeavors were more in keeping with the Pre-Raphaelite reverence for the
past and for the fantastic. Ford actually started his career at age eighteen with
the publication of *The Brown Owl* (1891), one of three fairy tales he would
produce before his twenty-first birthday. *The Brown Owl* was originally illustrated by his grandfather and sold more copies in Ford's lifetime than any
of his other works, despite being generally overlooked by critics then and
now (Hearn xxiv).

Like Morris's prose romances, Ford's fairy tales help to illuminate his
complicated views on gender dynamics. While this chapter will mainly focus
on Ford's writing, it is worthwhile to briefly touch upon his biography. Ford
apparently "admired independent outspoken women" and following the
demise of his marriage to Elsie Martindale in 1908, he "formed serious attach-
ments" to at least three who were self-supporting, including novelist Violet
Hunt and artists Stella Bowen and Janice Biala (Lurie 132–3). Still, Ford

never actually divorced Elsie and is also known for being fairly prolific in his love affairs, suggesting a less than reverent attitude toward the opposite sex. Ann Barr Snitow sees the ironies in Ford's fiction as "a bottomless succession of unresolved attitudes towards the experiences he describes" and a function of a narrative voice that is "almost always double ambivalent, self-questioning" (2). Robin Peel points out how in *Women and Men* (1923) Ford implies that "the way that men in a patriarchal society learn to construct the difference between [the sexes] is through reading literature" (67). As illustrated in the previous chapter on Morris, the writing of literature can produce this same effect for the author. Most often the questions emerging in and from Ford's work revolve around the same societal upheaval that also plagued Morris, whose sense of "living under a system that makes conscious effort towards reconstruction almost impossible" (Morris "How We Live" 566) did not stop him from considering how such an effort might be made. In *The Brown Owl* (1891), Ford uses one of the Pre-Raphaelites' most favored forms, the fairy tale, to take a first step in addressing *fin de siècle* gender dynamics.

Echoing his life experience, Ford's approach is decidedly uneven — even contradictory, at a time when the term "feminist," which "first came into being just at the point when a mid–Victorian consensus was breaking down," created an increasing "diversity of views, not only about feminist strategies and goals, but also about the nature of women and about what their emancipation meant" (Caine 144). Ford may have had what Timothy Weiss calls "a fascination with the feminine principle" (27) that plays out to an extent in *The Brown Owl*, but the tale is less than a ringing endorsement of female equality. Ford's Princess Ismara is assertive and clever, but Ford paradoxically makes her transformation into an effective ruler the result of masculine authority and manipulation.

The Brown Owl does not acknowledge an Other-world, nor show physical movement between worlds à la the cleft in the cliff wall that we find in Morris' *Wood Beyond the World*. Rather, Ford sets *The Brown Owl* in a traditional fairy-tale universe where he uses a version of magical agency in co-existent animal and human forms, each carrying significant implications both within and beyond the text. Through his guidance and downright interference, the Brown Owl — her father in disguise — becomes the porter by which the young heroine navigates her emotional and physical pathways toward maturity and power. By having the Brown Owl/king try to manipulate Ismara toward understanding her own needs by testing her own abilities, Ford alternately supports and undermines the fairy-tale princess archetype that has long been a topic of debate.

Interrogating the Fairy-Tale Princess Paradigm

In her essay "On Princesses: Fairy Tales, Sex Roles, and Loss of Self," Jennifer Waelti-Walters defines the traditional fairy-tale princess as an icon of subjectivity "systematically deprived of affection, stimulation, pleasurable activity, instruction and even companionship ... a totally powerless prisoner" (1). This paradigm remains common in fairy-tale scholarship, with Deborah L. Thompson, Elizabeth Heilman, Lucy Armitt, and others often finding fault with contemporary authors — most notably J.K. Rowling — for portrayals they see as confirming and perpetuating sex-based stereotypes. Yet increasing numbers of other critics are quick to point out, as Joyce Thomas does, that "anyone intent on finding sexist elements in the [classic] fairy tales will undoubtedly find them; unfortunately such a myopic concentration reduces the tale to a single dimension, just as its cartoon versions do" (32). In her look at *Kiddie Lit*, the genre's sometimes-denigrated reception in academe and the ways in which that "reception reveals the construction and deployment of childhood" (15), Beverly Lyon Clark reminds us that "attitudes toward children's literature are ... always complexly connected to attitudes associated with gender or class" (75). Deriving from the folk tale, the fairy tale does not become "children's literature" until after childhood itself becomes established as a distinct phase of human development in the late eighteenth century, but the association remains. This is particularly true due to both genres' inescapable associations with women, not only as mothers and the original tale-tellers, but in the traditionally female-dominated professions, as librarians and teachers. Within children's literature or more broadly as a fantasy convention, the fairy-tale princess continues to incite conflicting viewpoints — from those who see her as a dangerous threat to gender equality to others who believe she displays admirable assertiveness and authority — which serves to illustrate the complexity of the issue.

Looking at the fairy tale and the fairy-tale princess is likely even more relevant in relation to Ford's time than our own; and to late nineteenth-century fantasy in general, produced when the shifting social and political framework furnished a fertile ground for an artist to explore alternate visions of male and female identity. Jack Zipes sees this phenomenon as part of a Utopian vision: "For many late Victorian authors, the writing of a fairy tale meant a process of creating an *other world*, from which vantage point they could survey conditions in the real world and compare them to their ideal projections" (*Victorian Fairy Tales* xxix). Such "conditions" included a small but increasingly vocal female contingent "with dangerous designs on equality" (Honig 44). Marked by a tension between the real-world version of the Waelti-Walters's model and a more liberated woman often labeled as "masculine," this milieu gave birth to an altered fictional female, an emancipated fairy-tale princess transcending the classical and somewhat slippery stereotype of the "totally powerless prisoner."

For various reasons, however, the power such a protagonist wields often fails to free her from the limitations most of her imaginary predecessors and real-world counterparts experienced. Examples of this more independent fairy-tale female abound in late Victorian writing, particularly by women such as E. Nesbit, Christina Rossetti, and Juliana Horatia Ewing, whose heroines are often "credited with an ingenuity and resilience" more in keeping with the matriarchal culture of oral tale-telling tradition (Auerbach 15). Superficially at least, Ford's Princess Ismara in *The Brown Owl* stands among these exceptions to the fairy-tale princess paradigm designated by Waelti-Walters and others. In working to restore order in her father's kingdom after his apparent demise, Ismara exhibits some conventionally masculine traits and undergoes challenges associated with the usually male *bildungsroman* protagonist of both classic and Victorian fairy tales. At the same time, though, Ford is always careful to define her power as coming from an external source, making Ismara a problematic version of the "new" fairy-tale princess.

The Brown Owl and the Fairy-Tale Princess

To fully illustrate how the portal concept operates to simultaneously aid and undermine female power in Ford's work requires first identifying the way he defines Ismara's position in the kingdom. Early in the story, Ford places the princess within the patriarchal society where her father has been the sole ruler for "nine hundred and ninety-nine and a half years." The narrator opens with the standard "Once upon a time," then explains that Intafernes's kingdom spans "the whole of the western half of the world," with the rest being "divided into smaller kingdoms ... ruled over by separate princes" (261). Unlike in Morris' *Wood Beyond the World*, no queens or empresses reign here. Thus Ismara's assumption of the throne is in itself significant, calling attention to the idea of female power as an issue in the tale. Ford acknowledges the concept of power in general and aligns Intafernes's kingdom with his own Britain by incorporating late Victorian class structures, as the narrator explains, "in this [Intafernes's] country, as in all other countries, the rich magicians had the upper hand over the rest" (261). The line also establishes hierarchy as a deeply ingrained tradition, one that easily extends to the social hierarchy of male dominance and female subjectivity.

This notion of hierarchy is borne out in the opening section when the narrator stresses that, even though Intafernes and the male aristocrats possess magical powers, Ismara does not. Since no other female in the story even comes close to occupying a position of authority, the disparity between the powerful and the powerless signals a clear division between male and female status in the kingdom. A prime example occurs early in the tale when the narrator explains how Ismara responds when, while lying near death, the king instructs her to move his bed so he can look out the window: "The Princess did as she was told. Now from this you must not imagine that she was a very strong princess — for she was no stronger than most ... but the old king ... made that bed easy for her to move ... he knew that it would please his daughter to be of service to him" (262–63). Here Ford insinuates not only Ismara's subservient position to do "as she was told" but also her physical weakness in comparison to her father, who as a man — even one in his death throes after nearly one thousand years of life — indulges her by letting her help him. The passage also foreshadows how, in the shape of the Brown Owl, the king will aid Ismara even after he is gone. Confirming Ismara's female disadvantage, the passage echoes Ford's late Victorian society where most middle- and even upperclass women occupied a subject or servile position to her male relatives. Indeed after the king's death, the narrator repeatedly refers to Ismara as "the Princess" instead of the queen, implying the continuation of her father's presence. Even the story's title reinforces her secondary status, putting forth the Owl/king, not the princess, as the main or most important character.

Ismara inherits her father's crown; but in standard fairy-tale fashion, her actual assumption to the throne remains in question until she proves her ability to resolve a series of conflicts, her *bildungsroman* tests. Before supposedly passing on, Intafernes tells Ismara, "[When] the soul will have left my body ... the power will be thine. But above all cherish the Owl. Never go out of its sight, for if thou do, some harm will happen" (263). The king intimates that his magic will automatically transfer to his daughter, but his qualification that she keep near the Owl defines the process as occurring vicariously *through* the magical bird. In other words, Ismara will only have control if she keeps her promise to her father. As the embodiment of the promise, the Owl becomes the porter that will carry Ismara through her development, a role Ford repeatedly emphasizes in the story. She remains a subordinate, not only because she has not yet proved herself worthy to lead, but also because as a female she simply cannot rise beyond a certain standing, even if her official role immediately denotes control and probably would provide such power to a male heir.

Reinforcing Ismara's secondary status, her father's insistence on her proximity to the Owl also refers back to Ford. Again a brief look at Ford's

biography helps to provide context for understanding the Owl's porter qualities, as well as a point of entry into Ford's motivations in characterizing the
Princess as he does. While the revelation that the magical bird is a transfiguration of the dead king does not come until the story's end, the narrator continually hints at the doubling in descriptions such as "for it seemed as if the
Owl had become a companion to her that would take the place of her father"
(268). Critics including Thomas Moser view *The Brown Owl* as a family allegory, accepting the bird as a function of the author's impulse to comfort his
sister Juliet, who was only eight when their father Dr. Francis Hueffer died
(Moser 36). Read this way the tale signifies an act of "replacing" their father
as guide and protector with their grandfather, Ford Madox Brown, whom
the author called "the best person he had ever known" (Moser 31).

One of the few to even acknowledge Ford's fairy tales, Alison Lurie
treats this issue in *Don't Tell the Grown-ups: The Subversive Power of Children's Literature*, first by noting the similarity in appearance between Ismara
and Ford's sister Juliet, both blue-eyed blondes (132). Lurie conjectures that
Chancellor Merrymineral, who ranks second in magical power only to
Intafernes, represents Ford's uncle William Rossetti to whose home Juliet was
sent to live for a time after Hueffer's death. Rossetti's government post as
Secretary of the Inland Revenue and status as "the most practical and conventional member of a very bohemian family ... [whose] cautious attitude
toward money had displeased the already extravagant Ford" would make him
a prime target for his nephew's satire (Lurie 134). As a foil for Merrymineral in the tale, Ford's characterization of the Owl as a benevolent helper
supports the author's admiration for his grandfather, affirming the likelihood
of Ismara as a stand-in for both Juliet and himself as they worked through
their grief at their father's death.

Being fifteen, Ford would have been quite impressionable when Hueffer died, and given that the young man "felt a great gulf between his sense
of his own quivering self and his grandfather's blatant manliness," the use
of a female protagonist to represent his own feelings as well as his sister's is
certainly plausible (Moser 34). Lurie adds that Brown's illustrations for the
original edition portray the Owl with "eyes [that] resemble his own specta-
cles," suggesting the grandfather recognized the connection (133). Such evidence also verifies the idea that Ismara's reliance upon the magical bird may
stem from Ford's effort to help his sister, as well as himself, navigate a period
of loss just as Intafernes tries to help his daughter by guiding her via the
Owl's presence. This interpretation does ease the problem of Ismara's reliance
on the Owl, but also helps to buoy the bird's importance, and reading the
story strictly in biographical terms would unfairly reduce the larger meaning of a deceptively simplistic work.

Instead, it is necessary to go further by taking the Owl as a symbol in its own right. Vladmir Propp's groundbreaking study of folktale structure provides a helpful foundation to show how the portal concept works in *The Brown Owl*. In his discussion of types, Propp cites the animal as a primary shape in which magical agency manifests to the hero, a "donor or provider ... usually encountered accidentally" (39). While Ismara's introduction to the Owl occurs through the narrator's description of a struggle between it and her attendants, the bird's presence seems natural to Ismara. Upon awakening to the scene, she immediately remembers "her promise" to her father regarding the Owl (265). Here Ford only partially satisfies Propp's definition, though, since her father, as the "donor," is well known to her. Although she does not explicitly understand that he and the Owl are one, he has already explained the bird's importance, albeit somewhat cryptically, prior to his death.

For Propp the hero is "that character who either directly suffers from the action of the villain ... or who agrees to liquidate the misfortune or lack of another person ... who is supplied with the magical agent ... and who makes use of it or is served by it" (50). Despite being female, the definition fits no one in the story more snugly than Princess Ismara, whose bestowal of magical help from the Owl helps her to eliminate the threat to her kingdom posed by the villain Merrymineral. Clearly, Intafernes — whose name not coincidentally sounds like *interference*— satisfies Propp's definition of the magical agent's purpose. Instead of disappearing, though, the king lingers in the Owl's shape, unbeknownst to Ismara, but not to the reader who can see the resultant weakening of the princess' power. Propp explains that when a Magical Agent manifests as "a living creature," the Hero immediately uses it and "loses all significance" as an actor in the story. From this point onward, the hero "does nothing, while his helper accomplishes everything" (Propp 50). At the same time, "the morphological significance of the hero" continues because his (or her) "intentions create the axis of the narrative ... in the form of commands which the hero gives to his helpers" (Propp 50). Since Ismara assumes power via her father's death, her superficial goal involves keeping order and gaining her people's respect, rather than immediately rising to kingship as a male fairy-tale hero might need to do. From beginning to end, the Owl is central to this process, chipping away at Ismara's status as female hero. In a sense, she does give "commands," to use Propp's term, but her attempts at assertiveness are always couched by the Owl's protection.

In keeping with Waelti-Walter's fairy-tale princess paradigm, Ismara exhibits several stereotypical female tendencies throughout the story that magnify the problematic presence of the Owl. For example, after the king dies Ismara cries herself to sleep, awaking with "the wild impulse of calling for help" (264). When she discovers the Owl in her chamber and finds comfort in his presence, her next thought is that her "eyes must be quite red" and her hair "all ruffled" (267). While noting that Ismara was not in "the least conceited," the narrator admits she "liked looking at beautiful things, and so she liked sometimes to look at herself in the glass" (267). Coupled with an earlier description of Ismara's beauty (261), this passage casts her as the stereotypical, vain female whose role is primarily decorative. As Thomas points out, however, such an emphasis may be purely a function of traditional fairy-tale narrative, designating Ismara as the protagonist by singling her out as "special and different" from the other characters (34). Still, because she is female, her *way* of being "special and different" comes solely through her beauty, while a male hero would be typically described as brave, strong, and cunning, as well as handsome.

More importantly, and in a less troubling way, Ford's portrayal also defines the princess' immaturity in *Bildungsroman* terms. To be worthy of her new office, Ismara must develop the ability to look beyond the material and exhibit concern for others. Ruth Bottigheimer's definition of fairy-tale kingship also applies to the queen who "represents a high estate in the sense of a higher psychical development, a human being's maturation" (8). Validating the idea of Ismara's vanity as a flaw to be corrected as part of her maturation journey, Bottigheimer claims "self-control is a path to sovereign authority, a test for him [or her] who intends to exercise power beyond himself" (8). Still, Ismara's narcissism is problematic for signaling her acceptance of the female role in a patriarchal system that values woman for her beauty. By painting Ismara as an almost-willing participant in the process of male-domination, Ford's characterization of her again undermines the assertiveness with which he will endow her as the story unfolds.

"For I am but a girl": The Fairy-Tale Princess Fights Back (sort of)

The real conflict in *The Brown Owl* between the princess's character and the societal pressures undermining her progress emerges in the first meeting with Merrymineral, who, in a clear gender reversal, weeps and faints like a Victorian lady in trying to gain Ismara's trust. Instead of sympathizing, she laughs, orders him "to come to," and deems "[h]e must be punished" for disobedience (269). To counteract the harshness of her response, the narrator says the princess is "only joking" (270); possibly implying her immaturity. After being dowsed with cold water at Ismara's command, Merrymineral asks his fellow councilors, "'Are we ... the lords of the kingdom, to be governed by this schoolgirl, who is not even a magician...?'" (272). At first, Ismara agrees, saying, "I have no right to reign over you, for I am but a girl"; but when the lords follow her suggestion and take a vote, Ismara wins and the narrator says, "She had known all along what they would say" (273). Weiss sees Merrymineral as representing "the masculine principle of authority and privilege uncomplemented by the feminine principle of equality and cooperation" that would compel Ismara to try "to restore balance" (33). Extending this idea, the above passage from the tale demonstrates her effort to outwit an older, more powerful male enemy who, with her father, personifies the status quo of a society that mirrors Ford's late Victorian England. While her words "but a girl" obviously highlight her youth, the sex-based identification cannot be overlooked and seems to be deliberate given Ford's overall characterization of Ismara and of the men surrounding her, including the Owl/king.

Her most direct challenge comes from Merrymineral, whose name translates into "Glad Stone," a not-so-sly reference to one of the period's most well known British Prime Ministers.[2] We might then accept the meeting described above as an imaginative re-enactment of Victoria's experience as a female ruler working with her all-male Parliament at a time when, despite the precedent of Elizabeth I, women remained otherwise restricted from positions of authority. Aligning Ismara with Queen Victoria, who mourned her husband's loss for decades to the end of her own life in 1901, makes Ismara appear all the more potent for her assertiveness, particularly when placed against the conventional fairy-tale princess archetype. Yet we must not forget that Victoria was thought of as the "Great White Mother" and the "Grand-Mother of Europe." She publicly espoused a conservative view about woman's place in society, making ironic her position as leader of the most powerful nation on Earth at the time. As mentioned in the previous chapter, Victorian women (and men) were forced to reconcile in their queen what Gail Turley Houston calls "a deviant model of femininity that complicated the concepts of womanhood and sovereignty." Much like Ismara, Victoria's position was "endangered and endangering because she was queen" (Houston 32–3).

Ismara appears quite "endangering" in many parts of the story; for example, instead of awaiting rescue by a Prince Charming figure, she personally confronts Merrymineral, showing no fear. Nevertheless her power remains tenuous and inconsistent due to the male protectors Ford provides, so that Ismara's success implies women may rise, but only with the approval or guidance of the men who actually run things. Interestingly, while male opponents, such as *Little Red Riding-Hood*'s Big Bad Wolf or the wily Rumplestiltskin, do appear in the classic tales, most that feature a female lead make domestic circumstances the opposing force, driven by a female rather than a male antagonist (Thomas 37). For Waelti-Walters, such portrayals are in themselves problematic for pitting "women against each other in a thankless struggle to gain a master," which in turn makes "Dependency ... the only future offered" (4). Cinderella battles her stepmother and stepsisters, using her beauty to win Prince Charming; Rapunzel is held prisoner in a tower by an enchantress; Snow White is condemned to death by her jealous stepmother; and the list continues.

Of these brief examples, Snow White best compares with Ismara since she finds safety in the company of a group of men, the Seven Dwarves, who agree to shelter her as long as she "'will take care of [their] house, cook, make the beds, wash, sew,'" etc. (Grimm 252). By performing such stereotypical woman's work, Snow White earns her keep and some protection from the wicked Queen; her undoing comes at the hands of her stepmother disguised as an old beggar woman when the Dwarves are away (Grimm 255–6). Although as a political leader, Ismara's duties fall more accurately into the category of men's work, like Snow White, she gains the assistance of male helpers, chiefly the Owl, whom she must keep near in order to be safe. Ismara also moves beyond the classical model, however, for her more masculine tendency toward aggression that is generally absent in her predecessors. We can say then that she fits the fairy-tale princess stereotype to a point, but her divergence also carves a space for a new, more progressive variation. In this way Ismara exemplifies the same kind of tension felt by most women in late Victorian society.

She seems to bow to patriarchy in her early confrontation with Merrymineral by agreeing that she is "but a girl," but Ismara's actions throughout the story suggest that sees herself as much more. Even her coy identification of herself in that initial confrontation with Merrymineral implies she is using her femininity as a kind of weapon, to mask her true intentions or to get around her male adversaries. This in itself is troubling, but the real problem lies in the fact that her power and identity as a leader rely upon the Owl always standing ready to protect her. As a powerful king's daughter, Ismara could be innately brave; however, even in her initial meeting with Merrymineral, she carries the memory of her father's promise that she will avoid harm as long as she remembers to "cherish the Owl" (262). Weiss makes the point that all three of Ford's major fairy tales include a magical bird, which in *bildungsroman* tradition "symboliz[es] ... a power within the psyche that the heroine must explore and develop before inner fulfillment or outward peace can be achieved" (32). Following *The Brown Owl*, both *The Feather* (1892) and *The Queen Who Flew* (1894) allude to being airborne in their titles.

Also, in both of these tales (and in *The Brown Owl*), the protagonist is a female ruler compelled by circumstances to outwit a male foe or foes. In *The Brown Owl* the bird emblem projects an added dimension of paternalism (Weiss 34). Ford repeatedly links the creature with Intafernes, a father as well as a king: both roles traditionally associated with wisdom and leadership, for a family or a nation. Consequently, Ismara's reliance upon the Owl undermines the expression of her courage, more often placing her in the dependent position Waelti-Walters indicates rather than in the dominant role her assertiveness might suggest.

From the time she awakes after Intafernes's death through the end of the story, Ismara *never once* appears without the Owl. Weiss rightly calls *The Brown Owl* "the least feminist" of Ford's tales, noting that Eldrida (*Queen*) and Ernalie (*Feather*) "control their own fates" with only limited or initial outside assistance (34). Eldrida's helper, the bat, only steps in to tell her about the magic wind-flowers that subsequently enable her to fly (Ford *Queen* 12–13). After this, Eldrida takes off on her own and the bat reappears only briefly, first as an adviser and later to accept the throne, which she abdicates to him (Ford *Queen* 72, 76–77). Likewise, in *The Feather*, Ernalie becomes invisible via the quill lost by Jupiter's eagle, the agent for her movement from "the happy valley" to the troubled land of Mumkie (Ford 37). Even more than Eldrida, Ernalie progresses mainly due to her own ingenuity, since her bird helper plays only an initial role in her subsequent heroics. Ernalie has control over her own destiny, as she "can choose whether or not to wear" the feather, which Weiss reads as a symbol for "spiritual power within [her]" (26–7). The Owl serves a similar function for Ismara, but unlike Ernalie who acts more independently, Ismara has some idea of the magical bird's relation to her father, as well as its importance to her survival.

The feather, through its power to enable Ernalie to save Treblo's life and his father's kingdom, links Ernalie to a prince; but only as a vehicle to her future happiness, not a necessary tool for keeping her from harm. In fact, Ernalie takes the initiative and risks *her* life to help Treblo more than once. The feather provides her with a feeling of security and control, but only through its magic, not its relation to any male person. Also, since Ernalie activates the magic by touching the feather to her hair, Ford defines its power as essentially female, particularly since the princess is its primary user. Instead of turning to the mirror to look at herself the way Ismara does, Ernalie seeks the glass for proof that she *cannot be seen*. The portrayal reverses *Brown Owl*'s emphasis on female beauty as an instrument of power (*Feather* 35–36) and exchanges Ismara's vanity with Ernalie's more intuitive approach to problem solving.

These examples from the classic tales and Ford's own experiments in the genre illustrate his weaving of traditional fantasy and real-world experience into *The Brown Owl*, while also diverging from the stereotypes in some important ways. Ann Barr Snitow's point hits the mark, then, that Ford provides a "bridge" between his pre–Raphaelite and earlier Victorian fantasy predecessors. While making an effort to engage with the ancient past in his tales, Ford maintains his belief "that an artist's moral duty is 'to register [his] own times in terms of [his] own time'" (quoted in Snitow 21). Ford often paints Ismara more in keeping with the increasingly emerging, more assertive Victorian heroine one finds, for example, in Princess Alicia of Charles Dickens's *From the Pen of Miss Alice Rainbird*, more commonly known as *The Magic Fishbone*. Published in 1868, the story predates Ford's by more than twenty years, yet Alicia exhibits a similar capacity for courage, making Dickens's take on the fairy-tale female a helpful model by which to gauge Ismara's independence in regard to actual Victorian social progress.

In some ways, Alicia exactly parallels Ford's princess since she also has an external source of magic at her disposal; however, while Ismara looks to the Owl for help, her younger counterpart refrains from turning to the magic fishbone given to her by Fairy Grandmarina. Like Intafernes, Alicia's father is a king, but one completely lacking in magical power as well as being void of any apparent leadership (not to mention parental) abilities. When her mother becomes stricken with a mysterious illness that suddenly overcomes her as she tries to "get out of bed in the morning" (Dickens 410), Alicia steps in to run the household. Unlike any of Ford's fairy-tale princesses, Alicia first prefers to use her own skills and ingenuity to approach each domestic difficulty, rather than resorting to magic. Not until after she and her father have "tried very hard, and tried all ways" to fix things does she give in to wishing on the fishbone, even though she is aware of its power all along (Dickens 415).

Because she is only seven, Alicia's success in overseeing the care and feeding of nineteen children and two useless parents makes her a more remarkable female force than Ismara. Still, it is important to recognize that while the initial need for her to take over results from her father's lack of funds to run the kingdom as well as from her mother's incapacity, Alicia's duties follow the Snow-White model in being mostly domestic. In contrast, Ismara actually rules an entire kingdom; her concerns involve the fate of a nation, placing her in a more traditionally masculine, political arena. Alicia's example remains important, though, for showing that with Ismara Ford was perhaps following an impulse by Victorian writers in general to remodel the traditional fairy tale for their own age. In this way both Dickens and Ford incorporated a "new 'feminine quality'" in their tales that Jack Zipes sees as part "of the general re-utilization of the traditional fairy tale motifs ... by utopian writers to express the need for a new type of government and society" (*Victorian* xxvi). Dickens and Ford offer similarly progressive visions of femininity; however, each provides a familiar Victorian fairy-tale and novel ending: the efforts of both Ismara and Alicia are rewarded with marriage. For Alicia, this plays out as a kind of side-effect when she finally wishes on the fishbone and in addition to relieving her father's financial distress, she finds "Mr. Pickles' boy ... (entirely changed by enchantment)" and goes off with him to "live happy ever afterwards" (Dickens 415–6). Ismara's path to fairy-tale marriage is not nearly as uncomplicated.

War and Matrimony: The Fairy-Tale Princess Comes of Age

Arguably Ismara's most striking display of intrepidness under the Owl's guardianship occurs during the battle waged against her kingdom by Merrymineral when, like her classic and Victorian counterparts, she must confront the idea of becoming a wife. As it turns out, the now-former Chancellor Merrymineral was only temporarily banished by the Owl in the initial conflict. He re-appears, vowing to annihilate Ismara's forces unless she agrees to marry him. For a moment, she considers the proposition, thinking of her people's welfare, but because Merrymineral "is such a very unpleasant sort of man," she decides she will instead try to defeat him by force (286). Here Ismara rises above the traditional goal of the fairy-tale princess by choosing to fight. As usual, Ford undermines her appearance of strength by revealing that her refusal to use marriage as a political tool has more to do with her love for another man. Ismara indulges her emotional side in hoping to marry for love rather than for security, and in the process puts her whole kingdom at risk, which does not say much for her leadership. Even in this case, though, there may a positive way to view her decision.

Eldrida makes a similar choice in *Queen*, rejecting Blackjowl and a host of other suitors, all of whom she views as *un*suitable. Eldrida's negative replies seem to be even more appropriate than Ismara's given the circumstances. After all, one of the Queen's proposals comes from a neighboring king who, just before "shaking her violently," threatens, "If you don't marry me ... I'll have you thrown from the top of the highest tower ... and smash you to pieces," which he subsequently tries to do himself (29). While Ford makes Eldrida's decision to stay single appear eminently reasonable, the more important idea to take from the comparison is the vision of marriage she and Ismara share. Since neither woman wishes to place duty or politics over love, both exemplify rejection of patriarchal female commodification and a centuries-old tradition of marriage as a function of politics and economics. While Eldrida's choice partly comes from an effort to avoid violence committed against her, Ismara's decision *leads to the necessity of violence* in broader terms. By choosing war over marriage, Ismara displays a more conventionally masculine way of thinking. Her decision to don the armor also fulfills the *bildungsroman* tradition in which a young man engages in battle as part of his maturation journey.

Ford again emphasizes Ismara's divergence from the fairy-tale princess norm while also reiterating the Owl's importance as a male porter for female development when she encounters her second and more direct protector. Sir Alured, the Prince of India, fights in Ismara's army but tries to dissuade her from participating because "the battlefield is no place for a girl." Ismara responds that her "place is with the army," implying that she views herself as her father's replacement, regardless of her sex (279). Later the princess argues, "I will not be bullied by you, my lord, even though you are old enough to be my father. I know what you are going to say ... I won't be called a girl, for I'm nineteen'" (281). This last line is ironic given that she called *herself* "but a girl" in the scene with Merrymineral, but confirms that the earlier reference to her girlhood is meant as evidence of the princess' irreverence toward the men in her father's government. While emphasizing her youth in the scene with Prince Alured, Ford seems to uphold Ismara's courage as she vows to restore order at the risk of her life; however, reading further, one discovers the source of her daring again stems from her belief in the Owl's protection. Ismara explains to Alured, "Once before the cherished Owl has defeated [Merrymineral] and he may do it again" (280). Moreover, Alured joins the princess's security team: "Your Majesty will always have a protector while I am alive" (281). The addition of the Prince, whom Ismara acknowledges as "old enough to be [her] father," means she now claims two powerful male allies, making her courage appear to depend even more upon these outside sources rather than her own character.

A similar example of Ismara's illusory strength occurs later when her chief advisor, Lord Licec,[3] tries to dissuade her from grabbing a sword and leading her army. Entreating, "please don't say I mustn't go," Ismara sounds like a child trying to obtain permission to go unaccompanied to the park. Ismara later tells Alured, who appears "astonished" to see her on the battlefield, "you see if I only beg hard enough he'll [Licec] let me do whatever I like." While again spotlighting Ismara's immaturity, this passage carries more weight for suggesting that her bravery comes from an awareness of safety, especially since she had previously told Licec, "the Owl will protect me ... I'll promise to keep near the Prince of India, and he'll protect me, even if the Owl can't" (287). Certainly Ismara exhibits impressive determination here and reinforces her stereotypically masculine interest in solving a problem through force. True heroism, however, usually involves forging on in the face of insurmountable odds and great personal danger. Ismara shows bravery by wanting to engage in a traditionally male realm of the battlefield, but again Ford undercuts Ismara's more nontraditional fairy-tale princess traits by having her acknowledge the male protection continually surrounding her.

This idea becomes most pronounced in the story's second half. Structurally, the narrative undergoes a major, exceedingly significant shift following the battle scene in which the Owl intervenes yet again, sending Merrymineral soaring through the air to presumed oblivion (292). Based on this apparent victory, one might assume Ismara's coming-of-age journey is complete, but she continues on toward a more female-oriented goal. Ford emphasizes the significance of marriage as a female accomplishment by extending the tale beyond the battle scene, as the narrator describes Ismara and Alured "march[ing] back to the town at the head of the army" (293). Instead of ending here with Ismara's return to rule her kingdom and a simple union with Alured, Ford introduces a new plotline entirely. Now identifying marriage with female maturity, the rest of the tale pointedly concerns the princess's romantic life instead of just comically alluding to it, as in the first half. Before she can take over her father's kingdom, Ismara must prove herself worthy not only on the stereotypically male battlefield, but also in the more female-oriented, domestic sphere of love. In one way this aligns her with heroes such as Morris's Walter, who becomes king and marries the Maid almost simultaneously, making Ismara progressive for her time, but again not without qualification.

Although Merrymineral's vanquishing after the war seems a bit too neat, his reintroduction in the guise of the Knight of London in the second half more significantly enables a classic chivalric contest, with Ismara as the prize. As mentioned in Chapter One, folktale tradition, from which the fairy tale emerges, upholds the marriage bond as a symbol of "balance between masculine and feminine elements within the hero and his world" (Thomas 39). In other words, the convention of the marriage ending transcends the notion of female subjectivity. For Ismara, however, the tournament to decide the most worthy groom also makes her into a trophy to be won, reinforcing her secondary place in her (and in Ford's) society. Ismara's path toward marriage finds her once again displaying stereotypically female traits, such as her fickleness in abandoning Alured after he loses the tournament to the Knight of London (300). She acts coy when Licec suggests she marry Alured, replying, "He would never do; besides he would have to ask me, and he won't do that," upon which the narrator takes her blush in saying so as a sign of insincerity (294). Her comment that Alured would have to ask for her hand before she could seriously consider him also confirms her subordinate status. Despite the fact that she rules her own kingdom and fights alongside him in battle, social etiquette demands she subvert this kind of power, refraining from the display of any romantic interest in Alured. Instead, she must wait to be chosen.

The most significant function of Ismara's progress toward a union with Alured also illustrates the Owl's role as the porter for her maturity. Like the rest of her progress, the princess's marriage is largely orchestrated by her magical helper; he almost literally carries her forward. Ismara favors the Knight of London in the joust and afterward, but refrains from agreeing to marry him, even though as the contest winner he should rightfully become her husband. Using her position as a convenient reason to indulge in stereotypically feminine indecisiveness, Ismara tells the Knight, "I can't promise until the Council have given their consent, for you see that would be unconstitutional and I can't be that even for you" (300). Given her earlier tendency to favor her heart over politics, this passage marks a contradiction, showing Ismara's immaturity as well as her fickleness. Ismara's wavering also enables another Owl intervention into the plot by delaying her marriage.

Later, believing the Knight has been victimized by the Magi while on a hunting trip, Ismara cries to the Owl, who says she "wouldn't like it" if she knew the truth about the Knight (305). The bird carries Ismara deep into the forest where she eavesdrops on a conversation in which the Knight, whom she learns is Merrymineral in disguise, tells a witch about his plan to "kill the princess, and make [himself] king by force" (307). Returning home, Ismara quickly resumes her affection for Alured and helps him by questioning the Knight's tournament victory so a new contest can take place before Merrymineral has time to implement his treachery (308–9). Ismara concocts a plan, which "she had to think of it herself—for the Owl would tell her nothing" (308). That the princess conceives of a way to outwit Merrymineral while the Owl stands silent here proves her increasing maturity. Still, the princess would have lacked the information enabling her to reach this point without the Owl's intervention. As a result, when Ismara reveals to Alured her discovery that the Knight's armor is impervious to every substance except paper (a nod to literary power coinciding with the name *Allyou-read*), her use of ingenuity remains clouded by the Owl's presence (313).

Signaling the culmination of Ismara's journey, Alured's defeat of the Knight allows the Owl's transformation back into Intafernes, who commands the villain transform back into Merrymineral. Before banishing him permanently, the king quickly levels a series of charges: "You have broken your oath ... And you have rebelled against my daughter? ... And you have intended to murder her? ... And you tried to marry her?" (313). Humorously parallel-ing Merrymineral's intention to "murder" Ismara with his attempt to marry her, the king's accusations reflect the significance of marriage as part of her maturation journey. More importantly, the Owl's transformation back into the king's shape suggests that even after Ismara seems to have solved her own problem of banishing Merrymineral, her power remains insufficient to restore order absolutely. Instead, the king must return, albeit briefly, to conquer Ismara's enemy once and for all and help her to recognize Alured as a wor-thy husband.

Each step of the way, Ismara's more nontraditional fairy-tale princess traits become challenged by her reliance upon her father/the Owl and later upon Alured. Ford seems to be determined to counterbalance the bravery and cleverness he so carefully provides his princess by juxtaposing these traits with her stereotypical feminine vanity, fickleness, and easy reliance upon male protection. Merrymineral appears to be driven off at times by Ismara's resistance, but only meets actual defeat when Intafernes returns to take care of matters personally. Read this way, through the lens of the portal concept, the tale takes on new meaning, so that all events, from the king's supposed death to Merrymineral's final defeat, become a function of Intafernes's orchestrations to marry off his daughter rather than to help her to become worthy of running his kingdom.

Ending the tale so traditionally, Ford plays up Ismara's marriage rather than her assumption to the throne, as Intafernes tells the couple he "shall come and see [them] every seven years," implying a system of "checking up" to make sure his kingdom is being run smoothly (316). The marriage ensures Ismara will have a male partner to rule alongside her, providing her with more of the kind of help she enjoys throughout the story. Rather than imply-ing maturity by placing her on the throne on her own or with a lowlier con-sort, Ford insists Ismara marry an older man not unlike her father. In the end Ford suggests that her process remains incomplete, or that an adult female is immature or ineffective compared to a male. In many ways Ismara exemplifies true progress as a fantasy female forging her own path, but Ford's insistence on highlighting her less flattering character traits and her reliance upon male helpers also serves to perpetuate the feminine subjectivity schol-ars often debate as a major flaw in the fairy-tale princess archetype.

PART II

Charms, Places, and
Little Girls: Portals
in Children's Literature

CHAPTER THREE

E. Nesbit and the Magic Word:
Empowering Child and
Woman in Real-World Fantasy

There is a curtain, thin as gossamer, clear as glass, strong as iron, that hangs forever between the world of magic and the world that seems to us to be real. And when once people have found one of the little weak spots in that curtain which are marked by magic rings, and amulets, and the like, almost anything may happen.

The Enchanted Castle [Nesbit 170]

So far this study has considered works from two sub-categories of fantasy, the romance and the fairy tale. With E. (Edith) Nesbit, we encounter some new considerations: a female writer, working at a slightly later time and more specifically targeting as her audience children as well as adults. As Nesbit's narrator so eloquently expresses in the above epigraph, the primary concern of "modern urban," "real-world," or what is most commonly called "low fantasy," is the connection "between the world of magic and the world that seems to us to be real." By the 1890s, when William Morris and Ford Madox Ford were producing interesting albeit fairly traditional fantasy inspired by the past, a cultural shift occurred with fairy belief becoming almost synonymous with modernity and a revolt against authority (Silver *Strange* 205). Out of this shift emerged a sub-genre using "settings that seem to be real, familiar, present-day places, except that they contain magical characters and impossible events" (Attebery 126). When such a tale shows movement via a door or gateway between Primary and Secondary worlds, it may be characterized as "portal fantasy," but this term tends to mislead since, as I have shown in the previous chapters, the portal can occur in shapes and variations that do not require physical travel to or from an alternate space at all. Since Nesbit's time, and largely due to her influence, the low/portal variety has become a staple of modern fantasy for its flexibility in being able to challenge "established orders of society and thought" (Attebery 1).

As is the case with literary fantasy in general, those tales that acknowledge the real world are especially attractive to those who feel marginalized, particularly "the woman writer, who is already defined by her culture as the irrational, the disruptive, the formless, the Other" (Attebery x). Like Morris and Ford, Nesbit's personal life frequently contradicts her public persona. At a time when women were gaining ground toward active participation in the capitalist system, Nesbit was a working mother and the primary breadwinner for her family. Yet she remained conservative in her opinions on women's issues, making "[h]er various roles, whether imposed or willingly assumed ... often difficult to reconcile" (Briggs xvi). On the one hand, Nesbit publicly expressed opinions parroting those of her husband Hubert Bland, who was known for his extreme conservatism in regard to the Woman Question. On the other, Nesbit's personal choices opposed late Victorian convention. She was nearly seven months pregnant when she married Bland and accepted an open arrangement (mostly on his end), raising two of her husband's children to his mistress Alice Hoatson, who also lived with the Blands as the wife's companion (Briggs 50, 118). Nesbit cut her hair short, refused to wear the tight-fitting, figure-emphasizing fashions of the day, and even rolled her own cigarettes, which she smoked incessantly (Bell 28).

Given her status as a female writer who resisted woman's fight for independence, Nesbit's portrayal of gender roles continues to create debate, with many finding with Stephen Prickett "no hint of Nesbit's own unconventional lifestyle in her writings" (2). Unlike Prickett, and also Colin Manlove, who believes her "books do not ask more than a literal level of reading" ("Fantasy as Witty" 115), I find Nesbit's work to be rife with symbolism that gives clues to her true beliefs regarding sexual equality. Looking at her magical tales in this way furnishes unique insight into the situation for the *fin de siècle* woman writer while also demonstrating the portal's operation in children's literature, a genre that has also found itself "limited by its gendered specialization" (Lundin 21). Ironically, the place Nesbit and others like her carve, both for themselves and for their child characters, exists via a literary genre that is *prescribed to them* based on sex.

With "child care" as "their primary object," writing for the young was sanctioned as socially acceptable for those women who would insist on working. Thus "the literary marketplace ... rewarded women for adhering to stereotyped roles," but their show of conformity in "an age still free of psychoanalytic suspicion exempted their emotions from close inspection" (Auerbach and Knoepflmacher 1). What the woman fantasist actually succeeds in doing is turning *upside down* a system designed to keep her quiet by dismissing her to the nursery in the hope that there she can do no harm. As Julia Briggs explains, "[Nesbit] was conscious, as the children in her books are, of being a subject in a world where the rules are laid down by full-grown men — and where women, like children, are relegated to marginal positions and occupations" (399). By using child characters to convey ideas on contemporary topics, the female fantasist not only employs literature as a vehicle for change; she literally bestows control.

This chapter primarily considers two of Nesbit's best-known and regarded fantasies, *The Story of the Amulet* (1906) and *The Enchanted Castle* (1907), as well as to a lesser extent *The Phoenix and the Carpet* (1904), arguing that her use of portals in both concrete and metaphorical forms carries weight as social and political commentary from a female, if not exactly a feminist, perspective. As one of the most important architects of the portal device, Nesbit's signature brand of magical agency seeks to raise the societal position of the child, and by extension the adult female writer, making the book itself into a portal of power.

The Fabians, Feminism, and the Female Writer

Nesbit's membership in the Fabian Society, a pseudo-socialist organization her husband helped found whose object was "cultivation of a perfect character in each and all" (Pease 32), provides strong evidence of her closeted feminism, a logical place to begin considering the relationship between the real world and her children's fantasies. Similar to Queen Victoria, Nesbit publicly subscribed to Bland's belief "that nature had allocated men and women different roles to play, and that political and economic equality was unnatural ... and would undermine family life" (Briggs xviii). In a rare example of her Fabian participation, Nesbit gave a speech on "The *Dis*abilities of Women" (Pugh 108, emphasis added); yet she must have privately sympathized with the suffragettes, since through the Society she formed close friendships with women's rights pioneers Eleanor Marx, Charlotte Wilson, and Charlotte Perkins Gilman. Reva Pollack Greenburg posits that Nesbit's vague feminism extended only as far as "demand[ing] recognition for the exceptional female ... for the kind of girl she must have been and the woman she certainly was" (237). Known at the time and since as "armchair socialists" (Laybourn 20), the Fabians taught Nesbit "ways of circumventing rigid Victorian mores, without losing caste," which would have been useful information for such an "individualist" (Briggs 146).

This "circumventing" is nowhere more apparent than in Nesbit's children's fantasies, though debate continues as to what extent this is true. While earlier critics such as W.W. Robson suggest Nesbit "in no way anticipated modern feminism" and that she "directed [her stories] to boys rather than girls" (259), more recently Alison Lurie cites Nesbit's "implicit feminism" as an "especially radical, and at the time highly subversive" feature of her magical tales (105). Likewise, Auerbach and Knoepflmacher applaud Nesbit for "mocking earlier stereotypes of females magnified by male desire" (136) in stories such as "Melisande"; and Claudia Nelson finds that, while Nesbit might "valorize the masculine point of view" in the Psammead trilogy "when she seems most closely identified with the 'childlike' ... in her 'adult' persona she takes an essentially pro-feminine or androgynous stance" (2).

To Nelson's point, Nesbit creates some characters who try to buck tradition: for example, the assertive princess in "The Last of the Dragons" (c. 1900). When the time comes for her to choose a husband, this princess resists the usual ritual and suggests to her father, "Couldn't we tie up one of the silly little princes for the dragon to look at and then I could go and kill the dragon and rescue the prince?" (354). Here Nesbit demonstrates a tendency that began around the 1890s when women's fiction often "challenged conventional representations of gender roles" (Nelson 2). Supporting this, "Last of the Dragons" also challenges male stereotypes by presenting a "pale prince, with large eyes and a head full of mathematics" (Nesbit 354). Admittedly, Nesbit provides probably as many stereotypical boys and girls as she does their antitheses. For instance, in *The Phoenix and the Carpet*, the girls darn the worn spots in the magical rug while the boys go "out for a walk in the afternoon" (208). Reconciling such portrayals creates a similar challenge to deciding which defines her true nature: Nesbit's public condemnation of the New Woman or her personal exhibition of many of that Woman's most identifiable traits. In either case, to do so requires keeping in mind Nesbit's fondness for irony and satire, which infuse her portrayals of child characters confronting the social and political standards of Edwardian Britain.

Examples like the one above from *Phoenix* blatantly bow to established gender roles, but it is their very blatancy that suggests there may be more to them — that in her work Nesbit only *seems* to uphold Bland's firm beliefs about a woman's place, just as she *seems* to do in public. Over and over again, implicit yet pointed satirical challenges to the status quo bubble up just under the surface of the stereotypes. For example, in *Phoenix*, Anthea actually contradicts female convention by being the one to go on a mission by herself to see if the Cook (a woman) is doing all right on the island. Summoning her courage to leave, Anthea thinks, "It's my duty" (Nesbit *Amulet* 82), which suggests a masculine sense of obligation since a woman's duty at that time typically lies within the home. Also in *Phoenix*, Nesbit performs one of her characteristic self-reflexive moves when, out of his belief that his sisters lack a spirit of adventure, Robert says, "You girls will never be great writers" (143). Nesbit is supporting her family with her pen, so the line is a wink to the reader, her way of identifying and challenging in her work a conservative belief about which she refrains from speaking out in life. Her child characters both use and become portals and porters, occupying a power position for themselves and the writer at the center of conflicts around issues of gender, imperialism, and class felt by both children and adults, then and now.

Nesbit's Portals of (Girl) Power

Edith Lazaros Honig believes Nesbit's "confusion in her feelings about women's rights comes through ... in her portrayal of heroines who are adventurous ... yet somehow curiously bound to their time and their society" so that they appear as voices for her to attack or at least undermine sex-role stereotyping (98). In *The Enchanted Castle* Nesbit creates one such girl, an alter ego whose use of magic functions out of a drive to transcend the limitations society places upon her and upon the woman writer. The story begins with three siblings, Gerald, Kate, and Jimmy, facing a summer holiday at Kate's school with the French governess and a nurse as their only adult supervision. The children set out seeking adventures and stumble upon an old mansion that looks like a castle, where they find a girl asleep on a stone bench in the garden (13–28). When Mabel awakes, Jimmy is characteristically adamant in his disbelief that she is an "actual" fairy princess. She responds, "It doesn't so much matter what you believe as what *I am*" (27, emphasis added). Speaking her own identity into being, Mabel uses the issue of belief to elevate herself, not only above her class (and thus above the other children who socially outrank her), but also beyond the traditional limitations of her sex. In other words, in rejecting a boy's determination of what is "true," Mabel transcends social opinion. For these middle-class children, Mabel embodies the magic that will allow them to escape or at least reinvent the boring, adult-ruled world of Edwardian London. The ways in which she does so define Mabel as a porter, a magical transforming agent and a force for rebellion, not unlike Nesbit the woman writer.

Nesbit uses Mabel's first meeting with the children to define imaginative power as feminine. Emerging from an archway, they find the princess lying upon a "round grass plot" near a sundial (23). Mabel appears as magic personified, a "sleeping beauty" arrayed in "old fashioned clothes" (23), lounging in a garden "out of a picture or a fairy tale" (20). When they go inside, of all the treasures littering the shelves of the chamber, Nesbit reinforces the circular imagery by having Mabel choose the ring to wear, thereby initiating the magic. Although traditionally a symbol of marriage — a stereotypically female goal — as a portal for the children's adventures, the ring takes on greater significance. In physical terms, the ring is of course a gold circle through which one places a finger, and therefore a miniature version of the archway the children use to gain access to the castle and Mabel. Symbolically, the feminized imagery Nesbit uses to describe the children's path to Mabel, and by extension to the ring, links the entities of magic, power, and the woman writer's imagination. Nesbit earns money through her imagination, creating tales under a purposely-ambiguous name that, like the magic ring, bestows a kind of invisibility. Again like the ring, the book provides Nesbit with power: to speak her mind, to support her family, to meaningfully participate in society. Briggs cites Nesbit's "continuous awareness of the power of books, apparent in everything she wrote, [as] an endorsement of the power of imagination in life, and ... an acknowledgement of the writer's responsibilities" (220–1). As the primary user of the concrete portal (the magic ring) in the story, Mabel allies with her creator, transformed and transforming as a porter through which the other children, along with Nesbit in her authorship, take part in the world.

Mabel's assertiveness and desire to believe in magic attracts the other children, who are already eager to believe, except maybe for Jimmy. Mabel starts by serving them a meal in the manner of Hans Christian Andersen's "Emperor's New Clothes." Like the emperor and his attendants who fear embarrassment (and worse) if they fail to see the nonexistent garments, Gerald and Cathy go along with Mabel's assertion that barring "some secret fault the bread and cheese will turn into anything you like" (30). Even Jimmy only "feebly" challenges the idea, but when Mabel takes them to what seems to be an ordinary room, all three siblings doubt her claim of the existence of "treasure." Mabel actually frightens herself when she slips on the ring she says will make her invisible and finds it *actually does*. Again pointing up the power of belief, Mabel exclaims, "I was only playing at magic," and the children perceive the castle they "had believed in ... tumbling about their ears (42–3).

Ironically they accept "the invisibility of the princess" (Nesbit *Enchanted* 44), as all that remains of their fantasy, so that *not being seen* becomes the thing to define Mabel's power. In keeping with Bruno Bettelheim's belief that a child who feels insecure seeks "fairy tale solutions to life's eternal problems" (51), Mabel uses her imagination to acquire a sense of control in a dreary, old mansion where she is ward to a servant/aunt who ignores her. In doing so, Mabel literally disappears; her imagination is so powerful that what she feels about her own life becomes reality through the use of magic. Mabel's invisibility defines her sense of identity in the real world, as she expresses when Gerald tries to comfort her by saying at least she is under a spell in her own home: "What's the use of belonging anywhere if you're invisible?" (46). Here Nesbit expresses the child's feeling of powerlessness in an adult world while also implying the perspective of a woman who as a wife maintains a certain place in society, but remains invisible in terms of having any real social or political power. This idea even more readily applies to the female writer engaging in capitalism through her work while lacking the ability to voice opinions, vote, or otherwise influence that system.

Nesbit supports this reading by literally turning Mabel into an author of fiction when she composes a note to her aunt offering a made-up account of why she has to leave home (48–9). Here Jimmy and Mabel disagree over the difference between "lies" and "fancy," with Mabel preferring the latter term that further defines her as a stand-in for Nesbit (49). Her aunt embodies the antithesis of imagination and may be seen — quite ironically given Nesbit's own publicly professed views — as the highly conservative sort of woman who stalled female progress. In the scene where the children try to explain the situation, at one point actually telling the aunt the truth about Mabel's invisibility, she shows characteristic adult disbelief: "I detest untruthfulness ... in all its forms" (56). Being by all accounts very childlike even into her later years, Nesbit is more like Mabel. The aunt's dislike of "untruthfulness" makes her the epitome of a kind of adulthood Nesbit detests. The portrayal also aligns the aunt with those who would view fantasy as untrue and unworthy of serious attention, a stance the genre continues to fight even today. Nesbit, who "was always acutely aware of 'literariness,' of how reading experiences can affect the way readers, both young and old, think and act" (Briggs 175–6), elevates her children's stories by dealing with important issues of her day in a way that also celebrates imagination as an instrument of female power. In *Enchanted Castle*, Mabel's aunt equates the woman who *resists* such a move. While in public Nesbit herself appears to be just such a woman, her portrayals of Mabel and condescension toward the aunt subversively place the author on the "pro" side of the female power issue. Just as the ring provides the concrete symbol of Mabel's magical agency, the book serves the same purpose for Nesbit.

Published just two years later in 1906, *The Story of the Amulet* uses its magical charm in a similar way, but as an even more traditional portal that charges movement between worlds with social implications. The charm, being of "red, smooth, softly shiny stone" (26), suggests a woman's lips and a gemstone; according to the pawnshop clerk, "It was a Roman lady's locket" (30). With their parents away from home in separate locations, to achieve the "heart's desire" of having a whole family, the children need to fuse the halves of the charm, which easily read as male and female. For most of the story they possess what may be understood as the female half given the magic's operation. When the children use the portal for the first time, Jane holds the charm while Cyril says "the word of power," and as the charm begins to grow "tall and broad," Cyril notices "Jane ... just holding on to the edge of a great red arch of a very curious shape" (53). If its appearance, both as a charm and a gateway, are not enough evidence, Nesbit's narrator describes the amulet's "Voice" as emanating from "a faint, beautiful light in the middle of the circle" and sounding like "the voice of your mother when you have been a long time away" (44). In her child characters' hands the amulet transfers the power from its feminine source (mother/author) to the product of that source (child). When they travel through the amulet in search of its other half, the children symbolically reverse the birthing process, and in their repeated use of this pathway throughout the story they gain the knowledge that leads them "home" in the form of the reunion with their parents.

As with *Enchanted Castle, Story of the Amulet* places the bulk of the magic in female hands, those of another character who, like Nesbit, is the youngest of her siblings: Jane. Early on the Voice of the charm deems, "Let the last that passes be the one that holds me, and let him not lose his hold, lest you lose me, and so remain in the past forever" (48). Although the Voice uses the masculine pronoun, it is Jane who becomes the porter for the amulet, an object so precious that it is viewed as "sacred" by the ancient Egyptians and ends up on display in the British Museum. With each trip, Jane's voice becomes clearer and more decisive in directing the amulet's use. Their first journey into the past involves a clash between native tribes and the party cannot go into the village until Jane, after conferring with the Psammead, consents to the move (60). The adventure ends when Jane decides it is time to go (68); and her importance becomes even more undeniable in the next journey when she ends up separated from her siblings, carrying both the charm and the Psammead (107).

Jane can conceivably leave at any time, but without the amulet, the other children remain unable to get home. She becomes the guest of the Babylonian queen (another powerful woman) who unbeknownst to her holds her siblings hostage in a dungeon (127–8). Afraid Jane will refuse to go on any further adventures, after their rescue the children refrain from telling her about their experience and the next trip occurs when she chooses. Nesbit goes to some trouble in *Story of the Amulet* to elevate Jane from the least-likely status traditionally associated with the fairy-tale child hero. Given that in such stories "age and physical size are metaphors for power and knowledge" (Thomas 41), Jane would be the sibling least expected to show heroism, particularly since, besides being the youngest, she is also a girl. In keeping with Nesbit's strong, spirited girl characters, however, Jane overcomes the fear that after the first trip to ancient Egypt causes her to stereotypically exclaim, "I won't, I won't, I won't! If you make me ... I'll tell old Nurse, and I'll get her to burn the charm in the kitchen fire" (88). Later she proves her growth by finding little difficulty in conversing with Julius Caesar (who calls her a "prophetess") on the eve of his British invasion (Nesbit *Amulet* 194–6).

Claudia Nelson makes the point that, even though Jane holds the charm, "it is typically Anthea, as the child who feels the loss of the unified family most keenly, who suggests using the amulet" (10). The comment supports the importance of the maternal connection I discuss above, particularly since Anthea often acts as a surrogate mother to her siblings. Aligning Anthea with the amulet reinforces the argument for Nesbit's conservatism. Jane, on the other hand, provides a strong challenge to it. As the sister more closely corresponding to Nesbit herself, Jane's magic trumps Anthea's maternal power, providing the true agency that reunites the family. Confirming this, the author inserts an interesting exchange between Jane and her sister when the children take the Psammead to a lecture at Camden Town hall. A speaker trying to rouse imperial support among the young encourages, "I hope every boy in this room has in his heart the seeds of courage and heroism." In response to her sister's view that it is "unlucky that the lecturer said 'boys,' because now she and Jane would have to be noble and unselfish ... without any outside help," Jane says, "We are already [brave and unselfish] because of our beautiful natures. It's only boys that have to be made brave by magic" (270). Just after this scene, the children return to Egypt and of them all, Jane is the one who places her hand on the stone slab to retrieve the amulet's other (male) half, around which the entire story revolves (283). As a result of her adventures, by the end of the story Jane becomes a heroine not unlike *Enchanted Castle*'s Mabel, demonstrating the power of the magical tale to encourage the young reader to recognize the positive qualities in herself; or for a boy, to appreciate rather than trying to overpower them in the opposite sex.

Portals of Politics: Class, Imperialism, and Racism

As the above scene from *Amulet* shows, Nesbit's children's stories usually contain at least an underlying political concern. Manlove makes the point that "there must always be an element of 'class structure' in children's literature, not only because adults who write them or appear as actors in the stories have to be leaders and repositories of value, but also because the child's ... mental outlook is founded on rules, orders and stations" ("Witty Conceit" 110). Again, despite the directness with which she often handles this issue, Nesbit's views on class inequities and Britain's imperialist policies are not always so easy to unravel because of Victorian/Edwardian repressiveness and her own ambiguous sense of identity. In her children's fantasies Nesbit offers a complex and rich satire of a nation where as a woman she is barred from direct participation. In *Enchanted Castle*, Mabel becomes a kind of spokesperson for Nesbit to tackle the issue of female subjectivity as well as of social hierarchies more broadly.

Mabel first appears in the guise of a princess, when in reality as the housekeeper's niece she occupies a lower place than the middle-class child visitors she hosts at the make-believe dinner. Not only a girl, but a servant-class girl at that, Mabel might be expected to recognize her difference from the children and act accordingly. As a child with little adult supervision, she ignores or does not even know of such restrictions; she insists she is royalty and takes on a supervisory role with the other children via her connection to the ring. As a portal the ring empowers Mabel, allowing her to influence happenings in her world in a way she never could without it. In the process she also becomes a conduit for the other children to exert a similar influence. The ring's magic comes from belief in its power, making it a concrete artifact of Mabel's imagination. Thus her power occurs on a literal level that carries with it the added bonus of raising her social status, at least superficially, and also emphasizing the transformative capabilities of imagination.

Not unlike Tolkien's infamous One Ring, albeit in a much less sinister way, Mabel's ring equates an object of value, an idea she stresses by describing it as one of the "treasures" in the chamber. The ring makes wishes come true, and in doing so, usually brings the children into proximity with money. Most often this occurs when the ring becomes an exchange agent, such as in the first time the children purposefully use it, at the carnival after Gerald pragmatically points out that "[a]dventures are not always profitable" (Nesbit *Enchanted* 58). Gerald, the white middle-class English boy, blackens his face, dons a turban, and proclaims himself "a conjurer from India." Making a deal to "go shares" with a presumably white, woman vendor who sees through his disguise (60–1), Gerald tells the audience he has an "invisible accomplice" (Mabel) making their pennies disappear; however, they do not believe him (63).

In a sense here Mabel's invisibility commodifies her; she becomes a silent accomplice to Gerald's act, used by him to accomplish his goal of making money. Especially for the twenty-first century reader, Gerald's donning of blackface intensifies the negativity of what he is doing, which might further diminish Mabel, who in this scene is neither black nor white but altogether invisible, perhaps suggesting a woman's place in Nesbit's time. While Mabel's status as an instrument for Gerald's capitalist intention remains troubling in terms of Nesbit's possible feminism, one must keep in mind the author's overall portrayal of Mabel. Even though Gerald initiates and originally directs the scheme, Mabel is the one who saves the day in the end by giving the ring to him so he can "disappear" when the carnival goers start to get suspicious (66). The ring becomes stuck on Gerald's hand, giving *him* the chance to find out what it's like to be invisible (67), probably for the first time in his life.

In terms of Nesbit's politics, Mabel serves an important purpose in the carnival chapter by providing the ring that enables Gerald to enact a performance that implicitly criticizes British imperialist policy. Unlike the explorers who ventured into Asia and Africa under a guise of humanitarianism, Gerald reveals the "trick" of his conjuring. Effectively, he reverses the explorers' way of doing things by appropriating a "dark" face and telling the truth about his conjuring to make money, instead of pretending to be pure-intentioned and stealing the so-called "dark" continent's resources under the guise of friendship and Christianity. Similarly in *The Phoenix and the Carpet*, the children end up on a tropical island, where Robert suggests they "pretend to be missionaries" when the "copper-colored savages" seem on the verge of attack, and their wise magical guide the Phoenix advises against the idea because "it isn't *true*" (71, emphasis in original).

Nesbit's irony operates in a similar way in *Amulet* to offer an even more complex anti-imperialist stance by having the children continually greet the natives they meet in different times and (usually third-world) places by saying some variation of the speech Cyril gives to the ancient Egyptians in the first adventure: "We come from the world where the sun never sets. And peace with honour is what we want. We are the great Anglo-Saxon or conquering race. Not that we want to conquer *you*.... We only want to look at your houses and ... then we shall return to our own place" (61, emphasis in original). Stressing the relationship between real-world politics and children's make-believe, the narrator explains that Cyril conceives this speech from his impression of an article in the *Daily Telegraph* he had read while waiting for his father to finish with his solicitor. Cyril's appropriation of the newspaper headline makes him into an innocent vessel for satirizing adult ideas, not unlike the child voices William Blake uses in *Songs of Innocence and Experience* to expose the adult institutions that were exploiting impoverished children for financial gain. Along with the children in *Phoenix* and *Enchanted Castle*, Cyril serves the same purpose for Nesbit. Mavis Reimer's assessment of this reinforces the idea of Nesbit's conflicted personality: "If [she] appears at one level to be an enthusiastic agent of the empire-builders, at another level she seems to be mediating on the inevitable end of empire, a topic that also preoccupied many of her contemporaries" (48). Through Cyril's imperialist speechmaking in *Amulet*, Nesbit implies criticism of the actions and values espoused by the male-dominated status quo in her time in the same way she uses Gerald's act in blackface to communicate a negative opinion of colonial exploration and exploitation of native peoples.

One of Nesbit's most ardent admirers and self-proclaimed imitators, Edward Eager (1911–1964), tackles similar issues with his series of magical tales. Being American and writing about fifty years after Nesbit, Eager lives in a rather more open society, which brings new concerns to address and, one would think, new ways of addressing them. He clearly follows Nesbit in trying to address racism, an especially prominent yet thorny problem in Eager's time with the Civil Rights Movement gaining momentum. One of the most interesting examples of child characters confronting racism in Eager's magical tales appears in *The Time Garden* (1958). While spending the summer with an unusual aunt, the children meet a toad-like creature, the Natterjack, who accompanies them on adventures via the different varieties of magical thyme plants in their aunt's garden. In the chapter "Time Will Tell," the children and the Natterjack travel to "Civil War days" and use magic to aid a white mother whose house is a stop on the Underground Railroad. The children step in to help a family of escaped slaves, thus becoming porters — literally and figuratively — through which the black family is able to make their way toward freedom.

While the difference in time period and the fact that he is male should allow Eager more freedom from worry about public censure than Nesbit would have felt, his portrayals of interactions between characters of different races are in some ways more problematic than hers. He unfortunately tends to reinforce negative stereotypes, which undermines the power of any effort to illustrate the wrongness of racism. For example, in *The Time Garden* Ann uses the thyme to wish the escaped slaves to arrive in Canada at "a time when they served free dinner to all runaway slaves" (69), instead of sending them to a time when there is *no such thing* as runaway slaves. Before they go, the narrator explains how "the ex-slaves fell on their knees and kissed [the children's] hands in gratitude" (70). Here Eager makes the "ex-slaves" seem dehumanized and completely subjective — not only to white people, but to white *children*. While in one way Eager shows the children intervening in a situation they obviously see as wrong, in another way he reinforces racial stereotypes by presenting the African-American family as slaves rather than as people.

In *Amulet* Nesbit more than once conflates the poor with people of African descent. For example, the queen of Babylon inadvertently becomes transported with the children out of the past into their London. Touring the city she remarks, "How badly you keep your slaves." Jane corrects her, saying, "They aren't slaves, they are working people," to which the queen replies, "Of course they're working. That's what slaves are" (149). Again in *Amulet* Nesbit skirts the issue of color in the chapter "The Little Black Girl and Julius Caesar." The narrator is quick to clarify, "She was not really a little black girl. She was shabby and not very clean.... It was her dress that was black" (181). When they show interest in helping her, the children find themselves in Caesar's time because as the Psammead says, "You don't suppose anyone would want a child like that in *your* times — in *your* towns?" (186–7, emphasis in original). Here Nesbit upholds her positive identification of the children and of imagination/belief by having Anthea point out, "That's not our doing you know" (187).

Outside the issue of race, this chapter certainly supports Mavis Reimer's point that in *Amulet* "Nesbit articulates the new performative function of 'the child' in this phase of imperialism: 'the child' is the figure who 'conjures' home into being" (57). The children use the amulet to enable "the little black girl" to find a woman she identifies as her mother in an ancient time where the people's actions suggest "that a child was something to make a fuss about, not a bit of rubbish to be hustled about the streets and hidden away in the Workhouse" (191). Certainly by modern standards Nesbit could be viewed as "racist," but as Greenburg notes, "Her anarchic disdain for economic 'progress,' her aesthetic distress over the ugliness of modernization ... distinguish her brand of socialism from that of her husband" (205) and from the Fabians who showed "limited support for the war and for colonialism based on a Fabianized version of the 'white man's burden'" (177). Supporting this idea, Nesbit's Fabian work primarily focused "attention ... [on] the care and well-being of children, and the elimination of poverty and its attendant dirt and ugliness" (Greenburg 228). On the one hand, using the term "black" to describe the poverty-stricken orphan is troubling for its appropriation of racial identification and stereotyping as a means to dramatize the suffering of a white child. On the other, Nesbit's way of implicating race in a discussion of poverty in general, and of covertly arguing against her husband's opinions, may be viewed as progressive when taken in context.

Combined with the narrator's disclaimer, the title of the chapter makes one wonder why Nesbit would choose to use a white rather than a black child to illustrate the problem of poverty. The most obvious answer is that Nesbit assumes (unfortunately, but probably correctly) that the readers of her time will be more knowledgeable about and sympathetic to the suffering of a white child. Interestingly, in using such a strategy Nesbit parallels some nineteenth and early twentieth-century abolitionists, particularly Susan B. Anthony, whose famous "Women's Right to Vote" speech likens women to "slaves" and argues that "every discrimination against women in the constitutions and laws of the several States is today null and void, precisely as is every one against Negroes" (*American Rhetoric*). So while Nesbit herself avoided feminist participation, her associations with prominent women of the movement, including Annie Besant, whose name appears on an advertisement for a British Museum lecture in *Amulet* (147), apparently influenced her, at least subconsciously. Given her time and social position, perhaps Nesbit also felt unqualified or simply uninterested in directly tackling racism in a book that is ostensibly written for children.

Like Nesbit, Eager can possibly be forgiven to an extent. That he addresses racism at all places him among the early authors of postmodern children's literature, which began by "disrupting expectations of traditional storytelling modes, and acknowledging children as natural deconstructive readers" (Thacker 141) by tackling so-called "taboo" topics such as divorce, death, prejudice, sexuality, neglect and abuse. Even though Nesbit is cagier in her approach, Eager also follows Nesbit in providing an unexpected forum for confronting racism in public discourse, encouraging children to ask questions and to investigate their own understanding of difficult issues such as difference and inequality. Eager goes much further than Nesbit in performing what Karen Coats calls an "intervention ... a conscious assumption of our position as raced subjects combined with a conscious challenging and displacement of the secondary signifiers of Whiteness" (135). At the same time, Eager interrogates prejudice by imitating Nesbit, devising concrete and metaphorical portals through which his child characters engage in historical situations meant to reflect upon social and political conditions in his own time. His effort does not wholly succeed; his awkwardness in handling the sensitive subject matter undermines the effect, and occasionally ends up "turning Nesbit's radical socialist vision into small change" (Richey 268). Nevertheless, looking at his work in terms of the portal as a device for such intricate, volatile expression helps to intensify the power of Nesbit's achievement, increasing our understanding of the particular constraints that would have bound her voice and of her apparent effort to overcome them.

Child versus Adult: Imaginative Power and the Heart's Desire

Unlike Eager, who sometimes lets adults in on the magic, Nesbit "keeps the magical realm of children clearly off limits" to adults (Richey 259). As a function of her ability "to remember just what it felt like to be a child" (Bell 74), she places all of the magic in the hands of her young characters, making them porters for the transformation of adults and of society. One of the rare grown-ups who engage with magic in Nesbit's children's fantasies, the Learned Gentleman in *Amulet* provides a key example of her use of magical agency to elevate both the child character/reader and the woman writer. The Learned Gentleman was most likely fashioned after Wallis Budge, Nesbit's friend and possible lover, the British Museum curator who had the same "wide-ranging knowledge of early cultures." Budge helped Nesbit with her research for the book and the design of the charm's shape, as well as conceiving parts of the plot involving ancient Egypt and the Priest Rekh-marā (Briggs 246–7).

As his name implies, the Learned Gentleman represents the loss of imagination that results from overdeveloped adult rationality. When the children first befriend the boarder in the Old Nurse's house and seek his help in learning how to use the amulet, he thinks they are playing a game. His difficulty in saying "make-believe" causes the Learned Gentleman to sound like "one who recalls and pronounces a long forgotten word" (85). Earlier when they ask him to give his word not to create his own term that might override the word of power he gives to them, the narrator explains how "some faint memory of a far-off childhood must have come to the learned gentleman just then, for he smiled" (*Amulet* 39). In Wordsworthian terms, the Learned Gentleman has never reached his true potential because as an adult he has relied purely on empirical knowledge, represented by his very adult assessment that the "days of magic are over" (Nesbit *Amulet* 40).

As he spends more and more time with the children and even journeys with them through the amulet, the Learned Gentleman becomes more alive as he reconnects with a part of himself he had long forgotten. When the children take him to Atlantis, Anthea asks the Learned Gentleman for his name and he replies, "When I was your age I was called Jimmy ... Would you mind? I should feel more at home in a dream like this if I — anything that made me seem more like one of you" (*Amulet* 163). In this same episode Nesbit reverses the traditional roles when the children have difficulty in convincing Jimmy, who wants to see "the end of the dream," to leave Atlantis before it disappears into the sea. Sounding like a mother, Anthea threatens, "Oh, *Jimmy*! ... I'll *never* bring you out again!" (*Amulet* 176, emphasis in original). The Psammead confirms the child-adult role transposition after they return home, saying, "Never again ... will I go into the Past with a grown-up person! I will say for you four, you do as you're told" (*Amulet* 178). The Psammead's remark, rendered in a distinctly adult voice, reminds us that the adventurers are still children, making them relatable to the young reader who is also subject to adult authority. More importantly, the magical creature's refusal to "go into the Past with a grown-up person" identifies the children as more savvy in the ways of magic and by extension more powerful than those adults who normally preside over them. While their parents, teachers, and other authorities dominate the real world, children operate in and control the realm of possibility, a boundless place. The amulet is the concrete catalyst of the change in the Learned Gentleman as he finds some sense of the wonder he had lost, but the magic only works via the children's implementation and the choices they make to go to various places in search of the amulet's other half.

A problem emerges around gender and the child/adult power dynamic in *Amulet* since it is actually the Learned Gentleman's deepest wish rather than their own that the children satisfy by using the magical charm portal. The idea of the "heart's desire" occurs directly or indirectly in all of Nesbit's children's stories, usually as a goal to reunite with one's parent(s). Even in *The Railway Children* (1906), one of Nesbit's non-magical tales, the children's efforts hinge on their desire to help their father clear his name and return home from prison. In *Amulet*, Nesbit makes the objective clear from the start when the Psammead explains that if they can find the charm's other half lost somewhere in time, the children "will be able to have [their] heart's desire" (24). Anthea articulates this wish as "getting Father and Mother back safe" (25), which is exactly what occurs in the story's conclusion, after the children successfully fuse the two halves.

It is important to recognize that the union of the amulet's pieces actually occurs *after* the letter comes announcing the impending return of the children's parents and their baby brother The Lamb. Jane puts the letter in a drawer without reading it; so the children's "heart's desire" was already well on its way to being fulfilled long before the children even find the amulet's other half. In the end, the real "heart's desire" that comes true via the magic is that of the Learned Gentleman and his alter ego, the ancient Egyptian priest Rekh-marā. On the surface this is troubling since the story ends with the young adventurers returning to their mundane world and their parents' control while, as the amulet's keeper, the Learned Gentleman, a white man, takes on an even more prominent position than that which by virtue of biology he already occupies. A more careful study of this aspect of *Amulet*, however, illustrates that the children's role and use of the magic actually confirms the power position they hold throughout the story.

Upon returning to their own place and time with the long-lost treasure and Rekh-marā in tow, the children allow the amulet pieces to fuse by placing them next to one another on a quilt in the Learned Gentleman's room. After acknowledging that the children are already on their way to getting their "hearts' desire," Anthea asks Rekh-marā to describe his own. He replies, "Great and deep learning," but admits such knowledge would be "useless" back in his own time (287). Offering a resolution, the Voice of the amulet says, "a soul may live, if in that other time and land there be found a soul so akin to it as to offer it refuge in the body of that land and time." Upon hearing these words, "the eyes of Rekh-marā and the Learned Gentlemen [meet], and ... [promise] each other many things, secret and sacred and very beautiful" (289). The children use the amulet as a portal one last time to enable the two men to become one in the same way that the charm's two halves meld just prior to this scene (290). Here Nesbit indicates the final step in the Learned Gentleman's transformation is from overly serious scholar to one who now possesses not only "great and deep learning" but also, as a result of the children's influence, the imaginative capacity to turn it into something really useful.

In what is easily Nesbit's most sophisticated use of magical agency in any of her stories, the Learned Gentleman, representing a very adult, empirical approach to life, and Rekh-marā, personifying the children's efforts to retrieve the amulet's lost half through magic, come together to form a whole. The two men mirror the process by which the charm becomes whole, reinforcing its importance as a symbol and intensifying the children's roles as porters, the operators of the charm. This time, however, the end result is not an enchanted amulet, but something better: a whole person. As Claudia Nelson indicates, for Nesbit "completeness ... consists of combining the virtues of maleness with those of femaleness, not rejecting one for the other" (12). Given rationality as a stereotypically masculine quality, Rekh-marā becomes the "feminine," i.e., imaginative half in this union. Interestingly, there may be a racial implication here as well since Rekh-marā is Egyptian, but it remains difficult to determine whether Nesbit means an act of white colonization or a more progressive union of two parts that come together despite cultural — and even temporal — difference.

Regardless, we know that the Learned Gentleman ends up putting his new persona to good use because in an earlier episode the children journey into the future and find him holding the complete amulet. Surrounded by the evidence of his "fame and fortune" gained by writing books based on the "dreams" he recalled from his expeditions with the children, the Learned Gentleman says, "After you'd given me the whole of the Amulet ... somehow I didn't need to theorize, I seemed to know about the old Egyptian civilization" (244). The Learned Gentleman's success results from his young friends' use of the magical charm, and their influence on his life helps him to find a part of himself he seems to have sacrificed to his studies and to maturity, a lost part embodied by the ancient Egyptian Priest. When he is made whole, the Learned Gentleman contributes to the world's knowledge of past civilizations and, enlarged, Nesbit's portrayal of the children's influence on him elevates the child and the imagination to a place of power in society.

In *Enchanted Castle*, the ring enables a similar union between two individuals, although in this case the two parties are a man and a woman rather than halves of a single soul. The children's interactions with magic bring together the "castle's" owner Lord Yalding and his long-lost love, Mademoiselle, who use the ring as a wedding band. Here the magic initially appears much more as a part of the mundane world than it does in the case of the amulet, which in the end retains its mythical qualities as an object of antiquity in the British Museum. In *Enchanted Castle*, while standing in the Hall of Granted Wishes, Mademoiselle explains the history of the ring, which had been given to Lord Yalding's ancestor by a lady of her own family's house so "that he might build her a garden." The castle "is built partly by his love and partly by that magic" (238). In a voice that seems to be channeled through her from an eternal, magical source, Mademoiselle adds, "Except from children ... the ring exacts a payment.... Only one wish is free." Lord Yalding uses this wish, asking "that all the magic this ring has wrought may be undone, and that the ring itself may be no more and no less than a charm to bind thee and me together forevermore" (Nesbit *Enchanted* 238–9).

The story's ending implies a casting off of magic in favor of reality, but the narrator counteracts this possibility by saying, "A plain gold ring was used in the [marriage] ceremony, and this, if you come to think of it, could be no other than the magic ring, turned, by that last wish, into a charm to keep [Lord Yalding] and his wife together for ever" (240). As in the case of the amulet, via the children's implementation and ownership, the ring in *Enchanted Castle* powerfully enables a fusion of two souls who will presumably create one life together. The story implies that without the children's collective ability to imagine and enact the ring's potential, the reunion of two lovers originally parted by his family's rejection of her based on material concerns would not be possible.

Another way magic provides children with power over adults in Nesbit's fantasies is through words. As Lurie reminds us, "To a small child words are magical." An infant cannot communicate, so once he or she learns to speak, the new ability provides a perception of power, which plays out in fairy tales and fantasy in the form of spells and magic words (Lurie 197). In *Enchanted Castle*, Mabel uses a spoken "charm" of her own invention to reveal the treasures in the chamber (33), but an even clearer illustration of the word's importance in *Enchanted Castle* occurs when the children finally discover they have the ability to direct the way the ring operates simply by *saying* "what it is" (172). By figuring out this magic rule, they gain some control over the magic and begin to use it more efficiently; the power does not come without problems, however, as they come to discover that the exact wording of a wish is crucial. Nesbit transfigures the book into a portal in itself by defining language as having power to direct or alter the course of events, which she confirms in *Phoenix* and *Amulet*, where speaking a word invariably provides power.

The idea of telling tales occurs repeatedly, more often in *Phoenix* than in Nesbit's other fantasies, beginning with the title character's description of his history and his later narration of a story echoing *Sleeping Beauty*, a Nesbit favorite, while the girls are mending the magic carpet. Here the phoenix sounds like a stand-in for the author, complaining that "storytelling [is] quite impossible if people would keep interrupting" (Nesbit *Phoenix* 210). In *Amulet*, magic is defined as the "language that everyone could understand" (45), and the ritual of using the charm does not work unless the holder of the charm speaks the "word of power," a collection of symbols engraved on the charm (33). Given the amulet's maternal association (44), the link between power, imagination, and language reflects back to Nesbit, a mother and author who tells tales of magic in an approximation of her own voice. As such she provides herself with an outlet for revealing her innermost thoughts in a way she might not feel comfortable doing in a society where imaginative belief has been replaced by the motor-car and the electric light.

Invariably Nesbit's child characters use magic to influence adult behavior and to express perspectives on issues they themselves often do not fully understand. Echoing the confusion felt by their real-world counterparts trying to comprehend adult rules, Nesbit's children often misuse or misunderstand the magic, but they persist in believing such power exists. In contrast, the adults they meet almost always show unbelief, for which the children and their creator paint them as silly and unfulfilled until, through magic, the children show them the way. Using the printed word as a kind of magic wand, Nesbit rejects the idealized Romantic and Victorian stereotype by making her child characters imperfect but endowing them with power to which the real-world child can relate and aspire. Most significantly, she empowers herself as a female writer by showing how even a supposedly benign form, the "children's" book, can be used for a profound purpose, beyond simplistic moral instruction, to shape the ideas of the next generation (and those of their parents). In the process Nesbit frees her own voice and the voices of many subsequent authors in children's literature and fantasy more broadly, ultimately elevating an art form and means of political engagement whose power extends far beyond the illusory boundaries of childhood.

CHAPTER FOUR

Lost Boys to Men: Romanticism and the Magic of the Female Imagination in J.M. Barrie's *Peter Pan* and Frances Hodgson Burnett's *The Secret Garden**

> *Our birth is but a sleep and a forgetting:*
> *The Soul that rises with us, our life's Star,*
> *Hath had elsewhere its setting,*
> *And cometh from afar:*
> *Not in entire forgetfulness,*
> *And not in utter nakedness,*
> *But trailing clouds of glory do we come*
> *From God, who is our home...*
>
> —*William Wordsworth*, "Ode: Intimations of Immortality
> from Recollections of Early Childhood" [V. 58–65]

Although writing around the same time as E. Nesbit, J.M. Barrie (1860–1937) and Frances Hodgson Burnett (1849–1924) provide unique variations of the portal device by mixing conventions of children's literature and fantasy with interpretations of Romantic ideas on childhood, maturation, and imagination. While most of the work of the Romantics predates that of Barrie and Burnett by nearly a century, William Wordsworth (1770–1850) and his colleagues obviously influenced philosophies on art, education, politics, and human development throughout the 1800s and 1900s, and indeed into our own time. Barrie's *Peter Pan* and Burnett's *The Secret Garden* dramatize ideas about child versus adult perception, particularly in regard to memory and the creative process. Likening the concept of the Romantic sublime to the sense of wonder evoked by literary fantasy, David Sandner sees both as representing a "tearing of a veil between this world and another

*An earlier version of this chapter appeared as "Lost Boys to Men" in Deborah Bice (ed.), *Elsewhere: Selected Essays from the "20th Century Fantasy Literature: From Beatrix to Harry" International Library Conference* (Lanham, MD: University Press of America, 2003).

field of experience altogether." To achieve "the moment of unity," says Sandner, "requires ... a loss of the self" (52). Sandner's image of a "veil" approximates a portal and applies to *Peter Pan* and *Secret Garden,* both of which revolve around a young girl through whom imagination becomes a transformative influence on the males surrounding her.

Sandner goes on to explain Romantic "loss" as "a freeing of the self" that occurs "through two distinct kinds of forgetfulness ... two distinct states of being — the world and the world of spirit — each requiring one to forget about the other state" (52). In *Peter Pan* and *Secret Garden* this loss/freeing occurs to varying degrees for both the heroine and her male companions, but "the moment of unity" is really only achieved by the boys/men. Each girl's personal "loss of self" becomes permanent rather than transitional as the phases of her maturation resonate to enable the growth of the male figures in her life. It is important here to acknowledge that *Secret Garden* does not, of course, include magic in a *super*natural sense, but is generally classified among the "coincidence-filled" Victorian and Edwardian children's works accepted as "fairy tales ... whether or not magic and the supernatural literally enter the story" (Stolzenbach 25). In keeping with low fantasy convention, Wendy and Mary do travel via concrete portals: the Darlings' nursery window and the hidden gate of Mary's "secret garden." In both *Peter Pan* and *Secret Garden,* the metaphorical portal becomes a function of female creativity that is also bound to maternity as little girls become magical agents of re-birth for "boys" to become "men." Although they are most often viewed as minor characters, this chapter argues the importance of *Peter Pan*'s Mr. Darling and *Secret Garden*'s Mr. Craven in each story's portrayal of the female imagination as a kind of mortal magic. By moving between the realms of imagination and rationality, Wendy and Mary each perform an act for the men in their lives akin to that which the Romantic poet imagines doing for his society, but in a distinctly feminine fashion.

Although the Romantic ideal of the poet's unifying role implies a positive move, we must keep in mind that the most well-known Romantic poets — who were all male — tended to use the process whether intentionally or not to erase or appropriate "other" voices, especially of women who appear as subjects or silent auditors. Anne Mellor assesses that Wordsworth's women are permitted to "exist only as embodiments of an undifferentiated life cycle that moves inexorably from birth to death" (19). Wordsworth often uses his sister Dorothy as a silent emblem for nature, with the rationale being that as a woman she is closer to the state of childhood and therefore closer to pre-existence than the poet. For example, as the silent auditor in "Lines Composed a Few Miles Above Tintern Abbey," Dorothy is held up as a "less conscious being whose function is to mirror and thus to guarantee the truth of the poet's development and perceptions" (Mellor 19). In this way Barrie and Burnett are progressive in diverging from their Romantic tendencies enough to place girls into the artistic role normally occupied by adult men. Ultimately, though, *Peter Pan* and *Secret Garden* succumb to gender stereotyping in place at the time of their conception, by depicting assertive and inventive girl characters who in the end retreat to the background rather than taking credit for the men they "create."

Forgetting and Remembering

As M.H. Abrams describes in *Natural Supernaturalism*, for the Romantics, "division, separateness, externality, [and] isolation" are synonymous with "evil and death" as consequences of the biblical Fall. In humanist terms one might just as well add "adulthood" to "evil and death" here, since the Romantics also see such "division" from the divine as an unfortunate but inevitable condition of aging. According to Wordsworth's belief in a state of pre-existence ("Our birth is but a sleep and a forgetting") from which a person becomes increasingly estranged over time, the act of fusing memory and imagination to retain access to childhood perspective is crucial to healing the "division," and thus achieving healthy adulthood. For Wordsworth, this kind of imaginative re-creation can "enshrine the spirit of the Past for future restoration" (Bloom 161) as a way of dealing with or more fully experiencing the present. Recollections may be bittersweet or even frightening, but the ability to remember — and more importantly, to process memory intellectually and emotionally — are wholly positive for Wordsworth.

Since this process enables and usually occurs as a function of meaningful interaction between nature (i.e., life, the divine, the universe) and the human being, one who lacks the imagination or the inclination to keep childhood perspective alive appears stunted, rooted in present reality without the means to make sense of it. In *Peter Pan*, Mr. Darling and Peter himself provide prime examples, as do Colin and his father Mr. Craven in *Secret Garden*. While Peter does not change from the beginning to the end of the story (and therefore defines lack of growth as negative), Darling does change in a positive way, and the same can be said for Colin and Craven in *Secret Garden*.

Romantic philosophy helps to explain the "separateness" these characters personify by making the poet and/or work of art an intermediary in "a metaphysics of integration of which the key principle is that of the 'reconciliation' or synthesis of whatever is divided, opposed and conflicting" (Abrams 182). Put another way, the artist and his work together act as the agents of "integration" or healing in Society. The collaboration and its outcome are akin to the metaphorical portal/porter, a character, place, or object that serves as the conduit and as a magical agent linking Primary and Secondary space. In Wordsworthian terms, *Peter Pan* and *The Secret Garden* each highlight themes of forgetting and remembering, and perhaps more importantly, of *being forgotten* or *remembered* to symbolically represent in gendered terms this process of separation/integration as a function of human (male) development. The female imagination, individually wielded by Wendy and Mary, provides the agent of renewal or Romantic "integration."

Understanding the way Wendy functions as an intermediary for her father starts with a look at the consequences of not "growing up" as personified by Mr. Darling's antithesis, Peter Pan. For Wordsworth, memory carried both positive and negative connotations, an idea that informs both *Peter Pan* and *Secret Garden*. In Book Twelfth of *The Prelude*, Wordsworth speaks of the "spots of time / That with distinct pre-eminence retain / A renovating virtue," that furnish the "profoundest knowledge" and uplift a person in a time of sadness or uncertainty (208–9, 221). Yet in giving an example, the poet describes a memory of "stumbling on" a place "where in former times / A murderer had been hung in iron chains" (*Prelude* 234, 236), causing him to flee with fear (*Prelude* 240–46). The notion of memory as a double-edged sword appears most prominently in *Peter Pan* in the way Barrie characterizes the boy who refuses to grow up as both an emblem of youth and a harbinger of a child's death, or the death of imagination that prevents an adult from accessing Never-land. Euphemistically, children — that is, *boy* children — end up there by "fall[ing] out of their perambulators when the nurse is looking the other way" (Barrie 44). The name "Never-land" itself connotes a negative or "nothing" space from which one is unlikely to return. In other words, remembering too vividly or keeping too tight a grasp on one's childhood self equates to premature death, the failure of natural maturation, a state often attributed to Barrie himself.

Much has been said about Barrie's brother David and the probable influence of his early death on the story, so I will not retread that ground here. More important is to recognize how Barrie treats the issue of death by highlighting its contrary in *Peter Pan*. In this way the author also emphasizes an important connection between memory and feminine creativity. Peter's immortality hinges upon his insistence in not recognizing or remembering his biological mother, which compels his continual quest for make-believe mothers, principally Wendy, and presumably before her, Mrs. Darling. Here memory becomes inescapably tied to maternity. For example, when Wendy plays a game meant to encourage the Lost Boys to remember their mothers, Peter refuses to compete because "he despise[s] all mothers except Wendy" (109). While on the one hand, maternity constitutes an act of creation, on the other — for Peter at least — acknowledging a mother means becoming a real boy and thus relinquishing eternal creativity (life). Instead he chooses to forget his actual mother in favor of taking perpetual surrogates, all of whom grow up and forget about him, just as he does them. In this way Peter can be understood as enacting a Wordsworthian erasure of unpleasant or unflattering past moments.

The most significant illustrations of the connection between memory and female creative power in *Peter Pan* have to do with Mr. Darling, the primary recipient of Wendy's activity as a porter. From the beginning Barrie establishes Darling as the epitome of the Edwardian businessman, the complete opposite of Peter and of the author himself. Wendy and her brothers are able to fly after Peter through the window because their parents have gone away to a dinner party, effectively forgetting them for a while and leaving only Nana to insistently remember her duty (Barrie 50–1). The fact that a dog — a female one — shows more concern about the young Darlings' welfare than their father, who ignores her warning about Peter, suggests Barrie's estimation of the head of the household as he exists prior to Wendy's departure and return. Nana's recognition of Peter as a threat illustrates that even the dog has more imagination than the children's father, who has "a passion for being exactly like his neighbors" (Barrie 10). One might argue that accepting a dog as a nurse for his children takes more than a little whimsicality, but Barrie's narrator positions Nana's hiring as a function of economics: "As they were poor ... this nurse was a prim Newfoundland dog ... who had belonged to no one in particular until the Darlings engaged her" (10). In ignoring Nana, then, Darling represents not only a lack of creativity but also demonstrates his materialism, which causes him to forget what should be most important in life: his children, and by extension his own child self. By juxtaposing imagination with Darling's overwhelming concern for appearances, Barrie paints the ability to make-believe as more appealing and even virtuous.

The episode in which Wendy's father tricks Nana into taking his own medicine as a ruse to get Michael to take his (Barrie 27–31) offers an even clearer indication of the father's need of Romantic integration. Leaving him feeling "frightfully ashamed of himself" but unwilling to admit it, the incident is described by Darling as "only a joke." Rather than illustrating a child-*like* imagination, though, Barrie presents Darling as child-*ish,* and not a little vindictive in his attitude toward the canine nursemaid who seems to trump him in his children's hearts. The narrator explains Darling's behavior as "all owing to his too affectionate nature, which craved for admiration," but Barrie's characterization of Darling up until this point reveals this need for respect has more to do with misplaced pride, with his wanting to "show who [is] master of the house" and to maintain a certain position in his neighbors' estimation (30–1), since his bank account grants him lower social status.

Like Darling, Peter shows a similar tendency toward trickery and pride; his "crowing" is what really irks his nemesis and Darling stand-in Captain Hook, and Peter mirrors the medicine-switching act later in the story by deciding to shut the window so Wendy will think her mother has forgotten about her near the end of the story (221–22). The prank confirms that Peter "is not without his dark side" (Lurie 130). Likewise, in Romantic terms, Catherine Robson reminds us that in *The Prelude* Wordsworth "makes no attempt to represent ... [his childhood] as a time of moral innocence" (18). By designing Peter as the epitome of "youth" and "joy" (206), Barrie points up the childishness Darling will have to overcome if he wants to become a real adult, instead of merely an overly rational person. Barrie excuses Peter's joking, however cruel it may seem, while depicting Darling as a man and a father who should probably know better. Early in the novel, Barrie establishes the significance of Wendy's role by suggesting that Darling must recognize the difference between immature practical joking and real imaginative play, a difference that his children intuitively acknowledge through their disapproval of his behavior toward Nana. The medicine episode reveals how far Darling must progress toward Wordsworthian remembering in the course of the story, which intensifies Wendy's importance as the catalyst for this change.

Secret Garden even more explicitly conveys the experience of being forgotten in a variety of ways, both positive and negative. The story starts with Mary living with her parents in India but spending most of her time with her *Ayah* (nanny). When the cholera kills the *Ayah* and Mary's parents, she sleeps through the mass exodus and gets left behind because the adults are "too panic-stricken to think of a little girl no one was fond of" (Burnett 5). The official who finally finds her comments to his companion, "It is the child no one ever saw! ... She has actually been *forgotten*" (Burnett 6, emphasis added). Initially at least, Mary's situation does not greatly improve in England. Her uncle leaves her in the hands of servants at the big lonely manor in the rainy countryside that, despite being her homeland, feels completely foreign to Mary. In fact, Craven only remembers her existence after Dickon's mother Susan Sowerby, who has never before spoken to him, sees him in the village and asks about her. Dickon's sister Martha, a maid at the estate who becomes Mary's primary caretaker, relates the details of the encounter to her, saying Craven "forgot, but Mother hadn't, an' she made bold to stop him" (Burnett 114). The incident foreshadows the importance of Mrs. Sowerby as the only living biological mother in the story and supports remembering as a function of feminine creativity, particularly since Martha's mother accepts the children's "play actin'" in the garden, unlike the other adults in the story.

Being ignored by Craven leaves Mary to her own devices, which in turn leads her to the garden, a forgotten place that, as Martha explains, Craven had "shut when his wife died," burying the key in the ground (34). The lord of the manor treats his only son Colin similarly, keeping him "locked up" in his secret wing of the house. His father only visits when the boy sleeps and he forbids the servants to discuss Colin or even admit that he exists (Burnett 128–9). Phyllis Bixler makes the point that Colin and Mary are parallel "sufferers of parental abandonment and neglect" (44). The crying that leads Mary to discover Colin echoes "her own grieving self finally being heard from some unconscious recess" (Bixler 34). The intuition that attracts Mary to the lost garden also takes her to the lost boy, Colin. The three become tightly linked, creating the force that will eventually allow them to be remembered — not only by Craven, but also by society.

Without Mary's entrance into the manor, all three — Mary, Colin, and the garden — would presumably have remained "locked up," but being forgotten in *Secret Garden* also has its positive qualities, and these also hinge upon Mary's creativity. In a Romantic sense, her association with the garden (i.e., nature) helps Mary and Colin to *forget themselves* and become normal children. As Sandner explains, Wordsworth and Samuel Taylor Coleridge base their defense of the fairy tale on the rationale that "realistic children's stories only serve to make children more acutely self-conscious and prideful. It is better to release them into fairy tales and the imagination ... closer to the remembrance of the glory of the world of the spirit" (Sandner 53). Burnett illustrates this most vividly in the way other characters and the narrator describe Mary and Colin as miniature adults. When Mrs. Medlock first sees Mary she says, "But you are like an old woman" (Burnett 14), and Martha has a similar reaction later, saying, "Tha 'art a queer, old-womanish thing" (Burnett 72).

In the process of cultivating and of being cultivated by the garden, Mary almost magically transforms into her proper state as a little girl. She forgets her self-centeredness and develops a more external outlook that enables her to help Colin do the same. He acknowledges this by telling Dr. Craven, "When I lie by myself and *remember* I begin to have pains everywhere.... It is because ... [Mary] makes me *forget* that she makes me better" (Burnett 194, emphasis added). Again, in a Wordsworthian sense, Mary and Colin each connect to a childhood self that neither has ever really experienced. In their case, the claiming process is especially significant since their adult approach to life is unnatural for their age. In a book where nature represents such a positive force, anything that appears as *un*-natural is clearly broken and wrong, providing the "evil" in this realistic fairy tale. Mary finds her child self through her connection with nature, as her time outdoors stirs her imagination and physically strengthens her. Indeed she finds the key to the hidden garden gate with the help of the robin, an inhabitant as well as an emblem of spring and of the natural world (Burnett 74–75). Further, she has help cultivating the garden from Dickon, the Pan figure and veritable child of nature. In contrast to Colin, whom Mary notices continually talks about dying, Dickon represents life by spending most of his time outdoors, often rescuing and nurturing animals in need.

Rather than existing through some supernatural means, such as a wizard or fairy godmother, the long-ignored garden almost literally springs to life out of Mary's imagination. She creates her own portal to growth and change by cultivating the "secret" space, which only becomes possible because she can envision that it might one day bloom again. In representing "that which is dead or apparently dead in the past," the garden comes to illustrate "the illness and ill-temper which the children put behind them" (Koppes 210). Of course, as Phyllis Bixler Koppes acknowledges, the garden is inextricable from the memory of Colin's late mother and of the living father who locks the gate in an unsuccessful attempt to forget her. Certainly the connection to Colin's mother is important, but while she admits "the garden also represents the redemptive magic which can infuse the present and future" (210), Koppes underestimates Mary's importance as a creative force in the garden. Indeed, the "future" the garden has the potential to enable is a direct result of the girl's intrusion into the place that Colin's father purposely seals, in the same way that he conceals his son from the outside world. More than Colin's assertion that he will "live for ever and ever" (Burnett 214), Mary's recognition of the garden's potential, both to grow and to help transform Colin into a real boy, hinges on her creative vision and her ability to understand — to process in a Wordsworthian sense — the raw material of the garden's impact on *her*.

Such is the story's most important "sublime moment" in Romantic terms, not unlike the experience Wordsworth describes in Book Fourteenth of *The Prelude* when he ascends Mt. Snowden and recognizes a "transcendent power ... which Nature thus / To bodily sense exhibits" (80, 86–7). Mary feels a parallel awe as she enters the garden and for the first time realizes "she somehow [does] not feel lonely at all" (Burnett 80). For Mary finding the key "actually awaken[s] her imagination" (Burnett 67) and she sees the garden as "the sweetest, most mysterious-looking place anyone could imagine" (Burnett 78). As Mary takes in its "fresh scent of the damp earth" (Burnett 80), she begins to feel truly alive for the first time. Burnett positions this feeling as a trigger for Mary's imagination, which has been lying dormant within her, and which has been further stifled due to her being forgotten by adults. Imagination comes more naturally to a child such as Dickon, for example, whose mother shows love and encourages exploration.

Despite the superficial similarities between Dickon and Peter as "Pan" figures, the boy who more closely resembles Peter in *Secret Garden* is not Dickon but Colin, who rejects his mother's existence by keeping her portrait concealed behind a curtain in his room (Burnett 134–5). While Colin's situation is more dire, he and Peter share an association with notions of living and dying. Both live in fear: Peter refuses to grow up because he is afraid to lose his youthful freedom, and Colin has been conditioned to believe he will "not live to grow up" (Burnett 130). As a result, Colin shuns virtually every kind of experience that might be dangerous to his health — that is, until his association with Mary, Dickon, and the garden provide an antidote to the mischief his father — another Peter Pan figure — has done through his own refusal to really live after his wife's death. Unlike Colin and Peter, Dickon has an active, practical parent who appreciates her children's need to indulge their imaginations. Further, Dickon's obvious kinship with the natural world, one that includes death (defined in just one example by the case of the orphaned lamb he adopts) characterizes Burnett's Pan figure as one who accepts death's inevitability while embracing life, having the imagination to share Mary's vision.

Dickon clearly personifies nature, but it is Mary who opens the gate and sees the garden's potential, as the narrator describes: "She looked in the old border-beds and among the grass, and after she had gone round, trying to miss nothing, she had found ever so many more sharp, pale green points, and she had become quite excited again. 'It isn't a quite dead garden'" (Burnett 81). Later Dickon confirms Mary's belief in the garden's vitality when he notices the weeding she had done previously even though "[s]he did not know anything about gardening" (Burnett 81). When she shows him her work, he affirms her intuition, saying, "A gardener couldn't have told thee better" (105). Similarly, Dickon recognizes the garden's potential to help Colin, yet again he does this as a result of Mary's agency, after she has already thought of letting Colin in on the secret for his own good. When she tells Dickon "her story" of the other boy's plight, he says "we mun get him out here [in the garden].... An' we munnot lose no time about it" (Burnett 185). Here Mary speaks Colin's existence into being for Dickon, figuratively initiating the process by which Colin will become a real boy, and by extension forging his path to manhood. Mary's storytelling is similar to what Wendy does when she tries to help her brothers remember their father, as I discuss later in this chapter.

Since Mary refrains from telling Colin she has actually been inside the garden several times, her descriptions of it carry even more weight as creative output, for he thinks she is telling him a tale of how she *imagines* the garden to be rather than reporting how it really is. Through her stories, Mary's porter status intensifies as she creates the garden for Colin in the same way she creates India for him by talking about her experiences there. She helps him not only by cultivating the place that turns out to be the setting for his return to the world, but also by first making it live for him *through* her imagination. In this way Mary furnishes Colin access to this Other-world while he remains in bed. This makes the garden appear as even more a function of Mary's imagination than it does for her having found it and cultivated it in the first place. Her own transformation happens via her interaction with nature both before and after she finds the secret garden. When her recognition of nature's healing properties stirs her inherent, youthful imagination, she can pass on what she learns to Colin. In other words, Mary's transformation remains incomplete until she can apply what she has learned to save someone else.

Illustrating Burnett's unique combination of humanism and Christianity, the process calls to mind Thomas Carlyle (1795–1881), one of the foremost philosophers of the nineteenth century and a powerful influence on Romantic and Victorian thought. In *Sartor Resartus*, Carlyle approaches the problem of religious doubt through the experience of the fictional Professor Diogenes Teufeldrockh. The text follows the professor as he moves from "The Everlasting No," a state of alienation mirroring that felt by the citizen of the age, to "The Everlasting Yeah," when he decides that having found his ability to believe, such "conviction, were it ever so excellent, is worthless til it convert itself into Conduct" (Carlyle 984). At this point, the professor rejects self-centeredness in favor of concern for his fellow beings. In *Secret Garden* Mary mirrors this same process when she allows Colin access to "her" garden, first by using the imagination she has recently discovered within herself to show him the way to life. Later she makes an even more courageous and selfless move by actually taking him to the garden, a powerful gesture given her initial isolation and impulse to keep the place secret.

One of Burnett's "secularizations of the story about a saintly child who converts others" (Koppes 202), *Secret Garden* positions the path of conversion firmly in the realm of imagination. To be sure, Mary does not start out appearing "saintly," but it is her own need for growth that makes her effort to help others that much more powerful. Being initially remarked upon by others but totally unknown to herself, Mary's "disagreeable" nature can be forgiven based on her parents forgetting her virtually from birth. Mrs. Sowerby recognizes Mary's importance to Colin by saying, "It was a good thing that little lass came to th' Manor. It's been th' makin' o' her an' th' savin' o' him" (Burnett 249). Without Mary, Colin may otherwise have continued to waste away in bed, or fulfilled the unsubstantiated prediction of his untimely death. Supporting this idea, Burnett defines Colin as a true believer, "thankful to the Magic" he associates with "being alive ... being strong" (249). As the agent of this "magic" via her cultivation of the garden, Mary is the porter by which Colin becomes whole.

By extension, Mary's transformation of Colin also magically restores his father, which Burnett makes clear with a second intrusion into Craven's life by Mrs. Sowerby, one of the few adults allowed into the "secret" (Burnett 248). Her letter to Craven confirms his decision to return to Misselthwaite and the timing of its arrival roughly coincides with his son's growing health via his daily "exercises" in the garden (Burnett 288–9). Burnett's narrator describes how "the man who was 'coming alive' began to think in a new way and he thought long and steadily and deeply" (289). Thus even before returning to the Manor, Craven intuitively feels a change in himself, but he does not fully understand the feeling until he returns home to find his forgotten son walking around in the garden he thought he had cast aside forever.

Again in keeping with Carlyle's philosophy, Danielle E. Price recognizes that Mary's work in the garden represents the way her "strengths will be harnessed by patriarchal pleasure and imperial power.... [T]he beauty and comfort that Mary can provide are ultimately intended to serve another" (9). The idea also recalls the "Idealist Philosophy" of T.H. Green, a professor at Balliol (1870–1882), whose work underpinned what Jonathan Rose refers to as the "Edwardian Temperament." Rose glosses Green's ideas:

> The very existence of society ... is a tacit admission that man is a social animal and that the state can and should promote the common good.... Thought and society ... must logically have a uniting focus. That focus [Green] identified as God, or at any rate something like God — a "spiritual principle".... This philosophy made God the practical equivalent of man's social and intellectual achievements. He was therefore a finite and evolving God, continually enhanced by human progress, a God incarnated in history and immanent in all things [17].

In *Secret Garden* this "spiritual principle" is most obviously "immanent" in nature, but always with the added, equally important catalyst of imagination, the mechanism for processing all of the sensations and thoughts that nature evokes. Mary serves both Colin and his father, which Burnett's narrator supports by saying Craven "knew nothing of Magic [before returning home].... But the calm had brought a sort of courage and hope with it. Instead of giving way to thoughts of the worst he actually found he was trying to believe in better things" (290). Craven's transformation is even more

Wordsworthian than that of his son, since as a grown man he stands farther removed from pre-existence. Craven's name emphasizes his fearful avoidance of life, but like Colin, he finds a new self as a result of Mary's work in the garden. Without her intervention — a transgression akin to that of the biblical Eve, since Mary knowingly goes against Craven's edict sealing the garden — neither the man nor his son would become healed to the extent that they can take their rightful place and "promote the common good" (quoted in Rose 17) in society, which their aristocratic position demands.

"Those boys have found a mother": Mary and Wendy Grow Up

Although one is more firmly rooted in the real world, both the secret garden and Never-land are physical manifestations of female creativity, the place-type portals that become conduits for positive change, but only via the girls who conjure them. Mary's imagination is the agent of Colin's transformation from the time her stories about the garden intrigue him to such an extent that he focuses on her and on the "magical" place rather than on himself. His attention there remains especially appropriate since both he and the garden were forgotten at the same time, just after his mother's death ten years before. Through her vision of the garden as a place of renewed growth, Mary *reverses* the event that originally drove Craven to forget both the garden and his son. Again with a nod to Wordsworth, Catherine Robson sees the Victorian "idealization and idolization of little girls" as representing "not just the true essence of childhood, but an adult male's best opportunity of reconnecting with his own lost self" (3). Burnett carries out this concept in *Secret Garden*: both the forgetting and the remembering of Colin and the garden happen as a result of female agency. After his wife's death Craven closes the garden, which was her favorite place and originally cultivated by her; Mary's finding of the space eventually compels him to reopen both the garden and his heart.

Like Mary, who calls the garden a "fairy place," Wendy's imagination conjures Peter Pan, who only agrees to take her brothers to Never-land because of his wish to give the Lost Boys a "mother." Also like Mary, Wendy's storytelling provides the means for her and her brothers, along with the Lost Boys, to return to the real world. During their stay in Never-land, the children return the favor of their parents' forgetting about them for the evening by increasingly forgetting their lives at home, and especially their mother and father. As the oldest, Wendy retains the memory more vividly and for a longer period; in maternal fashion, she tries to keep that memory fresh for her brothers by telling them about home. Just as Wordsworth does, Barrie fuses imagination and memory by having Wendy use her mind to transform her diminishing impressions of her parents into a "story" that she tells the Boys. As a result, Wendy virtually creates Darling through her tale telling. She starts her tale, "There was once a gentleman ... [whose] name was Mr. Darling" (149–50), but ends with "See, dear brothers ... there is a window still standing open. Ah, now we are rewarded for our sublime faith in a mother's love" (Barrie 152). Wendy begins by reminding the boys of their father, but ends with the return home as a function of *maternal* affection. Here Barrie suggests the reintegration into the real world occurs in the same way as the child's initial entry into that world: via a mother whose love creates a "window," recalling the birth canal. In Wendy's case, the conjuring of her father's image in a story meant to stir her brothers' memories extends to Darling's simultaneous transformation while she is away. Mrs. Darling also plays a role in this process, but primarily as an older version of Wendy, an idea Barrie reinforces by making the girl so eager to play "mother" in Never-land.

Further reinforcing the transforming power of the female imagination in *Peter Pan*, Wendy stands at the center of the conflict between Hook and Peter, which imitates the opposition between Darling and Peter in the real world. It is widely known that from Barrie's time through today the same actor traditionally fills the role of both Hook and Darling, who never appear simultaneously. As the only other important adult male in the story, Hook approximates Darling's presence in Never-land. While Alison Lurie calls Peter and Hook "not so much opposites but two sides of the same coin" (131), the description seems more apt for Darling and Hook as real and imaginary icons of adulthood. As Lester Friedman points out, "By their very natures, pirates epitomize precisely the opposite of maturity as it is traditionally configured in our culture" (195). What Barrie does with Hook is to point up all of the negative and ridiculous qualities that define a *certain kind* of adulthood, which is being satirized in the novel's Darling/Peter and Hook/Peter juxtapositions. In other words, Hook performs a similar function as do the White Rabbit, Mad Hatter, and Queen of Hearts in Carroll's *Alice's Adventures in Wonderland*: to illustrate the absurdity of adults and of adult rationality from a child's perspective.

Further, by aligning the businessman (Darling) and the pirate (Hook), who both pursue profit-centered occupations, Barrie makes a clever commentary on industrial capitalism. The link between the two men (and the accepted view that Darling is a stand-in for Mr. Llewellyn-Davies) casts Darling as a socially sanctioned real-world pirate. Cecil DeGrotte Eby defines "a major theme of *Peter Pan* ... [a]s rejection of the traditional Victorian family, which placed the father as the central luminary around which wife and children revolved as dependent satellites" (Eby 131). In this way Darling "represents for Barrie the non-heroic, middle-class patriarch who measures the world with a stick calibrated in pounds and shillings" (Eby 131). The context provided by Darling's medicine-switching scene, Peter's defeat of Hook, and Darling's businessman/pirate personas combine to reinforce the opposition between Darling/Hook's adult materialism and Peter's youthful imagination. Once again Wendy's presence furnishes the catalyst for disruption and change.

Even though their animosity is long-lived, Peter and Hook do not actually square off and put an end to the feud until after Wendy arrives. Instead of seeing Hook as many critics do "as the serpent in the garden," Friedman rightly argues for "a more nuanced view [that] acknowledges the captain's sorrow as well as his malevolence: he is a desperately lonely, physically disabled, and emotionally damaged man who has focused his murderous rage on the person who maimed him" (216). Barrie makes this clear and reiterates Wendy's importance when Hook returns from a mission filled with "profound melancholy" and tells Smee, "Those boys have found a mother" (121–22). In fact, the final battle between Hook and Peter is brought about because the pirate kidnaps Wendy and the Boys. Just prior to this scene, Barrie provides a glimpse behind Hook's bravado, revealing the true source of the pirate's evil in his own words: "No little children love me" (187). Here Barrie collapses both Wendy's literal status as a child and her figurative role as a mother for the Lost Boys. Her presence creates such a difficulty for Hook that lashing out against Peter, the agent of her entry into Never-land, becomes inevitable. Hook destroys himself in the process, just as Darling seems to do figuratively when he tries to ignore Peter's threat against his children. As the pirate's real-world counterpart, however, Darling gets a second chance when Wendy finally leads her brothers back home.

Read this way, the battle scene takes on new importance. The narrator describes it thus: "Seeing Peter slowly advancing upon him ... [Hook] sprang upon the bulwarks to cast himself into the sea. He did not know that the crocodile was waiting for him; for we purposely stopped the clock that this knowledge might be spared him: a little mark of respect from us at the end" (Barrie 209). Since Hook exits by jumping overboard rather than being physically wounded by Peter, Barrie argues for balance, i.e., Romantic integration of imagination and rationality. Giving Hook such an end implies not that imagination should replace rationality, but rather that a healthy adult must try to avoid *all-consuming* materialism. Again Barrie seems to work within the context of Romantic philosophy, particularly as demonstrated in Wordsworth's *Prelude,* which generally "elects not to postulate a radical break between childhood and adulthood, choosing instead to see life as a continuum" (Robson 21). At first glance Peter himself might seem to be the instrument of Darling's transformation in these terms, but in actuality it is Wendy, not Peter, who provides the true catalyst, both for the story's events and for the change in her father. In this way Hook's jumping overboard, i.e., fully succumbing to Peter, represents a shedding of his adult self and foreshadows the transformation that Darling will undergo in the real world. The fact that Peter actually forgets Hook entirely when he returns to see the grown-up Wendy later in the story reinforces her importance in this process.

Through Peter's relationship with Wendy, and through the triangle of Peter/Wendy/Darling, Barrie further emphasizes "forgetting" as a key theme in the story. As mentioned above, Peter initially wants to lure Wendy alone to Never-land to provide a mother to the Lost Boys who "have no female companionship" (Barrie 44). Once there, Wendy establishes an ultra–Victorian household, spending most of her time doing traditionally maternal chores like darning, cleaning, and caring for the Boys as her children. After being told by Peter that his feelings for her are "those of a devoted son" (Barrie 145), she decides the time has come to return to her parents. Wendy takes the Lost Boys with her, which enables them to finally grow up as part of a real family (Barrie 226–27).

Back in the real world, Darling's discovery of Wendy's loss reminds him of her existence and his part in her leaving, so that he begins to forget his former self and becomes a new kind of father, the one who greets her so enthusiastically in the reunion scene. What really happens here is that Darling remembers or reclaims his imagination. Again conveying the power of female creativity, Barrie makes his ability to do so wholly bound by Wendy's loss/return. Essentially, Wendy creates her father as he becomes in the real world through the story she tells of him in Never-land; the two "stories" occur almost simultaneously in the text. Here memory carries both the negative and positive connotations with which Wordsworth endows it: her parents' leaving and Wendy's loss being negative; the final outcome of Wendy's return and her father's recognition of his shortcomings being positive.

Nearly every character in *Peter Pan* becomes transformed in some way over the course of the story, but Darling's change is arguably the most unexpected given Barrie's initial characterization of him. Barrie again reinforces Wendy's authority by naming the final chapter "Wendy Grows Up." The author also completes Darling's transformation by showing his response to his children's return and the prospect of finding space for the Lost Boys, as the narrator describes: "He burst into tears, and the truth came out. He was as glad to have them [all] as [his wife] was.... He went off dancing through the house and they all cried 'Hoop la!' and danced after him" (Barrie 227).

According to Carole Silver, the folk belief in the possibility of a child being stolen by fairies became a symbolic paradigm "for Victorian concerns with both loss of innocence and loss of self" (72). While Barrie's early scenes portray Darling as a "strong man" who "pooh pooh's" the existence of Peter Pan, by the end the he emerges as "quite a simple man ... [who] *might have passed for a boy again* if he had been able to take his baldness off" (216, emphasis added). The man who once calculated if he could afford to "keep" his own children now enthusiastically agrees to house, feed, and educate a large number of boys whose parentage and history are completely mysterious. The original Darling cares very much about "whether the neighbors talked" (12), but the transformed father tries to purge his guilt over scoffing at Nana by exercising his "noble sense of justice" by going "down on all fours and crawl[ing] into [her] kennel" (217), in which he insists on riding to and from his office each day.

While I agree with Allison Kavey that this behavior marks "a drastic departure from the world of acquired knowledge and evidence," her assessment that Darling's retreat "represents a return ... to the world of the imagined, rather than simply an expression of regret and shame" (100), needs to be qualified to account for Wendy's part in her father's transformation. I disagree that "by choosing the kennel, he is abandoning his role as a man," instead seeing Darling's taking to the kennel as a first sign of his move toward transformation into the kind of adult that recognizes the place of *both* whimsy and rationality. Admittedly, it is a silly move meant to provide comic relief, but the exaggeration is also necessary for getting across the idea of Darling's remarkable transformation. Although this change unfolds without Wendy's knowledge, her part in it is indisputable, giving her an implicit power few girls possess, either in fantasy or realistic fiction. Wendy retains this control through her memory; for in forgetting her parents she would forfeit her own ability to return to real life, a scenario Barrie clearly defines as negative. Also, while Wendy possesses the power to return home through the combination of imagination and memory, her parents must wait in ignorance and despair, believing their children to be lost forever. Barrie's narrator portrays the Darlings early in the story as they "sit there in the empty nursery, recalling fondly every smallest detail of that dreadful evening" when they had ignored Nana and opened the way for Peter to lead their children away (23). Lacking the child's ability to turn pretend into reality, the parents must wait until Wendy decides to shake off the forgetfulness of Never-land and take her brothers home.

Wendy's maturation coincides with Barrie's overall portrayal of imagination as necessary, but in moderation. Again this idea carries both positive and negative implications. Despite Wendy's importance, the story emphasizes Peter Pan as the central figure and the girl's role as primarily that of mother. On the island, Wendy is viewed this way by everyone, including Hook; and when she matures in the real world she happily settles in as a real wife and mother. In the end, rather than embracing Peter's refusal to mature as a positive idea, particularly in its treatment of Darling the story suggests that the imagination, while a splendid and valuable human faculty, cannot and should not take over one's life. Like Wordsworth, who believed the loss of "the hour / Of splendour in the grass" (*Prelude* 177–8) comes with the recompense of the "philosophic mind" (*Prelude* 185), in *Peter Pan* Barrie suggests the healthy adult is one who can accept maturation while tempering it with a sense that "the primal sympathy / which having been must ever be" (Wordsworth *Prelude* 213).

Peter Pan does indeed celebrate youth and make-believe, but also hints that "the childish imagination, splendid as it is, has the most terrible limitations, and can never (without growing up) come to terms with the real world" (Carpenter 179). These "limitations" are exemplified in Peter's perpetual return to claim a "new mother" in the form of the next generation of Wendys that he can indoctrinate into Never-land. Wendy herself matures to become a real mother, while instead of progressing, Peter remains trapped in a cycle of stagnation and longing. While a positive symbol of creative power and the freedom it provides, Peter is also isolated and lonely, which Barrie most poignantly reveals in the homecoming scene Peter watches from outside the window: "There could not have been a lovelier sight; but there was none to see it except a strange boy who was staring in at the window. He had ecstasies innumerable that other children can never know; but he was looking through the window at the one joy from which he must be forever barred" (225).

By upholding the power of female imagination as a transforming agent for male development, Barrie and Burnett offer progressive girl characters; however, their stories conclude either by returning the heroine to the contemporary status quo, or removing her to the background. The culmination of each journey suggests neither writer was thoroughly comfortable with or interested in absolutely overturning patriarchal authority. Many critics have commented upon the way Mary seems to be under-emphasized in the second half of *Secret Garden*, and the debate continues as to the validity of such a reading. Bixler notes that even though some "critics lament" Mary's reduced role in the latter chapters, it is important to recognize that Mary "does not ... lose all of her spirit." Rather, Bixler says Mary "continues to be an initiator of action" and that her transformation is remarked upon by Mrs. Sowerby, Mrs. Medlock, and even Dr. Craven (84). Gillian Adams reconciles Mary's diminishing role by emphasizing the need for the heroine to fully realize her own positive change by making a social contribution in the manner of Carlyle: "Although Mary is now able to 'like,' and has a secret kingdom of her own in which to work, to imagine a future, and to be happy, she must become less isolated ... before she is ready to use her caring and her imagination to heal others" (45).

These arguments carry weight yet do not fully explain why Mary's role so greatly diminishes by the end of the story. Mary powerfully and independently creates her own self, then uses her imagination and newfound strength to "save" first Colin, then his father. Both Mary and Wendy become transformed by their experiences in association with "Magic," but attention must be paid to the quality and nature of these changes. The idea of motherhood conjures the image or feeling of "home," which Robson identifies in a Victorian context as a feminized realm that had "not only the effect of creating that domestic, and now much vilified paragon, the Angel in the House, but also her ideal daughter ... the perfect little girl formed its most apt symbol" (8). In these terms Mary's transformation takes on additional importance: her original self, that of a "queer old-womanish thing," opposes the "perfect little girl" ideal constructed by the Victorian male. As if to satisfy this ideal, Burnett seems to allow Mary to change so that she can effect the more important transformation of the males whose strength will secure the continuation of (patriarchal) society.

Arguably Wendy's character is even more problematic, since Barrie actually shows her grown-up self interacting with Peter, who has now mostly forgotten her, near the story's conclusion. Barrie wrote at least "twenty variant endings to the dramatic story," but with each including "a future in which Wendy was changed by time and Peter remained constant within time. These sometimes stressed Pan's isolation, sometimes Wendy's age," yet the overarching theme remains that the girl "grows up" (Jack 204–5), as the narrator makes clear from the story's first page. While the Lost Boys and Wendy's brothers go on to pursue different career paths, Wendy, whose influence and guidance enables their integration into society, succumbs to its limitations for women. Once she discovers in Never-land that Peter's feelings for her do not promise a home-and-hearth kind of future, Wendy chooses to leave the world of imagination behind: "When they met again Wendy was a married woman, and Peter was no more to her than a little dust in a box in which she had kept her toys" (Barrie 233–4). As Kavey points out, all of the female characters in the story "share the desire to become wives and mothers" (101), including Nana the dog. Such a desire, particularly in Barrie's time, would be a definitive quality of little girlhood, but that it displaces or denies female imagination remains a most troubling aspect of *Peter Pan*.

Illustrating what may be called the "maternal porter," Wendy and Mary enable the major male figures in *Peter Pan* and *Secret Garden* to find their way "home." Without actually giving birth, Mary mothers Colin and his father, delivering them to manhood by filling the empty space created by Mrs. Craven's death. Likewise, through her departure, as well as by bringing back the Boys and reminding her father of his own shortcomings, Wendy figuratively gives birth several times before she literally becomes a mother. While R.D.S. Jack calls *Peter Pan* "a play about battles" (183), Harry Geduld says, "Barrie's emphasis is repeatedly on birth" (61). Both critics have a point; however, Geduld's view seems to be more apt given Wendy's importance in the story. I would extend his point to say "*re*-birth," a theme that pervades both *Peter Pan* and *Secret Garden* and which coincides with the Wordsworthian notion of pre-existence by which Wendy and Mary transform "boys" to "men."

Holmes sees the movement between Never-land and the real world as representing a "boundary between childhood and adulthood and the binary it creates" with its "many windows and gates ... open in various ways to users on both sides of the binary" (138). In these terms, their associations with the magical space enable Darling, Colin, and Craven to each achieve a Wordsworthian balance between imaginative vision and adult rationality/acceptance that enables him to take his place in society. Burnett confirms this in *Secret Garden*'s last scene, where the servants watch through the windows as "across the lawn came the Master of Misselthwaite.... And by his side, with his head up in the air ... walked as strongly and steadily as any boy in Yorkshire — Master Colin!" (298). Mary remains conspicuously absent from this moment, which confirms that she has taken her place in society's (and the book's) margins. Ultimately, *Secret Garden* and *Peter Pan* each make a female heroine the catalyst for ensuring that patriarchy continues, with each girl taking her place on its edges after having helped the men in her life to contribute to society in a more productive way.

PART III

Haunted Houses and the Hidden Self: Portals in the Gothic, Low Fantasy, and Science Fiction

CHAPTER FIVE

Confronting Chaos at the In-Between: William Hope Hodgson's *The House on the Borderland*

A hand that can be clasp'd no more
Behold me, for I cannot sleep
And like a guilty thing I creep
At earliest morning to the door
        — Alfred, Lord Tennyson, *In Memoriam A.H.H.* [VII. 5–8]

Each sobbing breath is but a cry,
My heart-strokes knells of agony,
And my whole brain has but one thought
That nevermore through life shall I
(Save in the ache of memory)
Touch hands with thee, who now art nought!
        — William Hope Hodgson "Grief,"
        The House on the Borderland [185]

In the introduction to *Frankenstein*, Mary Shelley writes, "Invention ... does not consist in creating out of void, but out of chaos ... it can give form to dark, shapeless substances, but cannot bring into being the substance itself" (23). Shelley's words, whose sentiment is echoed in both of the above passages, powerfully define the gothic sensibility in its confrontation with the most troubling facets of human experience. Of course Shelley writes about a century earlier than William Hope Hodgson (1877–1918), but chaos is obviously a universal, not a temporal condition. As I discuss in my own introduction, the late Victorian period through the start of the First World War was fraught with the kind of chaos that inspires Shelley to "invent," and which found its way into many subsequent fantastic works. As a prime example, *The House on the Borderland* (c.1908) blends elements of the gothic and science fiction in the manner of Shelley's *Frankenstein*. Up until now Hodgson has received little critical attention, but those few critics who have studied his novels agree with E.F. Blieler in finding that *House* is "more subtle, and more profound than [Hodgson's] other work ... [and] cries for an interpretation deeper than a summary of events" (423). Implicit in this chapter then is an effort to retrieve Hodgson from relative obscurity, by demonstrating the sophistication and social implications of his work as expressed in his approach to the portal concept in *The House on the Borderland*, whose title itself emphasizes the in-between as a theme and mechanism in the novel.

Comparisons with Tennyson's *In Memoriam* (1850), and George Mac-Donald's *Phantastes* (1858) and *Lilith* (1895) place *House* in historical and literary context. With most of their writing preceding Hodgson's by just a few decades, Tennyson (1809–92) and MacDonald (1824–1905) use fantastic elements and interactions between worlds in very similar ways. Like Hodgson, they infuse their work with their own intense personal interests in political, spiritual, psychological, and sociological processes, which often play out in a character undergoing a mystical, transformative experience. Following the previous chapter's discussion of Romantic philosophy at work in *Peter Pan* and *The Secret Garden*, here I do not suggest a direct influence of one writer upon another. This chapter, and the next on Edith Wharton and Oscar Wilde, show how the portal operates in the gothic and science fiction, revealing further uses of the device specific to social and spiritual tensions that increased as the nineteenth century transitioned into the twentieth. In *House* Hodgson uses concrete and symbolic portals to subversively speak out on nearly every issue of which other writers of the age showed equal concern: faith versus doubt, the frightening side effects of scientific progress, and the increasing female pressure for equality. Through the Old Man's travels between dimensions in *House*, Hodgson pessimistically represents the profound uneasiness felt by a man confronting the difficult birth of the modern world.

"Beyond the Veil": Faith and Doubt

Probably Tennyson's name is not the first to come to mind when one thinks of literary fantasy, despite the fact that his body of work shows great interest in and masterful use of the mode. From childhood Tennyson had what he viewed as mystical experiences stemming from an especially keen imagination, which caused bouts of depression, often making social interaction problematic for him. Poems such as "The Lady of Shallott," "The Kraken," "The Lotos-Eaters," and "The Palace of Art" powerfully depict such experiences with characters who have difficulty navigating the real world. Tennyson uses these portrayals to publicly engage the most difficult questions plaguing the individual in his society. As A.N. Wilson points out,

"More than any poet before or since, Tennyson openly exposed himself to the mood of his age, mopping up its angst and its excitements and triumphs, and transforming them into haunting lyric forms" (99). For Wilson and many others, *In Memoriam: A.H.H.* (1849) is the most vivid example of such expression. Tennyson's elegy for his friend Arthur Henry Hallam employs the central image of a "veil" separating life and death, easily read as a portal, a literal passageway between worlds and a figurative emblem of the human condition. Likewise in Hodgson's *House on the Borderland,* the Old Man who is the central character relates his experience traveling via his house to and from a spiritual plane where encounters with pagan deities, swine creatures, and his dead beloved stir him to complex questions. Told in the form of a manuscript found by two fishermen who come upon the ruins in a remote part of Ireland, *House* parallels *In Memoriam* in its study of a mortal effort to comprehend the incomprehensible: belief, life, death — and perhaps most confusing of all — love.

As my epigraph shows, despite differences in life experience and literary achievement, Tennyson and Hodgson have more in common philosophically than one might think. In fact Hodgson wrote a great deal of poetry, though much of it went unpublished. More telling evidence of a connection first appears in *House* with Hodgson's naming of the fisherman who unearths the manuscript: *Tonnison.* Hodgson spotlights Tonnison's importance by naming him while his companion, who is the frame narrator, goes unnamed throughout the novel (Hodgson 10). The fishermen even choose their vacation spot at Tonnison's suggestion, as he says he "stumbled on the place by mere chance the year previously," and it is his idea to make camp instead of taking lodging (Hodgson 1–2). His friend describes how Tonnison behaves strangely, with strong reactions to seeing the ruined house and to hearing the Old Man's story as related in the manuscript, which Tonnison unearths as if he knew it was there all along (Hodgson 9–10). He feels there is "something diabolical" about the area around the ruin, yet asks to hear the story "out loud" in its entirety, having his friend read it instead of doing it himself (Hodgson 12–13).

Such details indicate at least a nod to Tennyson in Hodgson's least obscure work, but the connection goes beyond the superficial with "Grief," the poem that provides a kind of epilogue, supposedly tucked in with the Old Man's manuscript. To date scholars have ignored "Grief," and while it may seem like an afterthought, its expression of what we can presume to be the Old Man's feelings, combined with its uncanny similarity to *In Memoriam* and with Tonnison's name, argue strongly in favor of the poem's importance.[1] Unraveling the threads of Hodgson's signature approach to the portal requires starting here — at the end of *House* rather than with the novel itself.

With both speakers wondering how to reconcile earthly loss in the face of spiritual doubt, the epigraphs to this chapter seem like consecutive stanzas from the same poem, instead of separate pieces composed more than a half-century apart. The most obvious similarity occurs in the way both poems focus on the deceased's physical body to illustrate their narrators' feelings of loss and guilt at remaining behind. In the passages from my epigraph, Tennyson and Hodgson refer to a hand no longer available for clasping, except in the speaker's mind. For Tennyson, the focus on Hallam's physical being creates a unifying motif for the poem as well as a way to measure the stages of the poet's grief. In the early stanzas Tennyson can not seem to break free from his fixation on Hallam's physical body, most prominently expressed in his concern that his friend's remains make their way safely across the water back to England. He worries "the roaring wells / Should gulf [Hallam] fathom-deep in brine, / And hands so often clasp'd in mine, / Should toss with tangle and with shells" (10.16–19), rather than finding their way "To rest beneath the clover sod" (10.12). Hodgson's Old Man, who presumably composes "Grief," echoes Tennyson's sentiment about Hallam's safe return by expressing his own inability to rest because the beloved is "naught," with no hand to touch. Like Tennyson who finds "all is dark where [Hallam is] not" (VIII.12), the Old Man views the remainder of his life with despair:

> Where'er I go I am alone
> Who once, through thee, had all the world.
> My breast is one whole raging pain
> For that which was and now is flown [186].

Here again the stress is on "that which was," referring to the woman's physical existence as well as to the bond between the lovers.

After Hallam's burial, Tennyson's material fixation starts to diminish as he moves toward accepting a spiritual explanation, or the possibility of eternal life "beyond the veil." Tennyson presents the stages of his grieving as a symbolic journey from doubt to near-reconciliation. I say "near" since, being human, he finds he cannot be wholly certain. Tennyson's prologue, which he wrote after completing the rest of the poem, still suggests lingering doubt in lines such as "Believing where we cannot prove" (1.4) and "He *thinks* he was not made to die," (1.10, emphasis added). Yet the drive of the poem is from skepticism toward at least a form of belief. The crux of this shift, usually pinpointed as coming just after the garden reverie scene in Stanza 95, corresponds to the poet's personal transition as he locates faith as a personal reality, which enables him to come to terms with his loss.

It is here, though, that "Grief" diverges from *In Memoriam* in an important way: while Tennyson's emotion *enables* him to believe, Hodgson's narrator sees his capacity to feel as a liability that *prevents* him from finding peace. In "Grief" the emphasis on the beloved's physical body not only represents the narrator's loss but also his inability to reintegrate himself into the world, to live on after she is gone. By the end of *In Memoriam* Tennyson finds a kind of reconciliation, reached in his epiphany, "I have felt" (124. 12–15), and confirmed by his sister's wedding celebration in the epilogue. In contrast, the narrator in "Grief" exits the journal/novel in a state of even greater turmoil, falling "Into the Blank where life is hurled / Where all is not, nor is again!" (186). The Old Man virtually disintegrates like the House itself, which near the end, in keeping with gothic tradition, "disappear[s] bodily ... [leaving] a stupendous pit ... in the place where it had stood" (183). The Old Man leaves no trace of his physical being, other than the journal/manuscript, "The House on the Borderland."

The difference between Tennyson's recovery and the Old Man's downward spiral can be partly explained based on a shift in attitudes toward faith over the more than fifty-year difference separating the two poems. As Jonathan Rose says, "The quest for secular religion forced the Edwardians to think along unconventional lines, and it gave the age its distinctive mental character: synthesizing, inventive, idiosyncratic, and sometimes sharply entertaining" (4). Thus Hodgson "explains his horrors as distortions of a psychic envelope surrounding the earth, but usually they are left mysterious and metaphysically portentous. In part suggestive of distorted upwellings of repressed unconscious, they are also products of raw supernatural hunger" (Manlove *Fantasy Literature* 82). In "Grief" Hodgson dramatizes such "hunger" in the narrator's desire to reunite with the beloved, particularly through his emphasis on the loss of her physical body and his inability to find or touch her in his trips to the other dimension. The Old Man's investigation of self leads only to the annihilation of that self, while Tennyson, writing earlier, finds room for redemption and rebirth. Certainly Hodgson's choice of genre plays a part in the pessimism, but no more so than Tennyson's elegy and subject matter. The despair in Hodgson's work can be more accurately traced to the impending World War, which marked a shift in the prevailing attitudes in science fiction as the "optimism about the utopianism" initially created by technology becomes "destroyed forever" (Moskowitz *Out of the Storm* 49).

Hodgson addresses the issue of religious doubt throughout the novel, especially in the narrator's journeys into the Arena of the other dimension. In his first vision the Old Man describes "being *borne forward*, floating across the flat waste" (19, emphasis added) until he comes to "a vast rift, opening into the mountains" (21). Moving into the Arena's "perfect circle," he confronts "a monstrous representation of Kali, the Hindu goddess of death." Circular images abound in the novel, suggesting eternal existence without a clear beginning or ending, as the narrator's almost seamless movements between dimensions reinforce. That the Old Man repeatedly describes being "borne," rather than moving of his own accord, emphasizes the obvious play-on-words making his experience a process of birth or re-birth. However, the more subtle implication is very telling: he retains as little choice over his own course as he has to understand — or even to recognize — the many options he has for belief. In this way Hodgson positions mortality at the mercy of a larger universal organizing principle. Being lifted into another world where he floats among "old gods of mythology" (Hodgson 22–3), the Old Man, a representative of Hodgson's time, confronts contrasting options for religious faith with no way to determine which "god" actually provides a guiding force for the human being.

The experience causes the Old Man to ponder, "Was there then, after all, something in the old heathen worship, something more than the deifying of men, animals and elements?" (24). After witnessing the swine crea-ture — a gothic double for himself/humankind — in the Arena for the first time, the Old Man rises back over the mountains and becomes "wrapped in an impalpable, lightless gloom" (26–27), suggesting his inability to answer the questions his journey evokes. Adelheid Kegel's assessment of George MacDonald and Emily Brontë helps to clarify Hodgson's expression of the faith/doubt dilemma. Referring to Plato's "image of space as an image for the soul," Kegel finds "the existential situation of [MacDonald and Brontë] and their time [is] that of experiencing the growing estrangement of the being from its foundation and origin, and the separation and isolation of spheres, once seen as a complex whole" (124). Such "estrangement" is a core concern of the gothic; Hodgson represents precisely this feeling through the Old Man's aimlessly floating in space and unsuccessful effort to rationalize what he sees in the Arena. His removal back to the "lightless gloom" in the initial journey and in subsequent travels reveals his human incapacity to process such vast, existential concepts. The outcome of his first vision, which returns him to his lonely study, also reinforces the "estrangement" Kegel describes.

One of the few scholars to approach Hodgson's work in some depth, Sam Moskowitz defines the "gaslight era" of the *fin de siècle* as the pinnacle of science fiction writing, and as a transition period defined by "an orgy of change and development; an incredible procession of invention and scientific discovery that was remaking the world beyond any hope of reversion" (*Science Fiction by Gaslight* 16). In *House*, Hodgson confronts this "orgy of change" by exploding scientific theory as the Old Man witnesses a massive acceleration of time and drifts through space without any ability to choose his course. These images represent the ultimate fate of humankind at the mercy of unknown and unexplainable forces. In his visions — if indeed they are such — the Old Man comes nearer to knowing than anyone can, but he simply cannot comprehend the enormity of the knowledge, or if he does, he abruptly leaves off the telling of it at the end of the manuscript.

Interestingly, the speaker's last words in the novel invoke Christianity: "Jesus, be merciful to me, an Old Man. There is something fumbling at the door handle. O God, help me now! Jesus —.... Somethi —" (178). Ending with "somethi[ng]" rather than with "Jesus," Hodgson hints that the Old Man finds no help in religion, that the answer is much weightier and more elusive than human-organized systems of belief can support or conceive. The Old Man's identity remains shrouded in mystery as the frame narrator explains in the final section when he and Tonnison try to learn more about the House and its inhabitant: "His identity is, as he seems to have desired, buried forever" along with the strange place in which he lived (Hodgson 184). The frame narrator echoes the Old Man's indecisiveness as his own final lines, which end the novel, express the human inability to find answers to life's most profound questions: "Sometimes, in my dreams, I see that enormous pit.... And the noise of the water rises upwards, and blends — in my sleep — with other and lower noises; while, over all, hangs the eternal shroud of spray" (184). A less mysterious ending might leave the reader more satisfied, but Hodgson's ambiguity here and throughout the story is apt for the genre/subject matter and illustrates his ability to "create ideas and images of awesome power ... [that] evoke high emotion" (Bleiler 423). The story must end this way to reiterate its main theme, that the mortal can never know what lies beyond the grave, or in Tennyson's terms, "behind the veil."

The Old Man's journeys make him a vehicle for Hodgson to dramatize the points of conflict where worlds, i.e., ideologies clash, reinforced by the story's numerous instances of the character moving from the Primary to Secondary dimensions where his questions become exaggerated and externalized. The Old Man travels via the house itself, the main concrete portal in the novel. With its remote location "on the borders of the Silences" (Hodgson 19), the house closely echoes Tennyson's "veil" as a way to represent the universality of human incomprehension. In *House*, the Irish countryside offers a perfect "Borderland," both in terms of a Tennysonian nexus point between life and death, but also in folkloric terms between the ancient past when people believed in magic, and the contemporary present when nearly every kind of faith stands in question. Hodgson reinforces the idea at the end of the novel when the frame narrator and Tonnison ask their driver to gather information for them. The driver returns with a tale from "an ancient man of the village" who relates a brief history of the House (182–3). The driver adds, "He had heard a rumour, *once upon a time*, of a great old house standing alone out in the wilderness; but if he remembered rightly, It was a place given over to the fairies" (181, emphasis added). As a magical "in-between" place overlapping life and death, the heath surrounding the ruined house equates the vastness of what the human being cannot know and, as a meeting place between earth and sky, becomes synonymous with the mortal drive to unlock these mysteries.

Of Men, Women, and Swine: Love and Power

The house itself as a concrete gateway shares an intimate connection with the porter character in the novel, the Old Man's dead beloved. Those few critics who have studied *House* agree with Blieler when he says the "third supernatural thread, sentimental communion with a dead beloved, is less important" than are the other "two interpenetrating motif-chains: cosmic visions that take the narrator beyond the bounds of reality and assaults by monstrosities from Below" (423–4). However, I find, that despite — and perhaps *because of*— her intangibility and lack of character development, the dead beloved occupies a highly significant place in *House,* bound up with the Old Man's effort to make sense of a rapidly changing world. Absences are central to the gothic, and the Old Man's beloved is defined by her non-being, by what she does not say. Like Tennyson, the Old Man filters his angst about her loss into poetry so that "Grief" actually becomes the core of the story, the stimulus for his journeys, rather than an afterthought. Elton E. Smith discusses the significance of Tennyson's mystical epiphany in his analysis of *In Memoriam*, viewing "canto 95 not simply [as] an extended metaphor; it is the *account of a rendezvous* (the letters), *a meeting, airborne oneness with the departed*, and a consequent mystic enlightenment concerning the nature of time, space, fortune, death, and resurrection" (4, emphasis added). Coming very near to describing the more expansive concept of the portal/porter, Smith finds that Tennyson's poem dramatizes "an inhabitant of the earth and a spirit from the other world shar[ing] a mystic vision of the entire world, of the meaning and the reuniting power of faithful love (4). This is exactly the kind of communion that occurs between the Old Man and the dead beloved in *House*. Like the letters that are a catalyst for Tennyson's epiphany, the Old Man's journal, which becomes *The House on the Borderland*, constitutes his way of working through his feelings after each journey to the other dimension.

In keeping with the gothic convention of doubling, Hodgson links the dead beloved with the house, which also becomes bound up with the relationship between the house and the Old Man. As the portal that allows the passages between dimensions and the stages of his internal quest, the house operates on at least two levels of meaning. Complicating matters, the actual house also has its own twin in the jade structure over which the Old Man floats in the other dimension. First, the house exists as a concrete structure through which the Old Man travels and as such represents the only means by which he can feel close to his lost love, an apt connection since the idea of home traditionally marks a female domain in Victorian/Edwardian terms. Besides the Old Man himself, the house and the beloved are the only real-world images that repeat in the other dimension. Hodgson makes the connection clear when the Old Man ponders why he does not simply leave the "very awful house" and reasons, "if I left, where could I go, and still obtain the solitude, and the *sense of her presence*, that alone make my old life bearable?" (97–8, emphasis added). Just after this line, the "editor," presumably the frame narrator, places a footnote explaining that the manuscript has heretofore not made any "previous reference ... to this matter," but that "it becomes clearer ... in the light of succeeding incidents," meaning the narrator's description in the following chapter when he journeys to "The Sea of Sleep."

In fact the Old Man records in "The Sea of Sleep" his contentment at having decided to stay, even though he alludes to one Secondary-dimension encounter that remains lost to the reader where his beloved told him the house was "long ago given over to evil and under the power of grim laws, of which none here have knowledge" (99). Again, given the conventional association between the feminine and domesticity, the beloved's warning carries symbolic importance, especially since she communicates the message from beyond the grave, where he can no longer reach (or control) her. Further reinforcing this idea, the speaker says, "How long ago, in the old-earth days, I had half suspected that, in some unexplainable manner, this house, in which I live, was *en rapport* ... with that other tremendous structure, away in the midst of that incomparable plain" (157). In other words, he had recognized in the early stages of his movement between realms that his house shares a relationship with the Other-worldly version, just as his view of the beloved corresponds to his interaction with her both before and after her death, or transition to another dimension.

Essentially the connection between the house and the beloved, as her comment about the place suggests, illustrates a perverted or dysfunctional domesticity that is a function of the speaker's loss, i.e., his inability to come to terms with his love's transformation from one state of being to another. Enlarged, his feelings equate with the uneasiness of the late Victorian or Edwardian male facing an increasingly vocal female demanding equality.

Read this way, the beloved's warning about the house becomes a rejection of the domestic frame into which patriarchal society invariably placed the female in Hodgson's time. Sally Ledger explains how the so-called "New Woman" movement became viewed as a threat to the status quo: "The establishment's desire to defend marriage as an institution was underpinned by a belief that, without conventional marriage and domestic arrangements, the social fabric upon which Victorian society was based would begin to crumble" (12). An independent woman challenged traditional concepts of partnership between male and female, thus undermining the family unit forming the foundation of "good" society. Hodgson leaves unclear whether or not the speaker and the woman were married, but his portrayal of the character's interaction with her now that she has crossed over clearly parallels the threat felt by the real-world male facing a female moving increasingly beyond his authority.

The Old Man's beloved also has a flesh-and-blood double in his sister who, along with his dog, furnishes the character's only companionship as well as a way of measuring his sanity. Hodgson's portrayal of the sister coincides with his overall approach to the male-female dynamic, once again with real-world implications. When the Old Man goes on one of his excursions through the house, checking to see if his fortifications against the swine creatures remain intact, he finds his "foolish sister ... actually unbarring the back door." He quickly reproaches her, saying, "Come, Mary!.... What's the meaning of this nonsense? Do you mean to tell me you don't understand the danger, that you try to throw our two lives away in this fashion?" She responds only by "gasping and sobbing, as though in the last extremity of fear" (60). While she seems to sense the danger seemingly motivating her brother's actions, Mary's apprehension is directed *at him*, not at the swine or any other supernatural force, since she never at any point in the novel admits seeing what her brother claims to see.

Believing *her* to be "mad," he locks her into her bedroom for her own safety and to prevent her from undermining his efforts by trying to unlock the back door again. Indeed Mary becomes a prisoner; she only receives permission to leave her room "on the condition that she [promise] not to attempt to leave the house or meddle with any of the outer doors" (69). Providing no definitive evidence that it is his sister, not the Old Man, who is crazy, Hodgson positions their relationship as a symbolic reversal of the speaker's connection with the beloved. The dead woman lies beyond his reach in the other dimension where she communicates with him or pushes him away as she likes. The living Mary, on the other hand, remains in the Primary, patriarchal world where he presides over her every move. His very presence evokes fear in Mary, and her sobbing and trembling coincides with the traditional, swooning Victorian lady. In contrast the beloved exhibits pity *toward the speaker* when he meets her on the Sea of Sleep.

The Old Man feels uneasy dealing with both women. By making a motion toward "unbarring the door," Mary symbolizes the female effort to move outside the domestic space, but the Old Man stops her in time and succeeds in preventing any future attempts through his characterizing her act as dangerous "nonsense" with the potential to ruin both their lives. Of course, since the beloved is dead and Mary alive, one might view her as occupying the more positive and powerful position, but Hodgson's depiction of death challenges such an interpretation. Although the other dimension includes the Arena full of awe-inspiring gods and frightful swine creatures, the speaker frequently expresses an "overwhelming ... joy" at seeing his love in the place he envisions as "paradise" (145–6). Further, the Old Man says he does not "fear death — as death is understood" (162). Instead he worries about something "intangible," an evil he associates with the house, not with the Sea of Sleep where the beloved dwells (Hodgson 162). In terms of Victorian and Edwardian society, the beloved occupies a space outside the male sphere where he can only reach her at her invitation and where dwelling alongside her requires a great sacrifice or transformation of his own state of being. For the Old Man, this sacrifice corresponds to his own death, which presumably comes when he leaves off writing the manuscript. For the real-world male in Hodgson's time, the sacrifice may seem more frightening and difficult to achieve since accepting a new role for woman means the "death" of his long-established role in society, compelling him to redefine himself and his intimate relationships.

The second level of meaning that may be attached to the house portal also corresponds to the Old Man's relationship with the beloved. In gothic terms, through its dark cellars and twisting, turning hallways, as a gateway to another dimension the house represents the Old Man's journey inward as a result of the beloved's death. Traditionally navigating Faërie most often equals an internal journey toward some form of knowledge as a character becomes forced to confront his own weaknesses or place in the world/universe. George MacDonald's *Lilith* (1895) provides a particularly useful example, as Raven illustrates when he tells Vane, "To go back, you must go through yourself, and that way no man can show another." The young man responds to this by thinking, "I had never yet done anything to justify my existence; my former world was nothing the better for my sojourn in it" (MacDonald 24). In *House* the Old Man feels the same lack of connection to the world, but being older his journey becomes an effort to reconcile his past action and experience, rather than to make his mark.

The narrator in *House* has heretofore avoided introspection, as he confirms in his search of the house in his own world as he tries to secure it against the swine. For example, when he initially turns to the door leading downstairs, he notes, "I doubt whether I had ever, before, been right through the cellars," and later he says, "It occurred to me how strange it was that I should be so little acquainted with my own house" (66). Vane utters words to the same effect in *Lilith* after he first visits the other realm: "The house had grown strange to me.... If I know nothing of my own garret.... Who, what am I?" (MacDonald 16). The young man's lack of self-knowledge leads to a coming-of-age journey through Faërie, but like Hodgson's Old Man, whose house seems to be a beacon for the swine, Vane identifies his dwelling as "an aerial portal ... ever open to creatures whose life was other than human" (16). While the Old Man spends most of his time fighting off the other-world creatures, however, Vane enjoys the protection of Mara and the Little Ones as he explores and increasingly accepts the oddities of the Seven Dimensions. Vane decides early on that he "could not endure the thought of going back [through the mirror] with so many beginnings and not an end achieved.... I would rather go on and on than come to such a close" (MacDonald *Lilith* 82–3). This thought drives him from this point forward, enabling him to complete the construction of self that seems to destroy rather than redeem Hodgson's narrator.

In the gothic, the house often becomes a "metaphor for the soul," with the "upper floor" marked by an abundance of "light" dispersing down through the lower levels and finally manifesting as fire in the "cellar" (Kegler 105–6), i.e., the seat of one's primal urges and conflicts. For MacDonald and Brontë the symbolic use of prisons, dungeons, cellars, stairs, etc. "throws some light on the[ir] existential situation ... and of their time: that of experiencing the growing estrangement of the being from its foundation and origin, and the separation and isolation of spheres, once seen as a complex whole" (Kegler 124). Kegler's comments also apply to Hodgson's *House* as the Old Man's second exploration of the cavernous rooms of the cellar reveal water, obviously a means of extinguishing fire, when he opens the trap door and realizes the house sits atop an "arched roof, of solid rock" that is part of "the Pit" (Hodgson 95). This discovery significantly occurs just before the novel's first mention of the beloved, preceding "The Sea of Sleep" chapter where the Old Man ponders his reasons for staying in the house and where he encounters the woman who seems to have directed this decision. Even though water, not fire, lies under the house, the idea of "the Pit" and the imagery that repeatedly associates the house with Hell support Kegler's view of the soul's light translating into fire in the "depths" of being, represented as part of the house metaphor through the cellar space. Kegler explains, "The space of the soul is also like a place of exile from where the lost, precious good may be measured only by intense desire" (105). Such desire also reads as a type of "fire" in the Old Man, manifested in his longing for the beloved and repeatedly dowsed by her pushing him away each time they meet in the other dimension. Moreover, fire literally appears in the first cellar scene when the Old Man burns his hand and then wards off a swine creature by scalding it (Hodgson 46–7).

In Hodgson's novel, as well as in *Lilith* and MacDonald's other major fantasy geared toward adults, *Phantastes*, the issue of "out" versus "in" provides a major theme in each protagonist's experience. Thus the house icon works as both an extension of the mind/body and a portal through which a person might find a sense of belonging and self-knowledge. For example, early in *Lilith*, Raven tells Vane, "There are places you can go into, and places you can go out of; but the one place, if you do but find it, where you may go out and in both, is home" (MacDonald 15). Vane's reference to his house as an "aerial portal" reinforces the idea, which MacDonald further illustrates in the young man's wondering during his first excursion: "How could I any longer call that house *home*, where every door, every window opened into — *Out,* and even the garden I could not keep inside?" (MacDonald 21, emphasis in original). Here Vane's implied definition of "home" is problematic, a function of the general lack of interest in people that largely compels his journey and slowly becomes corrected as he travels.

MacDonald even more emphatically uses the notions of "in" and "out" in *Phantastes*. In what is arguably one of the most interesting scenes of the novel, the cottage woman invites Anodos to pass through one of four doors in the center of each wall of her home. Before he disappears through the first, she tells him, "You will not see what you expect when you go out of that door" (136). This exit takes him to his childhood and a memory of his last day with his "favourite brother" who had drowned (136). Here MacDonald deals with one kind of grief, that for a lost family member, but when Anodos passes through the "Door of Dismay" on his third exit he experiences an emotion more closely akin to that which Hodgson's Old Man confronts in *House*. On a familiar street Anodos sees "a form well-known" and a face "unchangeably dear" (141). Entering another door he believes to be the way back to the old woman, Anodos finds himself "not [in] the mysterious cottage, but her home" and, believing his beloved to be away, he decides to "see the old room once more" (MacDonald *Phantastes* 141).

Instead he ends up in a church where he finds her tomb and exclaims, "If any of the dead are moving here, let them take pity upon me, for I, alas! Am still alive; and let some dead woman comfort me, for I am a stranger in the land of the dead, and see no light!" He is answered with a momentary hand-clasp from "out of the dark" and the feeling of a "warm kiss" on his lips before he somehow finds his way back into the old woman's cottage. The experience helps Anodos to recognize that "the veil between, though very dark, is very thin" (MacDonald *Phantastes* 142), echoing both Tennyson and Hodgson in terms of an almost-imperceptible but unyielding line between life and death. More importantly, Anodos' encounter with the woman, who reads as a lost love or perhaps a mother, supports the significance of the female in the young man's search for self. As in the case of Hodgson's recluse, the woman in Anodos' past remains frustratingly out of his reach. His feelings manifest in the aptly named "Door of Dismay" through which he gains only an unsatisfying, temporary access to her that evokes an even greater sense of longing, while also contributing to his emotional growth.

The presence of the female, whether physically or in spirit, even more vividly directs Vane's progress (and lack thereof) in *Lilith,* and also shapes the Old Man's visions in *House.* Unlike Anodos and Vane, whose encounters with women reveal what they have yet to learn about themselves, the recluse's movements between dimensions occur *because of* his loss. Recognizing this fact is crucial to understanding Hodgon's novel, especially in its social implications. While Vane has done nothing "to justify [his] existence" (MacDonald *Lilith* 24), and Anodos is eager "to see all that is to be seen" (MacDonald *Phantastes* 15), Hodgson's Old Man has yet to come to terms with what he *has done and seen.* The novel leaves unclear whether the separation occurred prior to or as a result of the woman's death, but the Old Man's descriptions reveal a decided lack of closure in the way he perceives the loss. Both for Hodgson's narrator and for MacDonald's Anodos and Vane, the house image furnishes the concrete gateway for an internal process that cannot go forward without the participation of the more figurative agent, the female porter.

In *Lilith,* MacDonald endows Vane with the ability to correct his former habits, which are strikingly similar to those of Hodgson's recluse. William Raeper calls *Lilith* "distinctly *fin de siècle*" and sees the title character existing "*between two worlds,* one patriarchal and resistant to change, the other subversive and mercurial" (46, emphasis added). The "tension" in the novel is between a "masculine drive to certainty and regulation and a feminine acceptance of openness and mystery, mainly represented by Lilith herself (Raeper 46). This description equally applies to *House.* In both cases the female both resides at the core of and embodies the chaos, in a space the male character can envision but can never fully reach or comprehend. In his first meeting with his beloved in the other dimension, the Old Man wants to join her, but cannot. This encounter begins with an exchange of glances not unlike that which he describes in his first face-to-face experience with the swine: "She looked back at me, with such a commingling of joy and sadness that I ran to her, blindly; crying strangely to her, in a very agony of remembrance, of terror, and of hope, to come to me." Yet while he cries, she keeps her distance and he notes, "In her eyes was the old earth-light of tenderness, that I had come to know, before all things, ere we were parted" (Hodgson 101). The Old Man remains incapable of making a move, but his beloved can touch him and does so; however, she ultimately pushes him away "with tenderly stern hands," leaving him feeling "abashed" (Hodgson 101–3). The effect clearly places power on the side of the beloved who, being firmly entrenched in the Sea of Sleep, i.e., death, possesses knowledge the speaker lacks.

His terror results not only from the possibility of losing contact with her forever, but also from his awareness that the only way to join her is to relinquish his hold on the primary world. Hodgson reinforces this blend of longing, confusion, and fear by placing the reader in a parallel position. An editorial note just after the above scene in the Sea of Sleep explains that only "fragments" of the rest of the speaker's descriptions of this meeting with the beloved remain as part of the "mutilated" and "undecipherable" portion of the manuscript. In this section, the speaker is forced to relive his earthly parting with his love, this time with the "noise of eternity" in his ears (102). Indeed this is not the only time he endures the moment of separation; later in the time-acceleration phase of his experience the speaker again meets the beloved and this time actually embraces her, but again she pushes him away (146–7). Each visit with her only intensifies his longing and frustration stemming from his mortal inability to join her and, more importantly, *to know what she knows.*

Hodgson's juxtaposition of contrasting feelings, "joy" and "sadness," "terror" and "hope," epitomizes the Old Man's internal conflict, which extends to characterize the man living in Hodgson's time. Just as Tennyson's sadness at losing Hallam ignites a combination of doubt and hope for the truth of an afterlife, the sight of the beloved drifting on the Sea of Sleep evokes both the Old Man's fear of the unknown and his longing to join her "beyond the veil." The terror he feels also recalls his initial encounter with the swine in which he feels simultaneously drawn to yet repelled by the creature that represents his own baser nature: "I realized, dimly, that the creature's eyes were looking into mine with a steady, compelling stare. I tried to turn away; but could not" (47). His response here equates with the feelings of the late Victorian and Edwardian male who finds increasing difficulty in comprehending and controlling the female bent on gaining independence from him. Like the swine creatures for the Old Man, such a woman appears at once both frightening and strangely compelling; as a case in point, in *Dracula*, Bram Stoker emphasizes Jonathan Harker's response of "deadly fear" mixed with "a wicked burning desire" when the vampire women prey on him at the count's castle (61). Kath Filmer makes a similar point in discussing Lilith as the "white leech" draining Vane's blood while he sleeps in MacDonald's novel: "For this sexual relationship is not born of human love but of power-lust. The seductress despises the seduced, just as those who wield power in an unjust social system despise those over whom they have control and from whose life and labour they derive their wealth and strength" (97).

While Hodgson gives *House*'s beloved an intangible form, MacDonald introduces Lilith as almost morbidly real for Vane when he first finds her "quite naked" with "all [her] bones ... as visible as if tight-covered with only a thin elastic leather" (96). His efforts to revive her seemingly lifeless body are directed by his thought, "But with the faintest prospect of a woman to my friend, I poorest of creatures, was yet a possible man!" (103). Here Vane links his construction of an identity to the need for partnership, implying a man requires a woman if he is going to be able to contribute to the world as a whole being. While Lona and the Little Ones certainly play their part, the true catalyst for Vane's slow growth is the title character, the one who most resembles himself in her greed and vanity. Again, when Vane tries to revive Lilith, he shows he is beginning to see outside himself: "To be enough for himself, a being must be an eternal self-existent worm!" (MacDonald 102). Vane's first choice of a woman to lift him from the "self-existent" state is thoroughly uninterested in the job; Lilith shows the opposite of gratitude for his revival efforts and repeatedly tricks him to get what she wants. Through her, though, he begins to see what is missing in himself and in his helping move Lilith to repent, Vane does so himself. As such, each becomes a porter for the other's journey, an unwilling one on Lilith's part.

The beloved in *House* does not seem to share Lilith's negative qualities, but she is equally important in the Old Man's process and their interactions illustrate a similar process of desire, avoidance, and prohibition. Like the Old Man in *House*, Vane begins to comprehend his own alienation and inadequacy. In contrast, though, Hodgson's narrator starts and ends with guilt, never reaching a more enlightened level of self-analysis and comprehension that is implied in Vane's willingness to sleep and his "journey home" (MacDonald *Lilith* 243–50). Hodgson's Old Man can only fight against himself, as shown in his repeated struggles to prevent the swine from entering the House. A self-imposed prison in which he can indulge his despair, the House becomes a perfect vehicle for the Old Man to commune with the beloved in visions brought on by too much isolation, study, and contemplation. That his story ends with the crumbling of the house and his disappearance confirms his failure in reconciling the "Grief" he describes in the poem and the guilt he shows through his cryptic descriptions of his sojourns to the Sea of Sleep.

In MacDonald's *Lilith* and *Phantastes* and Hodgson's *House*, the female soul emblematizes and directs the man's journey. All three novels use the domestic space as a concrete pathway into the self. More importantly, these works make the female element a supreme agent for a complex and intimate process, one that never completely reaches fruition for any of the men involved, least of all Hodgson's Old Man. Knowledge in these stories remains in feminine control and is doled out, if at all, only by the woman when and to the degree she chooses. Consequently Vane, Anodos, and the Old Man are left to follow, seek, and attempt, mostly without success, to understand her and what she knows. Death becomes an issue for all three characters, as well as for Tennyson, who often speaks as if to a female beloved *In Memoriam*, envisioning Hallam in death as dwelling in a place beyond his ken. Likewise in their tales MacDonald and Hodgson regularly convey the desire for the beloved or other female spirit around the idea of death as a transition to another state of being. Vane begins his journey in *Lilith* by refusing to "sleep" and ends up chasing she who also refuses. In both cases to "sleep" in *Lilith* refers to a kind of path to eternal life, only possible when one releases one's grasp on the material in favor of submitting to a higher authority, i.e., replacing love of self with love of a Creator. In *Phantastes*, MacDonald makes explicit a link between love and death through Anodos' thought, "The sign or cause of coming death is an indescribable longing.... When a youth and a maiden look too deep into each other's eyes, this longing seizes and possesses them; but instead of drawing nearer ... they wander away, each alone, into solitary places and die of desire" (81).

Applied to male-female relationships in Victorian and Edwardian society, these portrayals of longing that end in isolation and death represent each author's similar perspective on an increasingly confusing state of affairs. Hodgson's *House* stands at the center of a whirlwind created not only by conflicts around science and religion, but also more proximately in the relationship between man and woman. Unlike Tennyson and MacDonald, Hodgson died young at forty, killed in action by a German artillery shell on April 17, 1918. Thus his work remains — like the narrator's journey in *House* — unfinished. While analyzing its relation to the age through comparisons with other major authors and works should illuminate Hodgson's most important themes in *House*, his premature death in the war that helped to fuel the novel's pessimism leaves the author and *The House on the Borderland* mysteriously elusive, much like life (and love) itself.

CHAPTER SIX

The Society Insider/Outsider and the Sympathetic Supernatural in Fantastic Tales by Edith Wharton and Oscar Wilde

In the eyes of our provincial society authorship was still regarded as something between a black art and a form of manual labor.
— Edith Wharton, *A Backward Glance* [Wharton 68–9]

There is a fatality about all physical and intellectual distinction, the sort of fatality that seems to dog through history the faltering steps of kings.
It is better not to be different from one's fellows.
The ugly and the stupid have the best of it in this world.
— Basil Hallward, *The Picture of Dorian Gray* [Wilde 3]

Like William Hope Hodgson, Edith Wharton (1862–1937) and Oscar Wilde (1854–1900) use their writing to probe the reaches of the subconscious and to illustrate the pressure of outside forces on the individual. As established in my introduction, the interplay between internal and external helps to characterize the portal as a device of the in-between, as well as being a defining quality of the fantastic. This is especially true in darker modes such as the gothic, which dates back to Horace Walpole's *The Castle of Otranto* (1764), peaks with Mary Shelley's *Frankenstein* in the early nineteenth century, then undergoes a revival during the *fin de siècle* with the publication of iconic works such as Robert Louis Stevenson's *Dr. Jekyll and Mr. Hyde* (1886), Wilde's *The Picture of Dorian Gray* (1891) and Bram Stoker's *Dracula* (1897).

With its associations to Romanticism and revolution, from its emergence the gothic is defined by its socio-political and psychological concerns. As the gothic progresses into the later nineteenth century, "monsters" increasingly take the shape of "malign forces living in people's heads" so that "the haunted house" becomes "the haunted mind" (Smith and Haas xi). Also in the 1880s and '90s the rise of Occultism and its theories of "magically think-ing one's way into the interior of another" (Thruschwell 38) evoke anxiety about free will, further straining an already unstable relationship between the individual and Society. While Wharton and Wilde are best known for their realism, it is interesting to see how both authors tapped the symbolic nature of the fantastic to consider the more troubling aspects of this rela-tionship.

Since the gothic and one of its most popular variations, the ghost story, most often use Primary world settings, these modes remain rooted in the real world. Most of these tales do not rely on movement between worlds, but the portal concept still readily applies due to their juxtaposition of inter-nal and external space and their interest in psychological and social trans-formation. As I have shown in Chapter Five, Hodgson's *The House on the Borderland,* which uses concrete and metaphorical portals, fits into this cat-egory in its portrayal of the Old Man's travels. Hodgson differs from Whar-ton and Wilde, however, in that his personal experience (while colorful) did not include much association with society life. Born into a large family, liv-ing along the Irish coast, and heading off to sea at thirteen (Gullette), Hodg-son does not seem to extend his interest in gender roles to class-based power dynamics. In contrast, both in their fantasies and in their own lives Whar-ton and Wilde pointedly confront the problems of sex-based *and* class-based alienation. Invariably, they do so in their fantastic tales not through a con-cern with people transitioning from lower to upper but trying to *maintain or navigate* the pressures of prominent social status in light of being or feel-ing "different."

Wharton and Wilde use magical entities as porters for those living beings they identify in the manner of Coleridge's Ancient Mariner as being in need of aid or enlightenment. Transfiguring monster into victim, Whar-ton and Wilde illustrate the difficulties for unimaginative or helpless mor-tals who cannot escape or even recognize the perils of living according to corruptive, impossible behavioral codes. In their tales those who do resist end up dead or broken; in either case, haunting the living as reminders of a fall that comes with age, change, or loss of favor. While transformation is not always successful or positive in these stories, the effort is made; and the change that seems to be most important to Wharton and Wilde involves not the characters but the readers actually living the conditions being drama-tized. To illustrate how these portals/porters operate, this chapter focuses specifically on Wharton's "After Holbein," (1928), "The Lady's Maid's Bell" (1902), and "The Looking Glass" (1936), juxtaposed with Wilde's "The Fish-erman and His Soul" (1892), *The Picture of Dorian Gray* (1891), and "The Canterville Ghost" (1887).

Wharton and Wilde as Society Insider/Outsiders

In *Scare Tactics: Supernatural Fiction by American Women* Jeffrey Weinstock argues, "Ghost stories by women and individuals who feel themselves to be in some way or other alienated from their cultures ... need to be considered as expressions of desire" (17). Given her sex and his nationality and sexuality, this notion easily applies to both Wharton and Wilde. Their clever and often-biting social satire make these authors kindred spirits, but more importantly each represents an "Other" as well as a participant in the upper echelons of their respective American and British Societies. Many view Wilde as anticipating modernism, "a heroic but ultimately doomed castaway in an unsympathetic age, the very definition of the 'other Victorian' set against repressive forces" (Warwick 2). Similarly Jennifer Haystock does not identify Wharton as modernist per se, but sees her as having a related sensibility to this movement borne out of "feelings of isolation paradoxically combined with the inherent inextricability of the self from others, and the difficulty of relating experience in words" (17).

For Wharton these "feelings of isolation" are a function of being "out of place in traditional gender identities and dynamics. Most women, not having received the same education as men, could not offer Wharton the conversation she needed" (Haystock 76). Although a member of New York aristocracy from birth, Wharton recalls in her autobiography *A Backward Glance* a childhood in which her father's library and the family's travels helped her to understand the "Greater Inclination" that made her "too intelligent to be fashionable in New York" (119). When she finally "groped her way" to a vocation, she "felt like a homeless waif who, after trying for years to take out naturalization papers ... ha[d] finally acquired a nationality ... [in] the Land of Letters." There she "glorified" in her "new citizenship," yet never felt at home among peers whose greatest goal was being "a subject for adornment" (Wharton *Backward* 119).

Wharton's choice of words here is telling as the metaphor of citizenship further supports her insider-outsider status. Like her good friend Henry James, she spent much of her time in Europe and felt overwhelming kinship for Europeans, but her satirical gaze most often fixes the upper classes of her home country. Wharton wrote about Americans but "always denigrated one thing or another about the United States," which she associated with "crassness" and which led her to make Paris her home from about 1907 (Grenier 48). These feelings often find their way into her fiction, perhaps most vividly in her ghost stories, whose symbolic nature helps to mask her more volatile messages about an American aristocracy "blindly follow[ing] internalized cultural codes with disastrous consequences" (Dyman xiv). For the female writer on either side of the Atlantic in the nineteenth and early twentieth centuries, "the ghost story proved an ideal discourse for hidden agendas and deeper textual levels, as well as representing ... women's own marginalization, like the supernatural, to the realms of the irrational/Other" (Stewart 114). In Wharton's case the ghost story becomes a way "to utter the unutterable about sexuality, rage, death, fear, and especially the nature of women and men" (Fedorko ix).

An Irishman who dwelt precariously within and outside the English upper class, and a closeted homosexual nearly until the end of his life, Wilde had perhaps even greater reason to seek a means "to utter the unutterable." He produced what many believe to be his best work following his first homosexual experience, as Christopher S. Nassar explains: "[Wilde] definitely regarded homosexual contact as evil and [after 1886] wrote in full awareness of a demonic impulse within himself" (xvii). More broadly, Wilde's satire deals with being an outsider for his views on individuality at a time when conformity reigned. Shelton Waldrop makes the important point that "Wilde's own generative system of discourse was not so much about homosexuality—and its inevitable birth—as about the Attic Greek idea of liberty for the individual" (xix). Patrick Horan confirms this in his reference to a curtain speech from the opening night of *Lady Windermere's Fan* (1892) when Wilde "complimented the audience on the great success of *their* performance, emphasizing that ironically they were laughing at themselves and their own antiquated social manners" (31, emphasis added). Wilde cultivated a place in society and invented a persona for himself to that end according to the Decadent mode he largely established. At the same time, plays such as *The Importance of Being Earnest* and *An Ideal Husband*—produced in 1895 before he was imprisoned for "homosexual conduct"—offer pointed criticism of the ways men and women in that very society behave, singularly and collectively.

In implementing and reinventing gothic and fairy tale conventions, Wharton and Wilde create unique yet intriguingly parallel supernatural figures that are sympathetic and at times even pathetic. By definition a spirit occupies an "in-between" space, making it a supreme vehicle for considering the problems of the individual occupying such a position in the real world. With one foot among the living and the other in the hereafter or Faërie space, a ghost is an obvious porter, one that "link[s] the living and the dead in the present" (Weinstock 7). Other inhabitants of Faërie also fall into this category since Victorian folklorists found "the places of the dead and fairyland often indistinguishable" and "the rituals for dealing with both groups and prohibitions governing such relations ... identical" (Silver *Strange* 41). Further, the Occultist movement grew out of an impulse to prove "the supernatural ...

to be the natural not understood," thus aligning the faerie being with the ghost as a "natural" or "elemental" relative of the human (Silver *Strange* 56).

In their choices to occasionally work outside the limitations of realistic fiction and drama, Wharton and Wilde also support the argument for their insider-outsider status. Wharton believed "the faculty required for ... enjoyment" of the ghost story had "become almost atrophied in modern man" (Wharton *Ghost Stories* 8) and Wilde was "rebuked" by reviewers at the time of *Dorian Gray*'s publication "for its ostensible lack of moral import" (Womack 169). Yet she was convinced that "deep within us ... the ghost instinct lurks," writing to "celebrate those who have made [ghosts] visible to us" (Wharton *Ghost Stories* 8–9); and his novel has since come to be viewed as important for "exploit[ing] the fantastic elements inherent in the Victorian gothic as a means for fulfilling his decidedly *moral* aims" (Womack 169, emphasis in original). For both Wharton and Wilde the fantastic itself becomes a portal between the text and the world, the self and society, internal and external.

The Sympathetic Supernatural

Her abiding concern with conditions she personally experienced leads Wharton to favor a type of magical realism, making her ghost stories similar to her realistic fiction with an added element or accent of the supernatural. The choice of subgenre makes sense according to Lynette Carpenter and Wendy K. Kolmer, who see American "women writers [as] more likely to portray natural and supernatural experience along a continuum ... so that the supernatural can be accepted, connected with, reclaimed and can often possess a quality of familiarity" (12). The practice mirrors the way the portal bridges gaps between worlds: physical, sociological, political, psychological, etc. While not a ghost story per se, "After Holbein" is commonly accepted this way while depicting the corruptive real world of upper class, Golden-Age New York City, perfectly exemplifying her realist approach to the gothic and particular use of the portal/porter. The story centers on a pair of aging New York socialites, Mrs. Jaspar and Anson Warley, skeletons of their former selves and of a time that has passed away without their knowledge. Mrs. Jaspar has "bones" that have "remained impassive though the flesh had withered on them" (Wharton "After" 212). Once "New York's chief entertainer" (Wharton "After" 206), she now spends a death-in-life existence surrounded by servants who either humor or poke fun at her. Mrs. Jaspar's *guests* have become *ghosts*, imaginary presences whom her butler pretends to serve in an elaborate ritual (Wharton "After" 229–30).

As with the other examples in this chapter, "After Holbein" adds an interesting facet to the portal concept for its delineation of space in terms of social status as well as human psychology, an approach Wharton also favors in her more traditional ghost stories. Jaspar and Warley, who is her only real guest in the story, are porters grounded by the more concrete portal of her house. As is typical in the gothic, the remoteness of the house from reality contributes the "sense of claustrophobia, [whereby] the gradual exclusion of alternative options or explanations, felt by the character as the everyday world ... becomes obliterated by one growing certainty" (Manlove *Fantasy Literature* 107). This "certainty" has to do with the truth of Jaspar's and Warley's existence as her house also furnishes the nexus point where the myth of the New York elite collides with the reality, where the façade is pulled back to expose the ugliness beneath. Similar to Dickens's magnificently pathetic Miss Havisham, Mrs. Jaspar spends her last days in a veritable prison. The dinner party fantasy in which her servants participate paints her and Warley as doomed to repeat a ritual that is their only way of being in the world — which is to *not* be in it at all. In this way her house ironically juxtaposes the internal and external, representing the pain of being outside rather than the feeling of comfort normally associated with being inside, with feeling "at home." By emphasizing the pathos of the condition to which Jaspar and Warley have sunk, Wharton updates the traditional gothic, but upholds its usual abiding concern, to explore manifestations of evil in a society or a self.

Wharton also invokes gothic tradition in "After Holbein" through her use of doubling, first by splitting Warley's character, then by making his society self the perfect companion for Mrs. Jaspar. The narrator explains that the original, thoughtful Warley, "a rather remarkable man" (201), has been annihilated by "the other poor creature ... the lesser Anson" (202). The transformation represents the degeneration of the soul that results from prolonged conformity to society's roles and expectations. As the "lesser," the second Warley lacks all of the more appealing aspects of human nature, such as compassion and intellect. Like that icon of the gothic split self, Stevenson's Dr. Jekyll, the Warley who had sometimes "spent an evening with people who were doing or thinking real things" (203) slowly falls victim to the Hyde "creature" who prefers "anywhere where there's lots of racket and sparkle, places that people go to in Rollses ... and you have to pay a lot — *in one way or another* — to get in" (203, emphasis added).

In his heyday the "lesser" Warley delightedly "decline[d] the boredom" of Mrs. Jaspar's gatherings (208), but now finds himself drawn there as he goes through the streets with his brain in a muddle, trying to recall a destination. Apart from actual dementia, his difficulty stems from the fact that he simply does not have anywhere to go, no longer making the cut on fashionable guest lists. Like Jaspar, he remains incapable of admitting this to himself. The young maid Miss Cress wickedly reminds Jaspar that she "never invited Mr. Warley before," confirming that both of these relics have degenerated to the point where upholding a semblance of their former lives now requires associating with those they previously deemed undesirable. As Miss Cress demonstrates, little or no sympathy exists for aging aristocracy in a society where beauty is judged only superficially. Wharton published "After Holbein" in her later years, having spent her life as part of the upper class that virtually destroys Jaspar and Warley. Wharton uses her unique perspective to create two "ghosts" of a past way of life, or more accurately, two casualties of such a life. Exemplifying Wharton's use of the supernatural to evoke pathos rather than fear, Warley's attendance of Jaspar's dinner may be read as a sign of his redemption, that the "remarkable man" still lives. If this is so, the story becomes all the more tragic: just as in the case of Jekyll and Hyde, rather than reclaiming his life in the end the once "remarkable" Warley succumbs in the collision of his two selves.

Besides Mrs. Jaspar's house, Wharton more narrowly provides a second concrete gateway with symbolic implications in its front door, through which one virtually travels back in time to a world made partly of her own creation and partly out of a decadent past. It is on this doorstep that Warley meets his end. Wharton offers a pessimistic conclusion to "After Holbein," suggesting death as the inevitable and the *only* means of escape from such an existence. In the closing lines, the narrator explains how at the end of the evening Warley "issued forth from the house and drew in the first deep breath of night air" only to take "a step forward, to where a moment before the pavement had been — and where now there was nothing" (232). The "breath of night air" equates an epiphany toward which Warley heads in occasional lucid moments throughout the story, but one that comes too late to make a difference, at least for Warley. Like the vanishing sidewalk signaling Warley's loss of consciousness or death upon leaving Jaspar's house, the story argues the ephemeral life she and her guest have pursued. An existence dedicated to the worship of the material, the story seems to argue, ends very simply and poignantly, in "nothing."

A similar emphasis on superficial beauty and the perils of aging in Society drives "The Looking Glass," which may be even closer to Wharton's personal experience in its specific concern with the consequences for women. Like "After Holbein," this story lacks a literal ghost, but depicts the haunting of Mrs. Clingsland, whose name conveys her inability to let go of the earthly, to accept time's imprint on her face and in her relationships. Also haunted is the narrator Mrs. Atlee, who relates the story as a way of gaining the attention of her young granddaughter and reveals that her own past behavior continues to cause her suffering. Invoking one of the most ubiquitous devices both in gothic and portal terms, Wharton uses the idea of the looking glass to dramatize the tragedy for a woman trying to maintain her dignity in a materially obsessed culture.

Like Mrs. Jaspar, Mrs. Clingsland receives fewer visitors over time and increasingly relies upon Cora Atlee, whom she pays to do massage, hair, and makeup. Mrs. Atlee's main job, though, is to feed her employer's dwindling ego: "[Mrs. Clingsland] made me tell her every morning it wasn't true [that she had lost her beauty]; and every morning she believed me a little less" (258). In a vivid example of the porter at work, Mrs. Atlee *becomes* Mrs. Clingsland's looking glass, which Atlee makes explicit: "When her own people took enough notice of her to serve as looking glasses, which wasn't often, she didn't much fancy what she saw there" (262). Atlee is paid to make Clingsland happy, so she tells her what she wants to hear, becoming the means by which her employer engages with the world and keeps a tenuous grasp on her sanity. The illusion is both troubling and destructive as what Atlee really does is to encourage her employer's vanity, further perpetuating the problem and placing herself in an impossible position.

Wharton's "Looking Glass" subtly recalls an iconic, fairy-tale example of such a portal at work: Lewis Carroll's *Alice* books in which the title character can move back and forth between a land of imagination and "reality" because she is a child. Carroll makes this idea the crux of *Through the Looking-Glass*, but already raises the issue several times in its predecessor, *Alice's Adventures in Wonderland,* especially near the end when Alice starts to "grow" during the trial. She identifies some obvious illegalities in the proceeding as "stuff and nonsense," and when the queen orders, "Off with her head," Alice responds, "Who cares for you.... You're nothing but a pack of cards." Her expression of a lack of belief results in Alice's immediate return to her own place and time (Carroll 160–1). Contrastingly, in Wharton's tale, Mrs. Clingsland uses her "looking glass," Mrs. Atlee, as a way of standing still and avoiding the truth about herself. In leaving Wonderland, the little girl Alice illustrates the inevitability of "growing up," as painful as that recognition clearly is for Carroll himself. Being an adult in society, though, Mrs. Clingsland rejects this inevitability and ends up in a twilight world with the woman she pays to keep up the charade as her only companion.

Wharton confirms and intensifies Mrs. Atlee's porter status by adding a supernatural element to the story. Besides being a masseuse and cosmetician, Atlee professes that she has "a way of seeing things" (259). When Mrs. Clingsland shows her a "love letter" from the only man who ever "worshipped" her and who apparently sunk with the *Titanic,* Mrs. Atlee begins devising "messages" she passes off as his (263). The words are actually con-ceived by a dying young man Atlee befriends through another patient, yet she presents herself as the one transmitting messages from "Over There" (268). As a supposed medium, a psychic variation of a porter, Atlee bridges primary and secondary worlds. More importantly, she provides the conduit through which her employer clings to a memory that keeps her alive. Of course the whole process is a lie, just like the late nineteenth-century Occultist movement that partly inspires the story was quackery built from misguided belief and desire. The scientific challenge to faith caused people to search for meaning wherever they might find it, a compulsion Mrs. Clings-land would intimately understand, albeit for a more earth-bound reason. In hindsight Atlee admits this to herself and to her granddaughter, but feels somewhat vindicated about deceiving Mrs. Clingsland, reasoning, "What I was after was to make her believe in herself again, so that she'd be in a kinder mind toward others" (267). In fact, this does occur. According to Atlee, Mrs. Clingsland was partially transformed by the communications from her dead lover, becoming "less impatient with the people who waited on her" and "more understanding" with her family (269). Since the true author of the letters dies just after penning the last, technically Mrs. Atlee does receive at least one communication from the dead, which helps to soothe her guilt (273).

Combined, the story's being told by an older woman to a younger, its saturation of female characters, and emphasis on female beauty all point to Wharton's abiding concern with male-female power dynamics. The only thing that makes Mrs. Clingsland feel better is to have a man — even a dead man — profess his love for her. To make this happen, Mrs. Atlee compro-mises not only her personal morality, but also her religious beliefs ("I've been going against my Church and risking my immortal soul" 270). Even though men appear only peripherally in this story and the two main male charac-ters are dead or dying, what they think and believe drives the women's actions and responses. That Atlee is not in contact with "Over There" as she claims to Mrs. Clingsland reiterates the extent to which a woman — here both Clingsland and Atlee — would be willing to go to uphold social standards that corrupt and even kill women, while also having dire consequences for the men who establish and largely perpetuate these rules.

Beauty and its decay also form the basis for one of Wilde's most famous and complex works, *The Picture of Dorian Gray*. Here the looking-glass takes the shape of the painting into which the artist Basil Hallward pours his feel-ings for the title character. Wilde establishes the picture as a portal nearly from the story's opening as Basil describes, "While I was painting ... Dorian Gray sat beside me. Some subtle influence passed from him to me, and for the first time in my life I saw in the plain woodland the wonder I had always looked for and missed" (10). In one sense Basil views his painting of Dorian's image as creating a form of intimacy with his subject in an environment where a truly intimate relationship would be taboo. Lord Henry, being married and aristocratic, can freely spend time with Dorian, but the "poor artist" only gains access through his talent. Coinciding with Wilde's view of the artist's precarious position as an insider-outsider, Basil sees the painting as a gateway, a magical portal into the Society he otherwise avoids or is discouraged from joining. For example, in telling Lord Henry about an evening at Lady Brandon's, Basil says, "You know we poor artists have to show ourselves in society from time to time, just to remind the public that we are not savages" (6). Ironically it is the beautiful work of art, Dorian himself, who becomes the savage. Basil provides the conduit for this transformation by transferring his vision of Dorian, colored by his own inner turmoil, onto the canvas.

For Dorian the painting evokes what he fears most: losing his external beauty. When gazing at his likeness his first thought is "the full reality ... [that] there would be a day when his face would be wrinkled ... the grace of his figure broken and deformed" (24). Invoking the fairy-tale convention of the "foolish wish," Dorian muses, "If it were I who was to be always young, and the picture that was to grow old ... for that — I would give everything!" (25). His wish comes true and he does "give everything," but along the way he takes several others with him in a domino effect that such vanity creates in a culture where the external is all. The painting becomes the magical agent enabling Dorian to detach from his human conscience. With its existence, he can pursue whatever depravity he chooses — including murder — without showing any signs of wear.

In the end Dorian destroys himself in the presence of the painting. His death breaks the spell. The image on canvas immediately morphs back into its original depiction of "his exquisite youth and beauty" while the dead man shows a "withered, wrinkled, and loathsome visage" (224). The description suggests a transfiguration, reversing Basil's original and arguing the impossibility of a human achieving perfection or transcending mortality. In Jungian terms, of course, the painting can be read as Dorian's "shadow," or given its magical properties, as a "ghost" self. Although his soul physically decays, the picture still equals a positive agent in the story for nobly accepting the inevitability of mortality that Dorian rejects. The painting shows the grotesque reality of Dorian's character, and symbolically reveals the true nature of the society that produces him and many others like him. As his moral character degenerates, he feels himself slipping from his lofty position in that society, because despite his shadow/ghost self's sacrifices on his behalf, the living Dorian becomes less and less capable of hiding the truth of his dark nature.

While the painting represents the most obvious portal in *Dorian Gray*, an arguably more intriguing, metaphorical example comes in the shape of Sybil Vane. With her name revealing Dorian's interest in her, the actress captures his attention because he sees her as another kind of mirror, one that parallels Hallward's painting of him. Kathy Fedorko identifies "one of the most fundamental fears" in the gothic as that "deriv[ing] from gender identity and the mutual terror, anxiety, and dread that women and men arouse in one another" (ix). This notion operates in an interesting way in *Dorian Gray* as Sybil is not a mirror in the sense of a gothic double for Dorian, but a porter who helps bring about his reverse transformation at the cost of her own life. In Narcissistic fashion, her love for him means he sees himself reflected in her eyes, so that when with her he can continually gaze on *his own* beauty. This is why when she performs badly on stage he says, "You have killed my love" (86) and "without your art you are nothing" (87). He views her as he does himself, as a work of art. When she seems to stumble, she becomes mortal, less beautiful, and therefore less capable of positively reflecting *him*.

With its etymological associations to "artifice" and "artifact" the word "art" connotes fabrication, which also applies to Sibyl, at least as far as Dorian sees her. Harry makes this explicit after breaking the news of Sibyl's death: "The girl never really lived, and so she has never really died.... The moment she touched actual life, she marred it, and it marred her, and so she passed away" (103). The comment allows Dorian to quickly put aside any twinge of guilt. Sibyl becomes a "sacrifice" to his relentless pursuit of all things material, especially pleasure and beauty (Wilde 105). Thus she is for him both an example of art and in death an artifact. Had she lived he would never have been happy with her; even had she regained her acting ability, she would have eventually lost her looks. As a teenage corpse, she confirms the ethereality of her character by living in his memory as the lovely presence flitting across the stage. Perhaps even more powerfully than the picture of himself, Sibyl provides the supernatural agent pressuring Dorian. Her death haunts him to the end and provides the catalyst that compels her brother to revenge. Like Wharton, Wilde presents the ghostly Sibyl as sympathetic, especially in contrast to Dorian and the Society that destroys her and (for a time) preserves him.

Women figure even more prominently in "The Fisherman and His Soul," which although published in a collection of Wilde's fairy tales, actually offers a similar gothic/realistic hybrid to Wharton's "After Holbein," and "The Looking Glass," albeit with more obvious fantastic elements. Society is represented in Wilde's tale through the Priest, the Merchants, and the Fisherman's Soul after he cuts it from his body, thus sentencing it to wander without his heart. As with Dorian Gray, as well as Wharton's Jaspar and Warley, Wilde uses the Fisherman to explore the consequences of a human choice to pursue a particular kind of existence. In contrast to these other examples, however, in "Fisherman" Wilde shows an individual trying to *escape* rather than conform to societal dictates.

In "Fisherman" the object being pursued, the Mermaid, is consistently presented sympathetically, compared to the material pursuits that lead Mrs. Jaspar, Warley, and Mrs. Clingsland to self-destruct. For example, the Mermaid is captured by the Fisherman; she does not entice him. Aboard his boat she shows "terror" and pleads to be set free for the sake of her father who is "aged and alone" (130). The Fisherman tells her, "I will not let thee go save thou makest a promise that whenever I call ... thou will come and sing to me," so it is he who invites the act that in folklore would lure a sailor to his death. More significantly, though, the Mermaid, with her links to the sea, freedom, and immortality, is the object of the Fisherman's love. While Wilde often illustrates in his work a belief "that love relationships are rarely ideal" (Horan 74), true to his paradoxical nature, he nearly always upholds the act of loving itself as positive. In this tale, Society takes the shape of the Priest and the Merchants who refuse to aid the Fisherman in his quest to join his love in the sea. Both view the Soul in institutional and material terms: Christianity (Priest) and capitalism (Merchants.) While one system may be accepted as more virtuous, both the Priest and the Merchant define the Soul as a commodity and love as unimportant. Thus Wilde casts Society as negative and its failure to see the value of love as evil.

In keeping with the idea of the supernatural as benign, even the Witch shows concern in telling the Fisherman that to give up his Soul "is a terrible thing to do" (Wilde "Fisherman" 138). Despite her reaction she agrees to help him and her parting words, "He should have been mine ... I am as fair as she" (141), mark the Witch as a double for the Mermaid. Even though the Witch is aligned with darkness, through this doubling she also becomes a porter by which the Fisherman performs an act Wilde presents as positive. In seeking out supernatural aid, the Fisherman explicitly rejects societal authority by breaking the rules established by its two primary governing powers, religion and capitalism. Similarly, in loving the Mermaid, a supernatural being unencumbered by earthly limits or values, he becomes compelled to abandon the Society that will not allow him to indulge his passion.

In making his Faustian bargain with the Witch and her master the Devil, the Fisherman enacts a similar process to that of Dorian Gray, transforming his very nature by discarding his Soul. Again, though, in the Fisherman's case, the usual effect of such a bargain is reversed: It his Soul, not his body that manifests as his "dark" side. The Fisherman becomes the walking dead, a ghost of his former self, but for Wilde this shape creates a more appealing contrast to the Soul that is left behind. While the Fisherman joins the Mermaid under the sea, his Soul — now lacking the softening influence of his heart — wanders aimlessly and immerses itself in the seedy aspects of human life. The Soul adds a third supernatural double to those of the Mermaid and the Witch, but the fact that the Fisherman first tries to "sell" the Soul to the Priest and the Merchants reinforces the Soul's ironic link to the earthly.

The examples in this chapter are meant to show how both Wharton and Wilde use supernatural figures that help rather than frighten or injure the living. So to clarify here, the Soul *is* supernatural, but its association with the land defines it as a representative of Society, not of the spiritual. Because the Soul is not the Fisherman's whole being, but only a part of it devoid of feeling, it equates a soul-*less* Society that corrupts and even terrifies the feeling individual who dares or is forced to stand outside of it. In contrast, the Witch and Mermaid, who with their pagan associations, are in fact super-*natural*, enable the Fisherman to break his earthly bonds and achieve something more lasting, albeit less tangible. The Mermaid especially appears as a positive supernatural force due to her association with the water with its connotations of cleansing and rebirth, again in opposition to the Soul, "a concentrated symbol of evil and suffering that constitute the dry land" (Nassar 15). The Soul also equals the systems governing that "dry land" so that through the Fisherman's effort to detach himself from the Soul, i.e., mortality, Wilde shows that Society's corrupting forces are escapable only through great personal sacrifice, spurred by love.

In his Afterword to the *Complete Fairy Tales of Oscar Wilde*, Jack Zipes reminds us that Wilde loosely develops "Fisherman" as a version of Hans Christian Andersen's "The Little Mermaid," but re-imagines the original, since the Fisherman "gives up his soul ... to enjoy ... natural love ... [and] recognizes that his 'hedonistic' love is more holy than what society ordains as good." Zipes sees the Fisherman's reunion with the Mermaid as "an act of rebellion against traditional morality" (Afterword 212), which also coincides with Wilde's tendency throughout his work to depict the artist as a Christ-like and marginalized figure. The Fisherman partly fits this category, however, the love relationship in the tale adds a facet, as Zipes acknowledges (Afterword 212). Similar to Wilde, whose homosexuality placed him in a position of loving outside the norm of his day, the Fisherman stands on Society's fringe. In fact, prior to giving up his Soul, he lives mostly in his boat. Again like the artist Wilde, the Fisherman's vocation relegates him to a place *in between* sea (freedom) and Earth (Society). Once he meets the Mermaid he becomes obsessed to the point where his existence requires the boat, thus intensifying the outsider status he already occupies.

In the end the Fisherman and the Priest each gain knowledge, but the one has to die to achieve this end for them both. On the surface, viewing the Fisherman's demise as positive seems difficult given that he yields his Soul to the devil and so would be doomed to hell in Christian terms. Wilde's symbolism, however, begs a more complex reading. In death, the Fisherman "attain[s] a state of higher innocence and his place is now in heaven.... The higher innocence is again a world of love, but one that is all-encompassing" (Nassar 20). Wilde's version of the afterlife is absent of the judgment conveyed by the Priest, whose response to finding the Fisherman's and Mermaid's bodies is a vow to "bury them in the corner of the Field of the Fullers, and set no mark above them" (177).

Later the flowers that spring up on this unconsecrated burial spot suggest redemption and trouble the Priest to the point where, from that time onward he speaks "not of the wrath of God, but of the God whose name is Love" (Wilde "Fisherman" 178). With such an ending, the story finally argues that one who dares to challenge the norm does so at his peril, but that loss may be positive in that it paves the way for change. Wilde's protagonists usually "die through a sacrifice, either out of love for humanity or love for art," perhaps in keeping with the author's own feelings as he grew older and "became more painfully aware of the difficulties a 'deviate' artist would encounter in British society" (Zipes Afterword 211). In this way the Fisherman is both a martyr and a victim of Society's worship of the material over the spiritual, a condition that in the story even touches the Church and which would have deep personal significance for Wilde himself.

Like "The Fisherman" and her own "After Holbein," Wharton's "The Lady's Maid's Bell," argues that escaping Society may only be possible through a permanent severing of the human tie to the earthly, in other words, through death. As with "The Looking Glass," the issue in "The Lady's Maid's Bell" is decidedly one of gender dynamics; in this case, within the context of marriage. Given her own "passionless marriage to the neurotic socialite Teddy Wharton" (Grenier 52), it is unsurprising that the intricacies of the institution as it influences the choices and self-image of both sexes pervade much of her supernatural as well as her realistic fiction. Issues of female freedom and identity in particular centralize "The Lady's Maid's Bell," being primarily illustrated through the juxtaposition of three women (two living, one ghostly), and the deteriorating marriage that entwines their experiences.

Wharton builds the suspense around a motif of sound and silence, with the ringing of the "lady's maid's bell" as a supernatural "wake-up call." Unfortunately for all three, the silence through which it cuts always drowns them out, fulfilling patriarchal society's prescription that a lady should keep her opinions to herself. Emma, the ghost of the last lady's maid, tries to communicate but her efforts are ineffectual and vague. Seeing Emma "in her disembodiment and muteness ... [a]s a sign of the untold female story," Fedorko assesses the ghost as leaving "an emptiness where a resource should be" (31). Even though she is alive, the present maid Alice Hartley enacts a similar absence to that of the ghost as she repeatedly refrains from asking questions. For her part the lady of the house is the least assertive of the three and her death reinforces this point, amounting to a giving up or giving in to her husband's tyranny. By mirroring both Hartley and Mrs. Brympton, Emma poignantly embodies the frustration of and limited options for a woman who perceives herself as an insider-outsider in Wharton's Society.

Stories by other American women writers of Wharton's era, such as Kate Chopin's "The Story of an Hour" and Charlotte P. Gilman's "The Yellow Wallpaper," similarly posit death as the only means of escape for a woman of a certain class living in such a society, where even those who recognize and share her plight remain similarly chained. The ghost story is synonymous with the "tale of terror," particularly in women's writing, but a "commonality" often exists as "the messages brought by those who haunt their houses ... warn of the dangers of domesticity, frequently through connections between the ghost's history and that of the living woman" (Carpenter and Kolmar 14). Offering a perfect example, "The Lady's Maid's Bell" makes its supernatural representative, Emma, entirely sympathetic. When Hartley first sees the ghost she expresses no fear, viewing the "thin woman with a white face" as a living person (14). Instead Hartley associates her growing feeling of uneasiness with the *house* (Wharton "Lady's Maid's" 20, emphasis added). After learning the ghost's history, Hartley comes face-to-face with her and describes: "Afterward I was terribly frightened, but at the time it wasn't fear I felt, but something deeper and quieter. She looked at me ... and her face was just one dumb prayer to me —... I felt I must know what she wanted" (31). Personally relating to Emma's need to speak, Hartley feels a need to understand and help her, to "know what she wanted." In contrast, whenever Hartley encounters Mr. Brympton, she trembles and panics (24–6). Her fear of him is palpable and immediate, not an afterthought. In the gothic tradition Hartley, Emma, and Mrs. Brympton double each other, but sympathetically rather than in the usual way as good/evil sides of one personality. The two maids share an overwhelming concern for Mrs. Brympton and seek to break the bonds that prevent her from speaking for herself.

Their failure contributes to their mistress's death, but this does not entirely diminish the weight of the effort.

In a contemporary example of the sympathetic supernatural, *Tim Burton's Corpse Bride* (2006) uses a Victorian setting to similarly consider the destructive consequences when marriage is a socio-economic rather than an emotional transaction. The betrothed couple, Victoria Everglot and Victor Van Dort, are as charmingly naïve and unassuming as their parents are calculating and status-hungry. When Victor shows the slightest hesitation at the wedding rehearsal and ends up in the forest trying to get through his vows without stumbling, he finds his words taken literally by Emily, the Corpse Bride. In complete contrast to the living world, Burton chooses to make Emily's realm of the dead bright and colorful — in other words, *alive*. The dead sing and dance, being no longer burdened by earthly concerns about money, appearance, or social status. In a film that "is actually as much about life as it is about death" (Page 231), things climax when the dead go "upstairs." There the zombies find the living stoically seated around a long table, silent and lifeless at what is supposed to be a wedding celebration for Victoria and Lord Barkus Bittern, who takes advantage of her supposed jilting by offering himself as groom. The intrusion of the dead on the living in this scene supports Edwin Page's point that "in the real world the characters are ... like zombies following their social codes without question" (230).

The sense of freedom assigned to the dead world in Burton's film only partially applies to the Corpse Bride, whose heart is far from cheerful and free. Compared to Victoria, Emily has some say in whom she will wed; her efforts nearly lead Victor to suicide. In this way she parallels Wharton's Emma as a female ghost exemplifying the insider-outsider whose presence threatens the status quo. Wharton provides a kind of freedom to Emma, ironically making her the most *enviable* of the three women in "The Lady's Maid's Bell." Emma comes and goes as she likes and can see from an outsider's perspective the problems her living counterparts cannot, or that they feel unable or unwilling to challenge. Emma "haunts," but only in the sense of being a reminder that something is wrong. Paralleling the ringing bell, she echoes and thus intensifies the expression of pain felt by the real-world woman, Mrs. Brympton. As in "The Looking Glass," here Wharton stresses the extent to which a woman might go in response to such circumstances, but while Atlee and Clingsland try to work within the social limitations, the women in "Lady's Maid's Bell" move toward escape, just as Burton's Emily does. Emily's rotting wedding dress, her tale of being murdered by Bittern (the same man intent on marrying Victoria), her decaying beauty — not to mention the willingness of the other dead to defend her honor — all make the

Corpse Bride a grotesque yet pitiable and admirable figure. Even though she is initially unscrupulous in her determination to make Victor keep his promise, in the end Emily gives him up to her living counterpart. Within the gothic tradition Burton invokes through setting, lighting, music, and animation, Emily is Victoria's double, the physical manifestation of the toll that marriage takes on a woman when she is dealt with as a possession rather than a person.

Another role reversal mirroring that of the living and the dead occurs when Victor decides to sacrifice himself to keep his inadvertent vow to Emily, effectively shedding his hold on the living world. Confirming her porter status, he transforms as a result of her influence, as expressed in his newfound ability to say his vows in church and in her relinquishing of him to Victoria. She says, "This is wrong.... I love you Victor, but you're not mine.... You kept your promise, you set me free. Now I can do the same for you" (Burton). Here Burton emphasizes a theme of female solidarity that also pervades "The Lady's Maid's Bell." Emily's gesture enables Victor and Victoria to marry, and while this might suggest a perpetuation of the problem, it is clear from their interactions and the similarities of their names that they have found love despite the parental efforts to force them together — and also despite the supernatural efforts to keep them apart. The love match of Victor and Victoria suggests hope for the future, that their offspring will be more like their parents than their grandparents in their attitudes toward love and social standing.

In a nontraditional ending for a gothic/ghost story, the Corpse Bride exits by transforming into a glowing swarm of butterflies, a conventional symbol of transformation that also suggests she has found peace and true freedom. Unlike Wharton's Emma, who continues to haunt the Brymptons' country house, Emily insists on being heard; she even achieves vengeance on the man who made her the Corpse Bride. Despite this and the happy ending Burton provides, though, Emily's story remains a tragedy and a warning to the society that continues to produce Bitterns, Everglots and Van Dorts. While Burton's setting is Victorian, Emily updates the standard gothic female role for a twenty-first-century audience, so that in helping Victor and Victoria she also helps herself in a way that Wharton's Emma does not. Weinstock's point that "claiming ghosts and women are linked [in supernatural tales] by their disempowered status overlooks the inherent power that ghosts possess" (17), does not take into account the fact that the ghosts in Wharton's tales always seem to be bound by *earthly* rules. For instance, while Emma "defies death itself" and "possesses the capacity to inspire fear and awe," she shows very little power "to intervene in the course of events in order to effect material change" (Weinstock 17). In this way Burton's take on the Victorian gothic redefines the female ghost while maintaining its inherent quality of being and representing the insider-outsider.

Although certainly more lighthearted than "Lady's Maid's Bell," Wilde's "The Canterville Ghost" also dramatizes social marginalization through a supernatural figure acting as an instructional porter for the living. Isobel Murray makes a valid point when she says "The readiness of the English to believe in ghosts ... is mocked [in the story] as surely as the American commonsensical refusal to believe" (8). I would say, however, that the Americans are more often on the receiving end of the satire, as their response to the ghost of Sir Simon de Canterville actually intensifies to the point where they are the haunters. Indeed after a month of their residence, "his nerves [are] completely shattered and he start[s] at the slightest noise" (Wilde "Canterville" 218). In contrast to the Otises, Wilde makes the English ghost, Sir Simon, quite likeable and even worthy of respect. Thus Wilde pits ancient tradition and folk belief/superstition (England) against modern progress and scientific rationality (America) with the Ghost winning out in the end.

Despite being a murderer condemned to haunt his own former house, Sir Simon represents a sympathetic figure and a positive agent of rebellion in the story. He is repeatedly insulted and tormented by the Otis boys and their father, yet without fail pursues "his solemn duty to appear in the corridor once a week, and to gibber from the large oriel window on the first and third Wednesdays in every month" (219). The Ghost does "not see how he could honorably escape from his obligations" since he is "most conscientious in all things connected with the supernatural" (219). Wilde paints the Ghost's activities as a vocation; he is an ethereal businessman, a more appealing supernatural double for Mr. Otis. Sir Simon's disruptiveness therefore marks a productive challenge to the emerging modern status quo as represented by the United States Minister and most of his family. As Horan notes, in this story "the living haunt the ghost far more than the ghost haunts the living because he continually tries to understand why the humans are so inhumane" (80). Rather than being evil, the Canterville Ghost stirs fear in none of the humans and pity in the best of them.

The second porter in the story also bears a connection to the beyond and to a more concrete gateway between worlds. As the most appealing Otis, it is fitting that Virginia becomes the agent of the Ghost's deliverance. When she accidentally happens upon him she is "filled with pity and determined to try and comfort him" (223). Her innocence makes her a standard gothic heroine to contrast with the dark knowledge of the hero/villain; in this case, Sir Simon. Symbolically Virginia's interest in helping the Ghost again supports one of Wilde's major beliefs, one expressed in "The Fisherman" and in many of his other tales as well: the importance of compassion and love, particularly to those pushed to Society's borders. Epitomizing the idea of the "in-between," Sir Simon is marginalized from the "Garden of Death" but also from his own house, since the Otises have taken over and refuse to be frightened of him.

Virginia is the only one who can make this right as he tells her, "You can open for me the portals of Death's house, for Love is always with you, and Love is stronger than Death" (225). Unlike *Dorian Gray*'s Sibyl Vane, Virginia seems to gain something through her courageous effort on the Ghost's behalf. She enters the realm of death but her goodness protects her and not long after her return she marries, telling her husband, "Poor Sir Simon! I owe him a great deal.... He made me see what Life is, and what Death signifies, and why Love is stronger than both" (234). Since Virginia does not appear to need a lesson about love, the learning applies more readily to the rest of the Otises, who not unlike the Darlings in Barrie's *Peter Pan*, gain their own understanding through Virginia's loss and return. This becomes evident in the reunion scene when she says, "I have been with the Ghost. He is dead, and you must come and see him ... he was really sorry for all that he had done" (Wilde "Canterville" 20). While showing "mute astonishment" at her words, the rest of the family follow Virginia "down a narrow secret corridor" to a "little room" where his skeleton is chained to the wall. She prays while "the rest of the party looked on in wonder at the terrible tragedy whose secret was now disclosed to them" (Wilde "Canterville" 20–1). Being able to see Sir Simon's death as a "tragedy" equates with belief in the truth of his ghostliness. This idea is also supported by Mr. Otis' attempt to give the box of jewels left to Virginia by "his unlucky ancestor" to Lord Canterville, who has believed in the ghost's existence all along (Wilde "Canterville" 22).

As artists and social insider/outsiders Wharton and Wilde similarly embody the paradox of the artist's lot, which countless others have struggled to express and make sense of over time. How does one deal with and reflect the alienation and isolation from Society demanded for the artist to represent, and more importantly, to challenge it? Can a writer speak for the voiceless while sometimes counting as one of this number? In their fantasy work especially, Wharton and Wilde use parallel strategies to attack the institutions that also enable them to live among those toward whom their satire is aimed. By the end of his life Wilde was "an outcast from the same society that hailed him in the first half of the 1890s" (Horan 33). For Wharton, "life remained an exciting business till the end" (Auchincloss xi), but in an environment where ladies were not encouraged to give opinions, she lived in continual quest of what she called "my own spiritual kin" (*Backward Glance* 123). Wharton obviously fared better than Wilde, who died shortly after his release from prison on a sodomy charge, yet neither writer wholly succeeded in resolving their questions. The body of work each left behind continues to shape a critical understanding of both their era and ours, reiterating the book itself as a portal of power.

PART IV

Haunting History: The Portal in Modern/ Postmodern Fantasy

CHAPTER SEVEN

One World to Rule Them All:
The Un-Making and Re-Making of the
Symbolic Portal in J.R.R. Tolkien's
The Lord of the Rings

> *It seemed ... that he had stepped over a bridge of time into a corner of
> the Elder Days, and was now walking in a world that was no more. In
> Rivendell there was memory of ancient things; in Lórien the ancient
> things still lived on in the waking world ... wolves were howling on the
> wood's borders: but on the land of Lórien no shadow lay.*
> — J.R.R.Tolkien [*The Lord of the Rings* 349]

So far this study has focused on nineteenth and early twentieth-century writers and their influences to show how the portal operates as a magical transforming agent in the first golden age of literary fantasy. The portal
and its home genre have become even more prevalent in its second golden
age, from about the end of the First World War through today, but in wider
variation, subtlety, and sophistication. Pinpointing when fantasy becomes
"modern" remains difficult, but most agree on J.R.R. Tolkien as the author
who initiated a true evolution of fantasy with the publication of *The Hobbit* in 1937, and solidified this position with *The Lord of the Rings* in 1954.
For having "said something important, and meant something important, to
a high proportion of millions of readers" (Shippey xxvi) for well over a half
century now, Tolkien remains an inescapable presence for his successors,
including that other key fantasist who emerges in the 1990s, J.K. Rowling,
whose work I discuss in the next chapter.

Although Tolkien is commonly seen as an innovator, frequently overlooked are the implications of Middle-earth as an icon of the one-world
magical landscape. With Tolkien this approach becomes a defining trait of
modern fantasy, largely coming out of a desire for "alternative worlds that
we can treat as 'realities' while we read" (Manlove "Victorian and Modern"
17). To clarify, authors using the one-world setting present a magical realm

as a whole entity. In seeking to define "the dialectic between author and reader" in *Rhetorics of Fantasy* (xiii), Farah Mendelsohn uses "immersive" to represent a similar idea, saying, "We do not enter into the immersive fantasy ... [it] must be sealed; it cannot, within the confines of the story, be questioned" (xx). This is also true for the one-world concept, yet Mendlesohn does not go far enough to tease out the intricacies of immersive fantasy. Specifically, she overlooks that an author can (and often does) mark out dimensions *within* a finite, encompassing world so that a character does not have to — and indeed may not even be able to — entirely depart one to enter another.

Somewhere between Mendelsohn's categories of "immersive," and "intrusion," the latter being where the "fantastic is the bringer of chaos" into an otherwise "normal" space (*Rhetorics* xxi), stands the one-world fantasy. For example, as I discuss in chapter eight, only wizards, witches, and other magical beings are able to see Hogwarts, Diagon Alley, and Hogsmeade for what they really are, but these places *do exist* within the facsimile of our own contemporary world in which the *Harry Potter* books are set. Muggles just lack the power to reach them and/or the imagination to even notice them. Understanding the nuances of the one-world approach allows us to more accurately identify — as so much Tolkien (and Rowling) criticism resists doing — the presence and power of portals in works where travel between discrete worlds does not occur. Despite or perhaps because of his non-use of the more obvious, concrete variety, I submit that Tolkien is almost equally a master of the portal as he is "the author of the century," as Tom Shippey identifies.

Again, this claim holds up because of the malleability of the portal and the necessity of challenging the too-restrictive understanding of it as a concrete "door," as I have sought to illustrate in Parts I–III of this book for fantasists of the first golden age. Tolkien clearly understood the vast implications of magical agency in the fantasy text, though he did not specifically concern himself with the portal's operations as such. His insistence on the separation, insofar as it is possible, of Faërie from the everyday world not only serves to evolve and re-invigorate the genre, but also to further stretch the portal concept from its first major phase of development to its second. Recognizing this enables a richer, more precise understanding of Tolkien as the primogenitor of a whole category of fantasy writing, as well as of the category itself. First, this chapter sketches a working definition of modern fantasy in reference to Tolkien as sub-creator. Second, the analysis applies this understanding to illustrate the process of un-making and re-making within the singular world setting as a central motif in *The Lord of the Rings*. Altogether this chapter assesses Tolkien's almost-magical transformation of the device itself as he re-imagines the portal of power for the twentieth century and beyond.

From the Many to the One (and Back Again?): Tolkien's Middle-earth and Modern Fantasy

Not until fairly recently, in the last couple of decades or so, have scholars begun attempting a definition of "modern fantasy" as a distinct sub-category. This is unsurprising given the distance usually required for adequate generic labeling, which is tricky at best in the first place. In 1989, Colin Manlove makes an early useful effort in "Victorian and Modern Fantasy: Some Contrasts," postulating that nineteenth-century fantasy has little concern with the "threatened landscape" as appears later in the works of Tolkien and C.S. Lewis. Manlove also sees Victorian fantasy being "governed by patterns and by logic," while in the twentieth century the genre tends to be less concerned with "rules" and "more in touch with the unconscious roots of the form"; in other words, with myth and folktale. Manlove names Tolkien as the founding father in a more explicit definition, saying that by "modern fantasy ... we usually mean some post–Tolkienian sub-created world of idyllic nature in which elfish forces for good struggle against evil powers" ("Victorian and Modern" 12–13). Here "idyllic" may not be the most apt term for the clearly fallen state of Middle-earth, where Old Man Willow, Caradhras, and even the Ents can be destructive forces to be reckoned with. Still Manlove's definition helpfully marks the use of the singular Faërie space as the most significant convention differentiating first from second golden age fantasy. Also, because the one-world approach does not become a widespread trend in literary fantasy until after Tolkien, and for his highly original and complex synthesis of diverse mythologies, Middle-earth becomes "the standard against which all sub-creation is tested" (Mathews *Fantasy* 63).

Since Manlove, several others have sought to delineate some dimensions of modern fantasy. In 2001, esteemed Tolkien scholar Tom Shippey insists that fantasy is a "mode," not a genre, because it "includes many genres besides fantasy: allegory and parable, fairy tale, horror and science fiction, modern ghost story and medieval romance" (viii). A few years later in 2005, Jared Lobdel concurs with Shippey's assessment of folklore and other ancient forms of story as significant resources for twentieth-century fantasists. "Tolkien drank from the same stream as Langland and Bunyan," says Lobdel, "but rather than Piers or Christian, [he] gave us the Nine Walkers of *The Lord of the Rings* ... [and] the beginnings of fantasy as a new genre" (20). Lobdel provisionally dubs this "Tolkienian Fantasy," but supports Manlove in using the term synonymously with "fantasy" and "modern fantasy." In *From Homer to Harry Potter: A Handbook on Myth and Fantasy* (2006), Matthew T. Dickerson and David O'Hara also recognize the influence of past epic and folk traditions shaping modern fantasy. These authors see myth and fairy tale as "two ends of the spectrum" and find that "the literature of Faërie takes place where *the two worlds meet*" (50, emphasis added), which supports the idea of fantasy itself as a literary in-between as established in my introduction. With Manlove, Shippey, and Lobdel, Dickerson and O'Hara provide insights into the overall fabric of the genre; all firmly situate Tolkien as its primogenitor, albeit one whose own influences stretch far and wide, textually and temporally.

Still, my primary interest lies not so much in understanding how modern fantasy "came to be" (Lobdel xi), but rather in demonstrating how and to what effect the portal manifests and operates within this distinct mode, to use Shippey's term, whose concerns are both universal and contemporary. Mendelsohn comes close to acknowledging the more expansive use of the device but causes some confusion by defining a portal fantasy as "simply a fantastic world entered through a portal" (*Rhetorics* xix), then describing Tolkien's work as a "portal-quest fantasy" when no such entry occurs — at least not physically. She clarifies, however, by acknowledging Tolkien for "establishing a pattern for the quest narrative in which the portal is not encoded solely in the travelogue discovery of what lies ahead, but in the insistence that there is past and place behind, and that what lies behind must be thoroughly known and unquestioned before the journey begins" (*Rhetorics* 14). The portal can be more broadly understood, as Mendlesohn implies here; it need not bridge literal in-betweens but can function as a magical nexus for space occupied by concepts, traditions, time, and the "country" of the self.

This is precisely what Tolkien does in *LotR* and, although he may be best known for doing so, he is obviously not the first to use the one-world setting. Given his commonly known influence on Tolkien as well as his own signature use of the portal, William Morris provides a useful point of comparison to help illustrate Tolkien's debt to his predecessors and influence on his successors in expanding the uses of the device. In other words, part of Tolkien's achievement is as a porter for literary fantasy itself. Richard Mathews believes Tolkien "found in Morris ... the spark or connection [that] helped advance a new fantasy tradition" (*Fantasy* 86). This "spark" certainly informed Tolkien's perspective of fantasy as an art form, yet Morris's Victorian Medievalism causes his version of the one-world technique to diverge in at least one key way. In the prose romances such as *The Story of the Glittering Plain, The Water of the Wondrous Isles,* and *The Wood Beyond the World,*

Morris uses a singular setting containing discrete spaces within it,[1] but one that approximates the real world of the Middle Ages and Quest Romance. Morris' Faërie realm is, as E.P. Thompson specifies, "an organic pre-capitalist community with values … sharply contrasted [to] those of Victorian England" (59), but his characters are still cut from the knights, damsels, and sorceresses of the historical Middle Ages; his language a hybrid of medieval and Victorian prose. Rejecting the realist novel so prevalent in his time for "its preoccupation with the chiefly self-productive middle-class hero and heroine" (Silver "Socialism Internalized" 119), Morris creates what Carole Silver calls the "socialist romance" ("Socialism Internalized" 126). In this way his work remains in keeping with the Victorian penchant for placing the fairy-story in a recognizable setting, juxtaposing his own contemporary England and its Medieval past.

One might say the same of Tolkien: as a linguist and a philologist, he is famous for using his knowledge and love of ancient tales and cultures as a foundation for his work. In fact, with *LotR* he famously sets out to create an ancient history for Britain to replace the Arthurian legends mainly penned by the French. As Tolkien says, "Though I have not attempted to relate the shape of the mountains and land-masses to what geologists may say … about the nearer past, imaginatively this 'history' [*LotR*] is supposed to take place in a period of the actual Old World of this planet" (Carpenter *Letters* 219–20). Yet despite the similar nomenclature Middle-earth is *not recognizable* as an earlier version of our own world in the way one finds in the medieval sense with Morris. Superficially this is because we have no documented knowledge of such a place as Middle-earth existing in history, but this is just the point. Tolkien's universe is not only pre–Christian, but pre- or, more accurately, *a-historic*, populated by elves, orcs, wizards, and governed by naturalistic magic. The existence of Middle-earth is original and self-sufficient, never being explicitly contrasted against the extra-textual real world in the manner of Morris's "socialist romances." Seeing Tolkien as "the first to link the Celtic, the fantastic, and feigned history" (not to mention the Norse sagas and his own created mythologies), Lobdel explains, "Morris was not part of a Celtic stream, rather of a medieval stream which also had its origins in the growth of historical consciousness" (35–6). In contrast, Tolkien conjures what Mathews calls "a complete and self-contained reality" (*Fantasy* 92), presented as an epoch so distant as to be undocumented by historians, except by *LotR* itself.

I do not mean to suggest Tolkien's universe is original to the point where it denies the problems and ideas of his day. Such detachment from one's immediate surroundings is impossible for any writer, and in fact, quite the opposite is true for Tolkien. Fantasy as a genre — as its scholars including Tolkien and Shippey are fond of pointing out — can be more real than realistic fiction. By stepping outside the limitations of recognizable time and space, fantasy does not avoid but pointedly confronts universal *and* contemporary questions of the human condition: death, faith, love, good and evil, to name a few. Lobdel uses the term "Romantic Medievalism" in comparing Tolkien to Morris, which while slightly redundant, aptly recognizes Tolkien's abiding love of nature, use of the quest motif, and etc. One must not overlook, however, that *LotR* is also meaningfully shaped not only by Tolkien's medievalism, but also by his reaction to "machinery" in the "Robot Age," even more destructive than that existing in Morris' industrial era.

Not unlike what Morris did in his own time, Tolkien, with his modern medievalism as one might term it,[2] especially captured the imagination of youth in the 1950s and '60s who felt a "need for escape from the political and military tensions wracking the world and for stability in an increasingly unstable environment" (Chance 2). Being much less Romantic than he is pessimistic about modernity, Tolkien views any attempt to escape from it as positive, though he explicitly denies embedding any "inner meaning or 'message'" in *LotR* and emphasizes, "The real war [WWII] does not resemble the legendary war in its process or its conclusion" (Preface *LotR* xxiii–xxiv). Still, we cannot overlook that Tolkien initially conceived Middle-earth while serving in World War I, when he began filling notebooks with languages, tales, and history for what would become *The Silmarillion*, which he viewed as his most important work. While they may be familiar, the "scenes, characters, and actions [in *LotR*] ... are at the same time separate and distinct from ... reality; the reader's hopes and expectations are freshened once he or she is distanced from the jaded habits of response" (Mathews *Fantasy* 83). This freshening corresponds to Tolkien's notion of "recovery" or "seeing things as we were meant to see them," which he identifies as an important effect of the fairy-story ("On Fairy-Stories" 77). In this way Tolkien transcends the dreaded allegory, sub-creating Middle-earth as a singular realm with unique concerns that remain simultaneously remote and applicable to the facts of human history, to the modern *as well as* to the ancient and universal. Because his version of ancient corresponds to authentic as well as invented history and folk belief, Tolkien's work goes further than that of Morris, both in terms of its expansiveness and its sealed use of the one-world technique.

To the extent that it is possible to put Tolkien's influence and success aside for a moment, why specifically does the one-world approach become so ubiquitous in modern fantasy? Manlove considers the prevalence of the technique to be "a product of twentieth-century internationalism, the growing sense of Planet Earth made up of a potential community of nations"

("Victorian and Modern" 19). Certainly with two World Wars and a moon landing, in the twentieth century the idea of space itself uniquely captured the imagination. In turn this preoccupation greatly influenced the writers for whom the sub-creation of alternate realms is of primary consideration: fantasists. As the perceived threat to security in Great Britain and America shifted from the very real Nazi concentration camps and Pearl Harbor devastation to the much more elusive "Russian menace" of Cold War ideology, magical realms became more insular and self-sufficient. In her 2004 study *Readers in Wonderland: The Liberating Worlds of Fantasy Fiction,* Deborah O'Keefe offers a similar explanation, but with an emphasis on technology: "As fast travel and communication made the world accessible ... the fantasy books in this comparatively open world became ... comparatively closed. It's not that they are simple or tidy, but that the structures of many books now are tighter than those of the nineteenth-century fantasies" (15).

Returning to the source, as it were, one finds Tolkien's understanding of fantasy to be inextricably bound up with the issue of space, but for him this has more to do with authenticity and believability than with globalization. In "On Fairy-Stories," his speech originally delivered in 1939 as an Andrew Lang lecture and published less than a decade later, Tolkien coins the terms "Primary" and "Secondary" to delineate a boundary between mundane reality and the "Perilous Realm" of Faërie. He emphasizes the great difficulty for the fantasist to successfully bring to life "the indescribable" nature of Faërie, for Tolkien believes it "essential to a genuine fairy-story that it be presented as true," by which he means accurate to human experience, not scientifically or empirically provable ("On Fairy-Stories" 42). As noted in my introduction, virtually since Tolkien first uttered these words, "Primary" and "Secondary" entered the vernacular as a way to denote discrete realms within a story. Originally, though, he meant these terms to differentiate the spaces outside and within the text itself: the reader lives in the Primary world and (ideally) enters the Secondary in opening the book and starting to read.

In the Andrew Lang lecture Tolkien also establishes the trait that for him overrides all others in defining the fairy-story: setting. These are not, he says, "stories *about* fairies and elves, but stories about *Faërie,* the realm or state in which fairies have their being" (38, emphasis in original). Because a "genuine fairy-story ... cannot tolerate any frame or machinery suggesting that the whole story in which they occur is a figment or illusion" (Tolkien "On Fairy-Stories" 42), it makes sense that Tolkien's own tales unfold within a single world. The name itself defines Middle-earth as an in-between space. In a 1955 letter to his publisher, apparently responding to questions raised for an article in the *New York Times,* Tolkien explains, "'Middle-earth' ... is just a use of Middle English *middle-erde* (or *erthe* altered from Old English *Middangeard*: the name for the inhabited lands of Men 'between the seas'" (Carpenter *Letters* 219–20). Michael Stanton adds, "'Middle-earth' ... was the name for the Earth itself, imagined as suspended between the sky above and the void below, or as poised spiritually between Heaven and Hell" (12).[3] "Middle" also signifies the position of those who dwell in such a place, being between the Valar, representing eternal life, and "the void" or total annihilation. Events in such a realm cannot help but impact both extreme spaces, as confirmed by the departure of the elves and the return of Gandalf from the Abyss. Middle-earth occupies a portal position in itself, then, as a magical universe in which events unfold whose outcome resonates through to the spiritual/mythical realms on either side of it.

The destruction of the One Ring brings about the passing of the Third Age, with simultaneous loss and gain. The whole purpose of Frodo's quest and those of his friends is to un-make the One Ring in order to prevent evil from destroying all that is good in Middle-earth. At the same time, "the end of the Third Age means a loss of good works as well as evil ones" (Mathews *Fantasy* 78). Thus Tolkien seems to support Joseph Campbell's well-known belief in a "fundamental psychological transformation that everyone has to undergo ... [as] the basic motif of the hero's journey—leaving one condition and finding the source of life to bring you forth into a richer or mature condition" (124). Such creation-from-destruction forms an abiding motif of Frodo's "errand," even as it becomes fragmented into several physically separate quests performed by other members of the Company and their forces in "The Breaking of the Fellowship" at the end of the Book Two. Invariably in *LotR* this process of loss and recovery, un-making and re-making, is either initiated by or occurs through a magical object or character whose participation results in transformation in one form or another.

No traveler moves through time or space to reach Middle-earth à la William Morris's *News from Nowhere*, yet Tolkien's universe in *LotR* itself acts as a portal, one that both transforms and becomes transformed by the quests that unfold there. Also, one must not overlook that Middle-earth *does* house discrete and extremely difficult places that require some form of magic or special wisdom in order to reach. While they do not furnish access to separate spaces outside of Middle-earth, Tolkien includes some concrete magical objects and doors whose use results in transformation with great consequences felt well beyond the affected individual. In this way he acknowledges yet also overturns and reinvents, un-making and re-making the portal while he does the same for the characters in *LotR* and the fairy-story itself. To illustrate the intricacies of these processes, the rest of this chapter focuses on a few especially noteworthy objects/doors: Galadriel's mirror, the *palantiri*, and the One Ring, and their most closely associated users/beneficiaries. Likewise analysis of Aragorn's mustering of the Dead and Gandalf's and Frodo's respective "resurrections" reveal important nuances of the portal/porter concept as furthered by Tolkien.

Un-Making and Re-Making: Magical Agency and Transformation in Middle-earth

Across Middle-earth, many magical objects exist to telepathically link individuals (not always to their liking nor with their consent), providing passageways with remarkable transformative power. Apart from the One Ring itself, which I discuss later, perhaps the most obvious of these objects is Galadriel's mirror. In a sharp nod to the classic fairy-story, Tolkien places his version of the magic mirror in the hands of the most powerful female living on Middle-earth. Like Snow White's stepmother, probably *the* fairy-tale female most closely associated with a mirror, Galadriel uses the device to gather information. Yet, while she is certainly terrifying in her power and ability to see through facades into people's deepest desires and fears, Galadriel is no wicked stepmother. Also in contrast to *Snow White*'s queen, Galadriel does not live by or wholly trust in the glass; in fact, she counsels others that it is "dangerous as a guide to deeds" (Tolkien *LotR* 363).

Given its operations, Galadriel's version of the magic mirror is not a door, but a window, which she says "shows many things, and not all have yet come to pass" (363). Obviously, like a door, a window is a literal portal, a passageway between the inside and the outside, but with the added benefit of being able to see from one to the other and back again. As with the version in *Snow White*, Galadriel's mirror figuratively operates the way all good magic mirrors are meant to do, to make the internal visible; providing a tool for probing and bringing to light the viewer's own secret intentions and resolve. Here Tolkien's version has power far beyond that of the fairy-tale glass since, as Joyce Thomas points out, the gazing of Snow White's stepmother only illustrates the narcissism that ultimately leads to her defeat (72). The wicked queen does not really learn nor seek to learn anything important about her self. Her efforts to entrap Snow White only serve to magnify the young girl as an infinitely more positive (if highly conservative) version of femininity.

In contrast, Galadriel epitomizes self-sacrifice and humility as well as power. She turns her mirror toward Frodo and invites *him* to gaze instead of looking at or for herself, though it is clear that she does so on occasion. Frodo passes the test by agreeing to continue on his journey because of—

indeed *in spite of*—what he sees. Still Frodo's use of the mirror does not physically move him any closer to his goal of destroying the Ring, other than to give him the chance to decide if he will continue on with it; he does not penetrate the mirror à la Lewis Carroll's Alice. Nor does the mirror offer Frodo any real information beyond reflecting his fears about what might happen should he fail his quest, as well as those of Galadriel and Sam. Galadriel's mirror *suggests* a concrete portal, one that would provide physical mobility, but *behaves* more metaphorically by moving Frodo forward in his process of psychological transformation. Looking into the mirror Frodo confronts his own internal turmoil and begins to construct the kind of heroic self that will be needed, but which still lies largely dormant within him at this point. As such Galadriel's mirror becomes an agent of Frodo's coming-of-age process by testing his will to go on, just as it does for Galadriel (and for Sam), but in different ways specific to their characters and situations.

Much like the Rings of Power, especially the One Ring, Galadriel's mirror also acts as a magical communication device connecting the user to the consciousness of Sauron. The most trying image Frodo sees in the mirror is the Eye, which echoes the Ring's shape and becomes "so terrible" he stands transfixed, "unable to cry out or to withdraw his gaze" (364). The Ring pulls Frodo toward the water that is the mirror, and Galadriel cautions him not to touch it. She reveals, "I know what it is you saw ... for that is also in my *mind*" (364, emphasis added), which implies she is an extension or personification of the mirror. Her administration of Frodo's challenge in Lothlorién marks Galadriel as a crucial porter for his quest: she can and will magically influence transformative events, for Frodo and for all of Middle-earth. In addition to her use of the mirror, her gift of the phial with the "light of Eärendil's star" provides a "light ... in dark places" (376) and comes with her guidance as an added bonus. While they often do so intuitively rather than knowingly, more than once Frodo and Sam invoke her, receive her presence in spirit, and find courage and hope to go on when the quest seems all but failed.

The phial is pure goodness, untainted by any connection to Sauron. In contrast, the Rings of power, the *palantíri*, and the mirror create one open line of communication across Middle-earth, and as Anne C. Petty indicates, "Instead of magic, [for Sauron] the key to power over others involves psychology" (166.) Being a Ring-bearer herself, Galadriel is chief among Tolkien's Faërie females, and her test of wills against Sauron is inevitable for directing her own path and that of the elves, as well as for her part in Frodo's quest. Her porter status is further supported by the proximity of her own test to that of Frodo. After he looks into the water, he freely presents the Ring and Galadriel says, "I do not deny that my heart has greatly desired to ask what you offer" (365); yet she resists the idea of becoming "stronger than the foundations of the earth" (366). While gazing into the mirror carries its own risks, more dangerous is its ability to link consciousnesses with Sauron, as Galadriel explains: "I perceive the Dark Lord and know his mind.... And he gropes ever to see me and my thought. But still that *door* is closed!" (364–5, emphasis added). Here she becomes a foil for Saruman, who shares such a connection to Sauron through the *palantir*, but does not resist.

While Tolkien is sometimes chastised, or at least questioned for his lack of female presence in *LotR*, it is important to recognize that those he does include are powerful, wise, and supernaturally intuitive. Admittedly, it is problematic that the three women who meaningfully participate in the war against Sauron each give up their power before the end. Following her test against the One Ring, Galadriel joyfully yet resignedly says, "I will diminish and go into the West" (366). Arwen illustrates another, more profound diminishing when she relinquishes her immortality for love of Aragorn. Less troubling than Arwen is Éowyn, who although repeatedly told by Théoden and Aragorn to take pride in staying with the women and children, enters the battle and fights bravely. Still, she can only do so by disguising herself as a man, and ultimately accepts a place as consort to Faramir in his stewardship to Aragorn, her original love interest.

A comparison to Morris's *The Wood Beyond the World* might hold up here in the way Tolkien seemingly insists his females voluntarily renounce their power and be happy with subjective positions. Such a reading is faulty, however, for overlooking the supremacy of free will and self-sacrifice in Tolkien's universe. Galadriel and Arwen each *choose* their own paths, and in so doing illustrate brave gestures of sacrifice for love of something and/or someone other than themselves. In Galadriel's case the sacrifice is not even that significant for she only gives up illusory power represented by the One Ring in favor of the earthly transcendence implied by passage to the Undying Lands. Also, when she talks of being diminished, she says she "will remain Galadriel" (366), signifying an ingrained sense of identity that does not depend upon external influences to be maintained. While Arwen's choice may be viewed as submission to a stereotypical female role, she still makes her own decision against great pressure from two formidable men, her father and Aragon, both of whom argue that she should *retain* her power for her own good.

Likewise, even though Éowyn does not win the king she initially desires, Faramir is no mean second choice, arguably being the most admirable, heroic human of Middle-earth. More importantly, Éowyn's interest in Aragorn, as Faramir points out, remains unhealthily attached to her need "to have renown and glory" (964) in stereotypically masculine terms. On the battlefield she secures this glory for herself and therefore no longer needs Aragorn, enabling her to find her true match in Faramir. In defending her uncle as he lay dying, Éowyn outmaneuvers one of the most frightening and powerful of Sauron's forces, saying, "No living man am I! You look upon a woman.... You stand between me and my lord and kin.... I will smite you, if you touch him" (841). This scene provides all the evidence necessary to refute any claim of anti-feminism raised against Tolkien. Éowyn purposefully casts aside her male disguise, naming herself as woman and adversary to call out none other than the Lord of the Nazgúl himself. Combined with Tolkien's laudable characterizations of the determination, strength, and autonomy of Galadriel and Arwen, Éowyn's stand on the Pelennor Fields creates a triumvirate of female wisdom and authority, reinforcing the Lady of Lórien as one of the most valuable porters of Frodo's errand. In this way she helps to over-turn the problems inherent in Morris's female porters as discussed in chap-ter one.

The outcomes of the choices made by Galadriel, Arwen, and Éowyn also demonstrate the process of un-making and re-making that is so central to the meaning of *LotR*. However, in a book that is in many ways about states of consciousness, even more striking and complex illustrations of un-making and re-making in regard to the portal/porter concept play out in the related quests of Gandalf and Aragorn. Appendix B of *LotR* explains that about 1,000 years into the Third Age, the *Istari* or Wizards first appear, com-ing "out of the Far West [as] messengers sent to contest the power of Sauron, and to unite all those who had the will to resist him" (Tolkien 1084). While the wizards are "forbidden to match ... power with power, or to seek to dom-inate Elves or Men by force and fear" (Tolkien *LotR* 1084), as Tolkien identifies in one of his letters, they are "emissaries from the True West, and so mediately from God, sent precisely to strength the resistance of the 'good' when the Valar become aware that the shadow of Sauron is taking shape again" (Carpenter *Letters* 207). His race as well as his role in the war of the Rings, then, marks Gandalf as a porter; he is literally a go-between for the Valar and the tribes of Middle-earth. His magical agency becomes compli-cated by the restriction against directly challenging Sauron, but this only reit-erates his porter status, as he does not appear as a super-hero working on his own. Rather his guidance and good old-fashioned battle skills greatly *aid* in the transformation of Middle-earth. Gandalf's entire *raison d'etre* defines him as a dangerous weapon, not unlike the Ring itself, but "in the shape of Men" as Tolkien's appendix describes (*LotR* 1084).

More importantly, Gandalf's position points up that of Frodo. As the Ring-bearer, Frodo stands in between Gandalf and Sauron who "are of the same order of being, yet opposite: one fallen, the other unfallen" (Stanton

19). This position also aligns Frodo with the reader, i.e., a mortal constantly having to choose which side of our dual human nature to favor. In this way the importance of Frodo's own porter status, which is literal in his carrying of the Ring, becomes symbolic and magnified. His relationship to Gandalf and his own Hobbit nature tip the scales in favor of "good," though this is continually tested and reconfirmed as he struggles to carry out his errand under the increasing weight of the Ring. This idea becomes further illustrated in the fact that Gandalf is physically separated from Frodo; for most of his journey the hobbit believes the wizard to be dead. Yet Frodo repeatedly invokes Gandalf as he does with Galadriel, drawing courage and inspiration from his memory. What Frodo actually does in seeking Gandalf is to access these qualities within himself, which multiplies the porter concept by two.

If this were not enough to ensure his porter status, Gandalf's magical agency becomes un-made in Moria as he sheds one level of consciousness to attain another, higher level. While early in the journey he does not know the exact form this test will take, nor its outcome, that such a test is predestined becomes transparent when the Company are trying to decide on a course and Aragorn expresses fear on Gandalf's behalf, saying, "It is not of the Ring, nor of us others that I am thinking now, but of you, Gandalf. And I say to you: if you *pass the doors* of Moria, beware!" (297, emphasis added). Leaving the decision to the Ring-bearer, Gandalf accepts his fate as he and the others literally go *through* Middle-earth. In an example of one of Tolkien's more traditional portals, accessing Moria requires using speech to open the doors that "have no key," and it is Gandalf who solves the riddle (306–7). After they enter, this "gateway," as Gandalf calls it, slams shut so that "there is only one way out — on the other side of the mountains" (309). Later when the evil that Gandalf must confront finally takes shape, he emphasizes, "You cannot pass," as if he is standing in or personifying a doorway beyond which stands the rest of the company (330).

After his fall in Moria, Gandalf's re-emergence in Fangorn Forest is nothing short of "a glorious resurrection" (Mathews *Fantasy* 75). Aragorn, Legolas, and Gimli mistake him for Saruman and he says, "Indeed, I *am* Saruman ... as he should have been" (495, emphasis in original). Tolkien acknowledges, "Gandalf faced and suffered death; and came back or was sent back, as he says, with enhanced power" (Carpenter *Letters* 237), without which the wizard "could not have dealt so with Theoden, nor with Saruman" (Carpenter *Letters* 202). While a religious connotation is evident, Tolkien rejects the notion of Gandalf's process being inspired by the Gospels, for "The Incarnation of God is an *infinitely* greater thing than anything I would dare to write" (Carpenter *Letters* 237, emphasis in original). Nevertheless Gandalf's unmaking and remaking are commonly viewed in these terms, partly reinforced by the wizard's rather cryptic explanation upon his return: "I have passed through fire and deep water ... I have forgotten much that I thought I knew and learned again much that I had forgotten" (495).

Peter Jackson's film adaptation of *The Two Towers* (DVD 2003) brings to life what Tolkien implies and denies. Jackson often discusses in interviews his goal of staying true to Tolkien's most important themes, even if time constraints demand significant reduction of the original storyline. Often Jackson's choices actually magnify the subtler implications of Tolkien's portrayals. For example, *The Two Towers* film emphasizes Gandalf's transformation by repeating it: first in Fangorn when he is introduced in his new form to the other members of the Company; second and more importantly in Théoden's hall, where another kind of resurrection takes place. With Théoden under Saruman's spell, Gandalf enters the hall, arguing for the retention of his staff: "You would not part an old man from his walking stick?" (Jackson *Two Towers* DVD). In Tolkien's text, Gandalf begins what amounts to an exorcism. He starts with a song invoking Galadriel before "casting his tattered cloak aside" and "standing white and tall against the blackened hearth" (514). The stark contrast of Gandalf's whiteness against the "blackened hearth" equates the battle of light and dark unfolding, a scene Jackson masterfully interprets in *The Two Towers*.

Confirming the idea of the porter by doubling it, Jackson has Saruman taunt Gandalf by speaking *through* Théoden: "You have no power here, Gandalf the Grey." The wizard casts off his old cloak to reveal the blinding white garment underneath and responds, "I will draw you, Saruman, as poison is drawn from a wound!" The scene then echoes the wizards' duel that leaves Gandalf imprisoned at the top of Saruman's tower in Jackson's *The Fellowship of the Ring* (DVD 2002) by moving back and forth with shots of Théoden's hall and Orthanc. This time, though, the battle for possession of Rohan rages *within* the physical body and consciousness of its king. In both the text and film versions, Gandalf's rescue of Théoden provides another example of un-making and re-making in *LotR*, while also signifying the importance of the wizard's own transformation: in defeating Saruman, Gandalf tests his newfound power and strikes a crucial blow against Sauron. Théoden becomes both a vehicle and a recipient of magical transformation as his own resurrection furnishes another formidable foe for the Dark Lord, negatively impacting Sauron by weakening Saruman.

Again illustrating a shedding of one consciousness or identity to achieve a greater one, Aragorn's un-making and re-making contains numerous parallels to that of Gandalf. First, while the wizard is often viewed suspiciously for his association with conflict and danger, as a Ranger, Aragorn truly lives on the outskirts of society, fighting for good, but without acknowledgement from most of those who owe their protection to him, such as the Hobbits of the Shire. Also as one of the Dúnedain, Aragorn straddles the divine and the human, somewhat like Gandalf but mortal. Spending much of his boyhood in Rivendell, Aragorn was raised among the elves, with whom he shares a partial lineage. He is looked upon by Elrond as a son, and wins the heart of his daughter, but Aragorn is also a king of Men. Frodo and the other Hobbits frequently describe Gandalf and Aragon in similar terms, and like the wizard who opens the door into Moria, Aragorn acquires the "key" that identifies him as the king and provides access to a dark, isolated realm of Middle-earth where a major test of his courage unfolds.

While the seeds are sown much earlier in the novel, Aragorn's transformation starts with his identification as Isildur's heir at the Council of Elrond. Largely in response to Boromir's tale, Aragorn stands to present "the Sword that was Broken." Elrond identifies him as "descended through many fathers from Isildur" (246) and Aragorn resolves that "the Sword shall be re-forged" (248). In keeping with the tradition of the medieval knight whose shield and sword would bear markings to identify him on the battlefield, Aragorn's selfhood is bound up with a piece of weaponry, almost magical in its mighty history and for having cut the ring from Sauron's hand. An extension of Aragorn's physical body, his sword is primarily known for its association with his ancestors and their deeds, both heroic and otherwise. Indeed when along with the Hobbits we first meet Aragorn, Tolkien emphasizes his association with the sword and kingship through the verse Gandalf uses to confirm him as "the real Strider" in his note to Frodo: "Renewed shall be blade that was broken / The crownless again shall be king" (170). Up until the Council of Elrond, though, as Petty explains, Aragorn's "self-imposed exile ... isolates him from the community ... [and] forfeits his power for many years.... Once he acknowledges his ancestry and inheritance, and openly engages in bringing together the will of his people through trust and strength, his power is activated" (169–70). Supporting Petty's claim, Aragorn's mustering of the Dead to Gondor's aid illustrates his acceptance of his role and growing belief in himself as being capable of succeeding where Isildur failed.

The path to this process goes through a third fairly traditional type of portal: the Dunharrow gate. Before he seeks the Paths of the Dead, Aragorn finally reveals himself as the king to Sauron. As Isildur's heir he not only has claim to the Ring and to the Sword that was Broken, but also to the Stone of Orthanc. He announces his plan to pass through the Dunharrow gate, revealing to his friends how he confronted Sauron through the *palantir*: "In the end I wrenched the Stone to my own will.... Now in the very hour of his great designs the heir of Isildur and the Sword are revealed; for I showed the blade re-forged to him" (780). Here Aragorn directly links his own identity and heritage to two objects — one almost magical and the other clearly so: the Sword and the Stone. His use of them furthers the process that begins when he is named at the Council, preparing him for the next and ultimate shedding of his Strider persona, which occurs when he goes "on a path appointed" (783), passes the Dark Door into what Gimli calls "some other world," and emerges with the Dead following him through "a crack in the wall" (788). The words of Malbeth the Seer reinforce the portal idea as he predicts, "From the North shall he come, need shall drive him: / he shall pass the Door to the Paths of the Dead" (781). Being "summoned," the Dead follow Aragorn and his companions to the Stone of Erech where he says, "When all this land is clean of the servants of Sauron, I will hold the oath fulfilled.... For I am Elessar, Isildur's heir of Gondor" (789).

Jackson's film version again brings home the greater significance of these scenes and makes Tolkien's use of portals more easily understandable. First, in *The Return of the King* (DVD 2004) Jackson makes more of the sword's re-forging and its connection to Aragorn's identity by having Elrond personally deliver the blade, along with the sad news that Arwen is "dying." While Tolkien's text has the sons of Elrond remind Aragorn of the words of the Seer, in Jackson's film, it is Elrond himself who gives Aragorn the idea of taking the Paths, countering his fear and resistance by announcing the Dead will certainly "answer to the King of Gondor!" The second of Jackson's embellishments has a similar effect in highlighting the implications of Aragorn's journey, as he refuses to accept that "the way is shut" to mortals and says, "I do not fear death!" He passes through the door-like opening into the mountain and challenges the King of the Dead, who does not give in nearly as easily to Aragorn's summoning as in the novel, even after he raises the blade and identifies himself as "Isildur's Heir."

Third, and most tellingly, Jackson spotlights Aragorn's experience of being haunted by his fathers in a scene unfortunately cut from the theatrical release but included on the extended edition DVD. With Legolas and Gimli, Aragorn finds himself bombarded by and almost drowning in a crashing mountain of skulls that ejects them back outside. The extra scene reiterates Tolkien's implication of Aragorn's journey as "the symbolic death of his old 'ranger' persona" (Petty 275), in the manner of Gandalf's descent into Moria. Initially in the film Aragorn believes he has failed and nearly gives in to despair, sinking to his knees after exiting the realm of the Dead, whose king suddenly appears saying, "We fight." With the skulls as a test of Aragorn's courage, will, and blood-line, the film implies he is not doomed to repeat the mistakes of Isildur but has the strength to reinstate the majesty of the Kings of Gondor. Enlarged, Aragorn use of magical agents in the form of the Sword and the Seeing Stone, as well as the Dark Door, aids in Frodo's quest and therefore in the transformation of Middle-earth. Because he will be king of the most powerful realm if things go well, Aragorn is one of the story's most powerful porters: his own un-making and re-making are crucial to the transformation of Middle-earth.

While Aragorn and Gandalf have their individual quests, both work in service of the greater good, encapsulated by Frodo's errand. The Ring-bearer of all ring-bearers, Frodo is literally a porter and symbolically a magical agent of transformation for his world. His own death and resurrection occurs over and over in the novel as he is stabbed by one of the Nine on Weathertop and saved by Elrond's magical healing, then nearly succumbs to the Ring continually throughout the story. The clearest examples of Frodo's un-making and re-making occur in Shelob's lair and later at Mount Doom. Both of these instances echo the experiences of Gandalf and Aragorn as Frodo physically penetrates Middle-earth, battles great evil, and seems to die only to stand up again in fierce determination to carry out his mission. The first example, though, actually has more to do with the journey's transformation of Frodo's faithful gardener and companion, Sam. Revealing what may be termed an "unlikely porter," Sam's mistake in assuming Frodo killed by Shelob compels him to go "against the grain of his nature" (Tolkien *LotR* 733), don the Ring, and see if he might carry on in his Master's place. Sam follows Gandalf, Galadriel, Aragorn, and Faramir in resisting the Ring's pull, though for a moment he envisions himself "Samwise the Strong, Hero of the Age." The combination of love for Frodo and "his plain hobbit-sense" quickly bring Sam back to Middle-earth (901) and the task at hand: rescuing his master. With some relief he returns the Ring, but out of his willingness to ease Frodo's suffering, he offers to help carry it.

Here Frodo sees Sam transfigured as "an orc ... pawing at his treasure," suggesting that despite his "death" the Ring-bearer has borne the burden too long to be able to quickly exchange a lesser consciousness for a higher one with its temporary removal (912). Rather it is Sam who reaches deep within himself to find the heroic determination he will need to see his master through to the end. As they head toward Mount Doom, Tolkien provides a striking description of transformation catalyzed by Sam's journey into Shelob's lair. His loss of hope gives way to an increased "will" and he feels himself "turning into some creature of stone and steel that neither despair nor weariness nor endless barren miles could subdue" (934). Sam feeds on this feeling and becomes a supreme example of a literal as well as a more symbolic agent of transformation when he tells Frodo, "I can't carry it for you, but I can carry you and it as well!" (940). Without Sam, Frodo would likely not have made it even this far and his act of carrying the Ring-bearer nearly the rest of the way doubles and thereby intensifies the porter's importance, not to mention giving Sam his heroic due as a true contributor, not merely a sidekick, in the saving of Middle-earth.

Of course the Ring itself provides the clearest and most intricate application of the portal/porter concept, being the central concern of the story. While Sauron can use Galadriel's mirror and the *palantiri* to access those who wield them, his most powerful and direct line of influence is the One Ring, bound to him to such an extent that its destruction immediately results in his own. Sauron operates *through* the Ring hoping to corrupt all types of "goodness" it encounters. Besides this, the Ring enables its wearer to straddle parallel states of consciousness, as all portals invariably do in one way or another. Petty rightly identifies the Ring of power's "most unique and potentially dangerous feature ... as a *gateway between worlds*. The wearer of such a ring becomes invisible to those in the third-dimensional physical world but can at the same time see beings who were non-physical, such as wraiths" (155–6, emphasis added). As such the Rings, especially the One Ring, enable the closest thing to a physical separation of worlds in Tolkien's universe. Still, the separation is not absolute and the one-world technique is upheld because the dimensions exist in tandem.

In fact, Frodo's real shedding of identity occurs not in Shelob's lair but through his invisibility when wearing the Ring. At these times Frodo can still be detected and mortally harmed on either plane, so that the Ring bestows power but with extreme vulnerability. Also, wearing the Ring causes physical wasting away as we see in Gollum, to eventual extinction. The Ring begins affecting Frodo's life before he takes possession, and evidence of its influence occurs by degrees throughout the story. Vowing to take on the quest that passes to him by Bilbo means Frodo must continually resist the pull of the concrete emblem of that quest, the Ring. Further, while the power it bestows is obviously negative, a positive effect results from it, making the Ring a multi-faceted, paradoxical type of portal. Instead of furnishing true power, invisibility creates an illusion of safety while actually magnifying Frodo's mortal weakness, thus externalizing his sense of being unlikely to fulfill his quest. More ironic still, his status as Ring Bearer transforms him into a formidable enemy for Sauron, mostly because he tends to overlook the seemingly insignificant Hobbit, an idea reinforced by the Ring's power of invisibility.

Although Sam may be an unlikely porter, and Frodo the most obvious, Gollum is the most persistent, bearing the Ring for the greatest length of time (apart from Sauron) and providing a compelling, gothic type of double for Frodo. The combined portal status of Frodo, Gollum, and the Ring plays out most clearly near the end of the story when one loses his finger and the other his life in the final effort to destroy the "precious." While he might seem to be a fairly straightforward porter in the terms established here, Gollum actually offers a quite sophisticated example much like the Ring itself, being a magical conduit on competing levels. Particularly meaningful in regard to Tolkien's approach to the portal is the way Gollum inadvertently helps to destroy the object most "precious" to him. Sauron continues to work through Gollum when he no longer possesses the Ring, but since he was once a Hobbit, he retains at least a shred of his former self. Moreover, his worship of the Ring prevents him from siding absolutely with its maker. So while he wants the Ring for himself, Gollum stands as a thorny yet powerful weapon in the effort to topple Sauron, as evidenced by the numerous characters, including Aragorn, Gandalf, Faramir, and Frodo himself, who *avoid* killing him.

In a story where the mission is to destroy rather than to find something, what Stanton calls an "inverted quest" in which "Evil struggles to gain power; Good to relinquish it" (16), such avoidance is especially profound, upholding Tolkien's main themes of mercy, love, and self-sacrifice. Without Gollum, Frodo and Sam would presumably never find their way to Mount Doom. In spite of not meaning to do so, Gollum becomes the conduit through which Middle-earth becomes saved. By personifying Frodo's fears and weaknesses, Gollum creates a powerful incentive for the hobbit to do whatever he can to succeed on his quest. Jane Chance supports this notion in seeing "the grappling of Gollum and Frodo on the path to Mount Doom ... [as] a symbolic oneness, as if we are witnessing the darkest night of the soul and one side attempting to master the other" (120). In the end Frodo's journey overwhelms his good nature, but his previous acts of mercy leave Gollum alive. Reinforcing his porter status, the end of the quest is accomplished *through* Gollum; his demise coincides with the destruction of the portal of the Ring and allows Frodo to vicariously carry out his mission without physically dying in the process. I say "physically" here because Gollum's death also signifies Frodo's shedding — at least to the extent that he is able — of the side of himself that is intimately connected to the Ring. Even though he does not actually throw the Ring into the fire at Mount Doom, as a result of his porter role, Frodo becomes permanently transformed.

In keeping with the notion of un-making and re-making in *LotR*, Frodo returns to the Shire but finds he is unable to find peace there. Tolkien comes closer to a more traditional portal transition when Frodo and the others set sail for the Undying Lands from the Grey Havens. Still this does not completely satisfy either the traditional or more expansive notions of the portal, occurring as more of an actual physical journey in real space, similar but not equal to an "other" world transition ala Tennyson's notion of passing "beyond the veil," for example. In fact, as I discuss in detail in the following chapter, J.K. Rowling comes much nearer to this idea in the fifth *Harry Potter* book, *The Order of the Phoenix*, in a chapter actually called "Beyond the Veil," when Harry's godfather Sirius Black succumbs in a duel at the Ministry of Magic. While most critics see the departure for the Undying Lands in *The LotR* as a representation of death, this is inaccurate — at least if we accept Tolkien's view of it.

In a letter dated "19 January 1965," the author explains that "Gandalf was not 'dying,' or going by a special grace to the Western Land ... he was going home, being plainly one of the 'immortals,' an angelic emissary of the angelic governors (Valar) of the Earth" (Carpenter 354). The Grey Havens and the Undying Lands beyond are protected spaces; not just anyone can go there and many characters, including members of the Fellowship, *do not* go there. According to the history of Middle-earth Tolkien conceives, the Blessed Realm lies "removed for ever from the circles of the physical world" as a result of a "monstrous rebellion" by some Númenorians hankering after immortality (Carpenter *Letters* 206). The one-world technique still holds, though, because the Blessed Realm exists as part of Middle-earth. Much like Avalon in Arthurian legend, it just happens to be unreachable to all but the select few.

Again like Avalon but perhaps more of a function of Tolkien's Christianity than his medievalism, in Middle-earth the Grey Havens, the Undying Lands, and death itself, equate another phase of *life*, a seamless move forward and shedding of one consciousness for another, rather than a definitive separation from the primary world. Their philosophies slightly differ, but both Tolkien and Rowling illustrate how the one-world setting so ubiquitous in modern fantasy necessitates portals that are increasingly resonant and complicated. The next chapter explores Rowling's approach to the one-world technique as she creates portals linking the boy wizard's personal history and to that of his culture in the *Harry Potter* series.

CHAPTER EIGHT

Harry Potter and the Ultimate In-Between: J.K. Rowling's Portals of Power

[Dumbledore]: "Part of Voldemort's soul lives inside Harry... And while that fragment of soul ... remains attached to, and protected by Harry, Lord Voldemort cannot die."

"So the boy ... the boy must die?" asked Snape, quite calmly.

[Dumbledore]: "And Voldemort himself must do it, Severus. That is essential."

[Rowling *HP and the Deathly Hallows* 551]

With *The Lord of the Rings*, J.R.R. Tolkien opens up the possibilities of how elaborate, believable, and relevant a singular magical space can be. From about the 1960s through today, other fantasists such as Susan Cooper, Alan Garner, Neil Gaiman, and J.K. Rowling have not departed contemporary Great Britain or America at all in their stories, but divided it into discrete pockets accessible only by magic. So Farah Mendlesohn overstates the case a little when she says the *Potter* books "very rapidly transmute into almost archetypal portal fantasies" (*Rhetorics* 2). An "archetypal" portal fantasy would be one where movement occurs between distinct realms existing independently and apart from one another, in the manner of the multiverse Diana Wynne Jones imagines in many of her books. What Rowling does is different. While Tolkien makes his contemporary society an implicit after-effect of the events taking place in Middle-earth, enacting the "remove from our reality" Colin Manlove describes as typical of high fantasy (*Fantasy Literature* 4), Rowling's low fantasy engages that reality by partitioning a whole, alternate version of contemporary Britain into wizarding and Muggle regions. Because these regions co-exist within the real world of the text, numerous characters, especially Harry, move back and forth via magical devices rife with symbolic significance. Despite this movement, however, Harry's story — just like that of Frodo and the Fellowship — remains *within* the boundaries of the one-world setting.

There is no magical wardrobe à la C.S. Lewis that transports Harry and the other wizards to a distant, separate world. When he passes through platform 9¾ he does so at the real King's Cross Station; when he manipulates the bricks to access Diagon Alley, he is still in modern-day London. A Muggle happening across Hogwarts, according to Hermione's reading of *Hogwarts: A History*, would "see a moldering ruin with a sign over the entrance saying 'Danger. Do Not Enter,'" but the castle has to be "bewitched" to make this happen (*Goblet* 185) because it physically exists in Rowling's Britain. Likewise, Harry and his friends are very British, and Rowling maintains "British cultural centrism" since "the wizarding world overlaps and intersects with the Muggle world" (Anatol 167). Indeed, the wizards and other magical beings share the earth with the Muggles, often going to great lengths to keep their own realms hidden and protected. To Mendelsohn's point, wizards obviously do travel between magical and Muggle regions using devices such as platform 9¾ and a myriad of others that hearken back to the portals of nineteenth- and early twentieth-century fantasy, but Rowling plays with the conventions of magical transportation and transformation in a more expansive way and to a different end than the "archetypal portal fantasy" would do. Consequently her portals become part of the series' way of engaging the power dynamics being felt by the twenty-first century reader.

This chapter primarily focuses on Harry's quest for identity and the ways in which his role as a "chosen one/savior" for the wizarding world reflects upon real British culture. I will also unpick the implications of some of Rowling's more concrete magical nexus points: the Patronus charm, Marauder's Map, Invisibility Cloak, Pensieve, and Tom Riddle's Diary. Most importantly, given my definition of the portal/porter as a nexus point and an instance of magical agency, I will argue that Rowling uniquely stretches the concept by making Harry Potter himself the *ultimate in-between*. His operation as a porter illustrates the more recent evolution of the device by taking at least three important forms operating in tandem. First, Rowling works within fantasy tradition to sub-create Harry as a combination myth and folklore hero, marking him (quite literally in the form of his scar) as a carrier of information, memories, and cultural values between his own mysterious history, an idealized, mythical British past, and an uncertain present/future. Second, and more significantly in regard to the portal as a psychological and transformative construct, the battle between good and evil in the series most often occurs *through* Harry's physical body, consciousness, and decision-making. Third — and this is where the trouble begins — the battle not only involves Harry being used by Voldemort, but also *by Dumbledore* in ways that, while sympathetically revealing the headmaster's flawed humanity and making Harry appear even more heroic, also threaten Dumbledore's status as guide and hero.

Memories, Maps, and Mortality: The Magical Artifacts of Harry Potter's Father-Quest

While most Muggles remain blissfully ignorant and wizards insist on keeping it that way, Rowling invents an array of magical objects that enable Harry and those of his kind to get things done without attracting undo Muggle attention; or at least that's the goal. Most of these portals carry some minor symbolism; for example, the portkeys, "objects used to transport wizards from one spot to another at a prearranged time," appear to Muggles as "unobtrusive things" they would dismiss as "litter" (*Goblet* 81). The portkey contrasts the creativity of the magicals with the total lack of imagination of the Muggles — only a wizard would be able to see beauty, utility, and power in an old boot. Coinciding with an absence of belief inherent in modern society in general, the Muggles reject anything remotely out of the ordinary, beginning with the first book when the narrator describes the Dursleys as "the last people you'd expect to be involved in anything strange of mysterious, because they didn't hold with such nonsense" (*Philosopher's Stone* 7).

While the portkey is a straightforward celebration of imagination, most of the series' portals are more complex and often hinge on Harry's seeking some sort of relationship with his parents as a way of achieving a sense of self. Rowling acknowledges this as a major theme of the series, believing that in a story with "very few good fathers," one way to bring home the scope of Voldemort's evil is to illustrate its destructive effects on the family unit and on children in particular (Viera). In this way Harry's situation is nothing new, of course, as folktales and children's fiction are abundantly populated with orphans. Rowling explains, "When you are trying to show *the journey of a child into a man* ... a dramatic and poignant way of showing that journey is to strip him of the people closest to him" ("J.K. Rowling Press," emphasis added).

Since Harry loses his parents "before he could ever know them as living ethical guides" (Pharr 57), he has special difficulty establishing who he is, having no biological family members to observe and model (apart from Aunt Petunia who is obviously no help). Being an orphan in such circumstances would create a heightened sense of powerlessness and alienation. This might seem ironic given Harry's magical heritage and aptitude (flying, battling the Dark Lord, winning the tri-wizard tournament), but Rowling is careful to play up Harry's losses and imperfections so that the series "speak[s] to the dynamic and unconscious conflicts, fears, and wishes that arise when children set their sights on becoming adults" (Damour 15). The irony dissipates as the series progresses and it is in fact the choices Harry makes in using magic that become his way of carving an identity and a place for himself in the wizarding world beyond his status as "the boy who lived." Despite being continually reminded of a responsibility thrust upon him before he could even hold a wand, Harry's public and private selves remain separate in his own mind, at least in his first few years at school when he feels most puzzled by the attention. Boarding the Hogwarts Express, the Weasley twins know him by his scar, but Harry shows confusion as to what they mean when they say, "Are you? ... He Is! ... Harry Potter." He answers, "Oh *him* ... I mean, yes, I am" (*Philosopher's Stone* 72, emphasis added).

In *A Reader's Guide* to the series, Philip Nel characterizes Harry as "a child who survives through his ability to adapt to new surroundings and to fashion his own unorthodox but effective family structure" (47). The Weasleys furnish the most obvious and actually quite orthodox version of such a structure, but Rowling supports Nel's point with the many paternal surrogates she gives to Harry, particularly in his father's old friends Remus Lupin and Sirius Black. Harry's longing for his father most vividly plays out in his use of the Patronus charm, which he learns from Lupin in *Harry Potter and the Prisoner of Azkaban*. With a goal to rescue Sirius, Harry travels back in time and heads toward the lake where the Dementors are gathering with "no thought in his head except his father" and a desire to know if it was really James who rescued them (*Azkaban* 300). While he watches the Dementors close in on him and Sirius, Harry repeats in his mind, "He'll be all right. I'm going to go live with him" (*Azkaban* 280). Initially Harry mistakes the image of his own time-traveling self across the lake for his father. In going back, though, he finds it was actually he who conjured the *Patronus* and banished the Dementors (*Azkaban* 300–1).

Here Rowling plays with a standard phase of growing-up: Harry must stop looking for help from adults and find within himself the strength and sense of identity he seeks. Supporting this, all of his major father figures begin to disappoint him or are absent for one reason or another in *Azkaban*: he learns that Dumbledore and Mr. Weasley have withheld important information about his parents' death, Hagrid is preoccupied with Buckbeak's trial, and Sirius becomes a fugitive before they can get to know each other. As his godfather, a "survivalist whose skills and knowledge Harry needs ... [and] a direct link to the past Harry cannot himself remember" (Pharr 61), Sirius is the most obvious choice as a porter for the boy wizard's maturation process. Still, in the lake scene it is Harry who rescues Sirius from the Dementors.

As an extension of Harry and of his father-quest, the Patronus is the more powerful porter than Sirius, literally existing in a liminal state, visible but non-corporeal, and performing a *go-between* service of protection. By definition, the Patronus emanates from within, taking a form that is specific to the witch or wizard and acting as a "positive force" that makes it impervious to Dementors (*Azkaban* 176). In his ability to conjure a fully formed Patronus, which is no mean feat for a wizard of thirteen, Harry becomes the magical agent of his own transformation, which he acknowledges as he and Hermione fly off to free Sirius from the tower: "I knew I could do it this time ... because I'd already done it" (*Azkaban* 301). While Harry seems to be surprised by this, he proves he has the ability to find his own way as he effectively replaces his father and protects his godfather. The Latin "*patronus*" also implies ancient history and identifies the father of a nation as well as a more intimate family association. Keith Robbins reminds us how kingship "in the societies of 'Britain'" served a function of "linking past and present in symbolic fashion and of being the effective *locus* of power" (45, emphasis in original). By having Harry go back in time to make a step forward in establishing a sense of identity, both as his father's son and as his own man/ wizard, Rowling firmly positions Harry as a magical conduit between past, present, and future.

Given the notoriety and lingering consequences of his parents' death, they become almost mythical for him, particularly James, whom Harry often envisions as a hero. In *The Power of Myth* Campbell identifies the "father quest [as] a major adventure for young people," saying such experience equals "the adventure of finding what your career is, or what your nature is, what your source is" (129). For Harry, this also means coming to terms with who his father really was — a human instead of an ideal. The creation of "Moony, Wormtail, Padfoot, and Prongs," otherwise known as Remus Lupin, Peter Pettigrew, Sirius Black, and James Potter, the Marauder's Map provides a slightly more traditional portal for Harry's identity quest. In death James remains elusive, but the map allows Harry to quite literally follow in his father's footsteps. Rowling emphasizes the idea of inheritance when George Weasley says, "We bequeath it to you" as the twins hand down the map they stole from a drawer labeled "Confiscated and Highly Dangerous" in Filch's filing cabinet (*Azkaban* 142). Harry initially hesitates about using the map for an unauthorized Hogsmead visit, remembering the words of another paternal surrogate, Arthur Weasley, who warns not to trust any magical object "*if you can't see where it keeps its brains*" (*Azkaban* 145, emphasis in original). Making his decision "quite suddenly, as though following orders," Harry sees "that a new ink figure had appeared upon [the map] labeled 'Harry Potter.'" The map not only identifies him, but provides instruction: "The tiniest speech bubble had appeared next to his figure. The word inside said '*Dissendium*'" (*Azkaban* 145), giving Harry the magic he needs to unseal the portal — this time an actual doorway — that connects Hogwarts to Hogsmeade.

Not by coincidence, his first use of the map takes Harry to a place where he overhears the details of his parents' deaths and of Sirius Black's supposed betrayal (*Azkaban* 151–5). That Rowling provides Harry with a document whose traditional purpose is to guide and direct — as well as to shield the user from censure while shattering boundaries — reiterates his identity quest and its paternal connection. The Marauder's Map is an active portal by which to travel from one place to another in the present, but also operates as an artifact of and a magical link to the past. The map provides physical proof of his father's existence, while showing Harry the present as it happens. Being the map's current owner and primary user, Harry confirms his supreme importance to Hogwarts' survival and by extension to the "path" of the Wizarding world's future.

Harry's Invisibility Cloak, also handed down, but this time from his father through Dumbledore, similarly connects Harry to the past in terms of both his biological and Hogwarts families. In *Harry Potter and the Half-Blood Prince*, Dumbledore tells him to carry the cloak everywhere, and Harry uses it more here — in the book where he eventually loses his most powerful surrogate — than in the previous five books combined. Similar to Frodo's One Ring, the Invisibility Cloak places its wearer in between existence and nonexistence, a position Harry personifies not only in surviving Voldemort's first attack when he was a baby, but also in fending off subsequent attacks. According to the folklore of wizarding culture that is revealed in the final book, the cloak is "the third hallow," making Harry an heir to one of the original three brothers who sought to "conquer" death (*Deathly Hallows* 348–9). Harry's ownership of what turns out to be "the true invisibility cloak" from the tale of "The Three Brothers" (*Deathly Hallows* 333) increases his chances of staying alive, but does not ensure his defeat of Voldemort. In his struggle to decide between hunting Hallows or Horcruxes, Harry again follows in his father's footsteps but more importantly ponders who *he* is — which side of himself to favor, the dark or the light.

Invisibility also equates with the Cloak's original wearer, Death, as it makes a person virtually untouchable and seemingly absent, a kind of spiritual as opposed to a physical presence. Rowling cites death as a main theme of the series (Viera), and her handling of it in *Order of the Phoenix*, where Harry faces his first real loss as a young man when Sirius falls in the battle of the Order versus the Death Eaters, illustrates one of the most intriguing examples of her more traditional portals. The narrator's describes Sirius Black falling "through the ancient doorway and ... behind the veil, which fluttered for a moment as though in a high wind, then fell back into place" (*Order* 710–11). Rowling's "veil" comes very near to Tennyson's notion of death from *In Memoriam: A.H.H.* For Tennyson, the possibility of surmounting the physical separation from Hallam becomes bound up with his perception of faith and the immortality of the soul. Like Rowling, Tennyson finds a way to ease the pain of Hallam's loss by accepting the boundary as a "veil" rather than as a finite, unmovable obstacle. This idea, which Voldemort repeatedly refuses to even consider, becomes arguably the most important aspect of Harry's personal philosophy as he begins to accept the necessity of his own death to save the entire wizarding world from tyranny. In the famous Stanza 124 of *In Memoriam*, Tennyson says, "I have felt" (ln 16), sounding uncannily like Dumbledore telling Harry, "It was your heart that saved you" (*Order* 743). In other words, it is the ultra-human capacity to love that provides the most convincing evidence for belief. This is "old magic," the kind to which Tennyson returns in moments "when faith had fallen asleep" (Tennyson 124.9). Both in Tennyson's poem and Rowling's novel, the "veil" image marks a subtle, magical division between life and death meant to provide comfort as well as closure. Harry's confrontation with the "veil" through the loss of his nearest father figure echoes his earliest and most profound loss of his parents.

Just like the "youngest brother" who eventually "greeted Death as an old friend and went with him gladly" (*Deathly Hallows* 332), as the series progresses, Harry increasingly sees that he must overcome an all-too-human impulse to stay alive if he wants to finally eliminate Voldemort's threat. In *Deathly Hallows* when Harry accesses Dumbledore's final gift of the Golden Snitch, the Resurrection Stone calls up the spirits of those whom Harry loves to join him in a final, conclusive battle to save the wizarding world from being overtaken by Voldemort (*Deathly Hallows* 559–62). After he surrenders to his enemy, a "flash of green light" like that which scarred him as a baby sends Harry to a purgatory in the form of a phantom King's Cross station, the place where in book one he first meets the Weasleys and takes the train to Hogwarts to officially join the wizarding world. The scene ends with Harry making a choice whether or not to "go back" (*Deathly Hallows* 578). Before he decides, he asks Dumbledore, "Is this real? Or is it happening inside my head?" and receives the answer, "Of course, it is happening inside your head, Harry, but why on earth should that mean that it is not real?" (*Deathly Hallows* 579). Emphasizing an almost seamless link betweem internal and external, mind and matter, the scene reinforces Harry's porter position between two worlds. Throughout the series his continual navigating between wizarding and muggle realms has always equated his precarious position between life (wizards, magic) and death (muggles, lack of imagination), making him a supreme representative of the human condition. Although prior to reaching the phantom King's Cross, he chooses death, this choice only reinforces the value he places on life, particularly in regard to his friends and his society.

Harry's last conversation with Dumbledore, which significantly occurs *in between* life and death, mainly has the headmaster going back through his own past to provide Harry with information he needs to make a decision (*Deathly Hallows* 565–79). Along with his uses of the Marauder's Map and the Invisibility Cloak, these scenes remind us that Harry's search for who he is nearly always involves memory. Like invisibility, this faculty tends to be intangible, unreliable, and elusive, so Harry spends much of his time trying to decipher the past and decide where he fits into it. Another interesting magical artifact of the series, the Pensieve, embodies this idea, being a stone basin where one can put thoughts that become too weighty to carry around. The Pensieve is also a vehicle for time travel through which one can access his or her own thoughts, and those of other people. Roni Natov views Harry's falling into the Pensieve as "a descent into consciousness," one that is "visionary" rather than "cautionary ... [and] suggests connection, that we can participate in another's experience, explore another's past, albeit only through the subjectivity of our own vision" (138). For magically transporting a person from the present to the past, the Pensieve is a "liminal space" that helps one to "understand another's history ... [and] move beyond the established boundaries of self and other, represented by the indistinguishable states of matter" (Natov 138). Still, in keeping with Rowling's one-world technique, the Pensieve does not transport the user outside the primary space, only to a parallel echo of it, as if the past is always present through memory.

What the Pensieve provides is a more internal, psychological kind of portal than the Marauder's Map or the Invisibility Cloak, which again points up Harry's own position as an in-between. The Pensieve constitutes the concrete adjunct to Occlumency, "the magical defense of the mind against external penetration" (*Order* 458), and Legilimency, "the ability to extract feelings and memories from another person's mind" (*Order* 468). Whether conscious or not, Rowling's conception of the techniques are akin to "[t]he cornerstones of magical technique, which are believed to strengthen and hone one's Will" (Lewis 153). According to James R. Lewis, "Meditation is required to train the mind to still extraneous thoughts" and enhance focus, while "Visualization is required to form a clear 'mental picture' of the desired ends of a magical working, and to be able to sustain that picture throughout the course of the spell or ritual, even while one is doing something else" (153). That

Harry ultimately fails to learn Occlumency leaves intact his connection to Voldemort, while also preserving his status as a porter between past and present, both of which in the end enable him to finish (and win) the last battle.

In terms of a nation, memory corresponds to history. Like the Muggle world (and our own that it is meant to resemble) the wizarding world is not singular but scattered, existing in hidden pockets throughout Britain, and indeed the world; as we find out in *Goblet of Fire* when the Quidditch World Cup championship is played and the Durmstrang and Beauxbatons students arrive at Hogwarts for the Triwizard tournament. As Jennifer Sterling-Folker and Brian Folker note, "the conflict between Dumbledore and Voldemort is over how to socially construct the magical collective" (120). Harry Potter stands at the very center of this conflict and as its chief actor he also equates a vicarious filter through which ages of inter-cultural animosities most recently explode. The next section of this chapter expands upon Harry's personal quest for identity to illustrate the larger implications of his in-between position in regard to the Muggle/magical spaces and their historical/mythological associations for Rowling's Britain, and by extension, western society.

The Chosen Porter: Harry Potter and (British) National Identity

Again in keeping with the one-world approach, it is important to recognize *Harry Potter*'s environment "as an accurate reflection of British reality" (Anatol 167). One way Rowling accomplishes this is in her appropriation of real-world political and social institutions to show how situations in the wizarding world impact the Muggles. My favorite example is "The Other Minister" chapter, which opens *Harry Potter and the Half-Blood Prince*. With the Ministry of Magic finally recognizing that "You-Know-Who" is back, Cornelius Fudge stops in to brief the British Prime Minister (I always imagine Tony Blair), who already has "quite enough concerns" due to a recent string of bizarre catastrophes. Fudge points out, "We have the same concerns ... *we're* at war, Prime Minister.... I was sent here tonight to bring you up-to-date on recent events and to introduce you to my successor" (16, emphasis added). When Rufus Scrimgeour emerges from the fireplace, he reinforces the inter-relation of the magical and non-magical regions by promptly revealing that the Muggle PM's "excellent" secretary is actually a "highly trained Auror, who has been assigned for [his] protection" (*Half-Blood Prince* 22).

From the time he is a year old, Harry's personal quest for identity is bound up with the survival of the Wizarding world, which directly impacts Muggle Britain in the story and reflects upon cultural identity as it ebbs and flows in Rowling's own society. To understand how this works, it is first necessary to consider the relationship between the *Harry Potter* series and the mythology/history that always sources the fantastic. Jennifer Schacker explains that the "roots of folklore study have generally been traced to the quest for national identity and cultural purity that began in the late eighteenth century" in Europe with "nationalist movements" and "intellectuals" such as Hans Christian Andersen and the Brothers Grimm collecting tales in order to preserve the history and traditions of their countries (2). Similarly, Carole Silver points to the increased interest in proving the existence of fairies that emerged in the nineteenth century in a move to "reveal Britain's uniqueness and greatness as its global reputation increase[d]" (31). Silver's idea is probably best exemplified by Oscar Wilde's mother, Lady "Esperanza" Wilde, and by William Butler Yeats, both Irish-born folklorists whose collections continue to be invaluable cultural studies.

In her preface to *Legends, Charms, and Superstitions of Ireland*, Esperanza lists "the language, the mythology, and the ancient monuments of a country" as the "three great sources of knowledge respecting the shrouded part of humanity" (xi). Among these she denotes "the written word, or literature ... [as] the fullest and highest expression of the intellect, and culture, and scientific progress of a nation" (xi). As with *Grimm's Fairy Tales*, Esperanza's collection contains selections "obtained chiefly from oral communications made by the peasantry themselves," and, she emphasizes, "The legends have a peculiar and special value as coming direct from the national heart" (xii). In the twentieth century Tolkien performs a similar exercise to that of the Grimms and Esperanza, but by creating an *original* mythology drawn from a tangled combination of ancient sources and from his own imagination, rather than by transcribing from oral tradition. Rowling mirrors Tolkien's approach with a nod to the tradition of Andersen and the Grimms in the final book of the *Harry Potter* series by having Dumbledore bequeath to Hermione *The Tales of Beedle the Bard*,[1] which according to Ron Weasley is a staple of wizarding childhood (*Deathly Hallows* 113–14). Like the original folklore collectors and their informants, Rowling handles the magical tale as a cultural identity marker, particularly at a time when global political and economic tensions make national boundaries increasingly slippery and alliances fragile.

As is typical with cultural identity, historically, "Englishness has had to be constantly reproduced, and the phases of its most intense reproduction — borne as its finest moments — have simultaneously been phases of threat to its existence from within and without" (Colls 29). This was certainly true when the Victorians were seeking "proof" of fairy existence and remains equally true in today's technological age. Rowling's characterization of Harry as a likeable, flawed, "normal" teenaged boy facing extraordinary circumstances makes him "a potential representative of the monomyth; a magical figure growing up within the perimeters of a specific fictional universe that clearly needs new heroes" (Pharr 54). Harry remains highly relatable in what John Stephens theorizes as a "Postmodern" version of the Victorian "*fin de siècle* mentality" marked by "a cultivation of radical inter-determinancy; a preference in representation for transparency, for surfaces-without-depth; the return of surrealism." In such a milieu these "tendencies ... *may* create anxiety about the directions in which society is heading" as "we find ourselves more and more acting and thinking collectively and less and less individually" (Stephens 15, emphasis in original). With Voldemort's threat becoming increasingly difficult to ignore (though the Ministry of Magic does its best), the wizarding world faces a similar anxiety to what Stephens describes. Simply by being who he is, Harry embodies a magical meeting point, not only between the past and present in the books, but also between fictional and real political constructs.

Rowling's books and their film versions continue to break sales records around the world, confirming that Harry "speaks to the fears and longings of his millennial-era readers" (Pharr 54). The final installment in the series, *Harry Potter and the Deathly Hallows,* sold 8.3 million copies in its first day on U.S. shelves, more than 5,000 copies per minute (Italie *ABC News Online*). Excepting Peter Jackson's *The Lord of the Rings* trilogy, no other fantasy film franchise has come close to achieving such success, as the 2007 adaptation, *Harry Potter and the Order of the Phoenix,* attested by breaking the franchise's own previous records with $140 million at the box office in its first five days (Bowles *USA Today*). I do not mean to suggest Rowling's success is a direct result of Harry being a source of inspiration in an often-frightening modern society, but rather to support the relevance of the series in dealing with the extra-textual problems in a similar way as folklore and fantasy have done for centuries. Like Frodo Baggins, in both novel and film versions, Harry rises to a "call to adventure ... [that] come[s] as a threat to his homeland and his very way of life" (Petty 277).

While readers and viewers may not consciously seek Harry as a national identity marker, his heroism is inextricable from his identification with Britain, which is constantly being expressed in Rowling's use of the actual environment (weather, terrain, etc.), political systems, and place names as important sites of meaning in the series. Harry's position as the savior of his culture's values and its very existence aligns him with Frodo in a long line of Anglo-Celtic heroes dating back to Arthur[2] and Robin Hood, but with more powerful resonance for the twenty-first century reader since Harry's journey unfolds in a version of our own socio-political landscape. Scholars commonly want to compare Harry to Arthur; like the fabled King of the utopian Camelot, Harry upholds ideals of sacrifice, loyalty, and duty, while displaying human frailties that jeopardize his quest. Rowling actually puts a sword in Harry's hands in *Chamber of Secrets*, making him a combination Arthur/St. George figure as he confronts Tom Riddle and kills the legendary basilisk. Normally kept in Dumbledore's office, the sword originally belonged to Godric Gryffindor, a school founder and the namesake of Harry's house. In taking up the sword against the "king of serpents" (*Chamber* 316), Harry slays the dragon, rescues the damsel (Ginny Weasley, who in book six becomes his girlfriend), and implicitly accepts his role as mythical hero. Given the symbolic implications of *God*ric Gryffindor's name, and the lion that is the emblem for his house also being an icon for Great Britain, Harry is easily read as fighting for God and King, as well as for his school, i.e., his "country." As such he becomes the magical agent for transformation as his society faces a serious threat; neither he nor they can hope to overcome it without undergoing major change and loss in the process.

Read psychoanalytically, of course, the Chamber of Secrets equates the innermost recesses of Harry's self, and his victory against the serpent at the significant age of twelve marks another hurdle overcome on the path to maturity. Harry begins to unravel the mystery of the Chamber when he enters Tom Riddle's diary, effectively confronting his own darker side as personified by he who will become Lord Voldemort. By definition, a diary provides a place to record "secret" thoughts; Ginny Weasley uses Riddle's diary in just this way before she tries to throw it away in Moaning Myrtle's bathroom (*Chamber* 228–9). Riddle's diary also links past (Tom Riddle, the Basilisk), present (Harry Potter, Ginny Weasley), and future (what Riddle will become, Harry's effort to save Hogwarts and his entire society). Rowling makes the temporal connections explicit by highlighting the similarities between Harry and Riddle/Voldemort that form a core motif of the series. Harry's act of destroying Riddle by stabbing the diary with the basilisk tooth, then, can be read as an erasure of less positive aspects of the past — for the boy, his society, and the real world.

For Harry this means trying to reject his darker nature as represented in the Chamber by Riddle. Such a nature dwells in everyone and usually begins to surface in pre-adolescence. Around this time Harry finds he can speak parseltongue and uses the language to open the portal into the Chamber of Secrets, where he fights the most direct and physical battle of the series up to this point. As the books progress, the idea of erasure also plays out in Harry's effort to reconcile less savory aspects of his father's character as expressed in "Snape's Worst Memory" and Sirius Black's recollections. While jealousy stemming from their rivalry over Lily furnishes the major catalyst, when the young James Potter attacks the young Snape, leaving him "hanging upside-down in the air" (*Order* 570–1), power is the issue at stake. Lily moves to intervene, saying James is "as bad" as Snape, and Potter defends himself by emphasizing, "I'd NEVER call you a — you-know-what!" referring to "Mudblood," the highly derogatory term for Muggle-born wizards (*Order* 571).

Throughout the series Rowling implies the past cannot be erased entirely, and one key aspect of this is the fact that the drive for power remains constant as a feature of human nature. As Harry matures, the books "gro[w] increasingly interested in questions of power: who has it, who has the right to exercise it over another, who has the moral authority to wield it, and how it should be exercised" (Nel 40). Voldemort hypocritically follows his ancestor Salazar Slytherin in his main concern to preserve racial purity, even though he himself is a Mudblood. Harry's quest, then, corresponds to the quests for power that have defined generations of wizards for "a thousand or more years," according to the Sorting Hat, at least since the time when the four original founders of Hogwarts envisioned their ideal students (*Goblet* 196–7). The beliefs underpinning their differences of opinion have obvious roots in the real world. As Anatol points out, while aiming to convey "ideas of global equality and multiculturalism, the stories actually reveal how difficult it is for contemporary British subjects ... to extricate themselves from the ideological legacies of their ancestors" (165). For example, even though most wizards find the term "Mudblood" offensive, they uphold a hierarchy in which wizards reign supreme, making laws prohibiting house-elves and goblins from carrying wands, and marginalizing the supposedly dangerous magical races such as the centaurs, giants, vampires, and werewolves. As Griphook explains in *Deathly Hallows*, "Goblins and elves are not used to the protection, or the respect ... from wand-carriers" that Harry shows when he pays tribute to the fallen Dobby (394). The décor of the Ministry of Magic foreshadows this idea in *Order of the Phoenix* when Harry goes for his expulsion hearing and notes that the fountain depicts a "centaur, goblin, and house-elf" who are "all looking adoringly up at the witch and wizard" (117).

Enlarged, such images implicate the real Great Britain (and western society in general), as an empire priding itself as the epitome of civilization, but with a class system that has been in conflict for centuries. In these terms, the destruction of the past means revision and even erasure of military defeats and acts of barbarism, often in the name of faith and always in the pursuit of power, that are as much a part of the nation's history as its naval prowess

and Victorian tea table etiquette.[3] In *Specters of Thatcherism*, Karin E. Westman finds that Rowling's ongoing portrayal of "tensions" among the various
magical races "echo the fervent tensions between race and class in the 'real'
contemporary British body politic of the Dursleys' suburbia and of British
readers' own experience" (307). Like Harry, who idealizes his dead parents,
modern Britain stands in the shadow of its imperial and mythical past, where
epic heroes such as Arthur are still remembered, but represent a consid-
erably waning, anachronistic source of inspiration in the twenty-first century.

Rowling's engagement with the real world also includes more individual experiences that have to do with growing up and "making informed
choices within one's cultural circumstances as opposed to following a destiny determined by biological difference" (Westman 316). As if to bring
things full circle and to tease out an underlying heroism in an otherwise standard sidekick, Rowling echoes the Chamber of Secrets scene in *Deathly Hallows*. In the iconic folktale setting of the forest, an in-between in its own
right, Ron Weasley faces the fears that have been dogging him for a lifetime
and which motivate him to leave Harry and Hermione to hunt Horcruxes
on their own (*Deathly Hallows* 253–4). When Ron realizes his mistake and
tries to return, he finds his chance to demonstrate his loyalty and courage
by retrieving Gryffindor's sword and Harry from the water. Because it is Ron
who pulls the sword from the pool, Harry keeps in mind what Dumbledore
taught him "about the incalculable power of certain kinds of acts" and reasons his friend is meant to be the one to annihilate the locket Horcrux
(*Deathly Hallows* 304). Shadow selves of Harry and Hermione emerge from
the locket, taunting and tempting Ron toward disloyalty by playing upon
his insecurities, yet he finds within himself the courage Dumbledore and
Harry have seen in him all along (*Deathly Hallows* 305–8).

The scene not only characterizes Ron as a worthy friend, but also
confirms the sword's Arthurian association. Among Snape's final revealed
memories, Dumbledore reminds him the sword "must be taken under conditions of need and valour" (*Deathly Hallows* 553). The image of pulling the
sword out of the water directly parallels Arthur's claiming of Excalibur and
his dealings with the Lady of the Lake, but more subtly, Rowling also plays
upon the love triangle that helps to bring about Arthur's downfall. Ron's
biggest problem with Harry, according to the *Horcrux* images, is jealousy
over Hermione. Given their positions in the story, Harry would fulfill
Arthur's part as the "king/hero," while Ron would equate Lancelot. Since
Harry was never romantically interested in Hermione, however, neither fills
Lancelot's shoes. In fact, Harry might be more apt as Lancelot since Ron
and Hermione have been inching toward each other since the Yule Ball in

Goblet of Fire and because Ron's jealousy of Harry is what causes a rift. It would be more accurate, though, to say that here in *Deathly Hallows*, Ron and Harry take turns at filling in for Arthur: each wields the sword and performs an act of courage and skill that contributes to the rescue of his society.

Rowling's revision of the love-triangle trope reinforces Harry's position as the larger-than-life mythical British hero, while simultaneously updating it to enable Ron — a decidedly "normal" English teenager, like many of Rowling's readers — to come into his own. The sword, and in this case the locket as an opposing power, become the magical agents for transformation, not only of Ron himself, but of Harry in his relationship with Ron, and in his own self-knowledge. Along with isolation, least-likeliness, and social marginalization as the traits creating the folktale "hero's appeal," Joyce Thomas says he who is the "most excluded from society becomes the one most capable of entering into relationship with other worlds ... [those] of nature and the supernatural" (22). Harry obviously fits this mold, but his status as the "Chosen One," his magical heritage, and his uncanny knack for staying alive, also take him well beyond the folktale hero into the realm of the mythic. As the youngest son from a poor family whose brothers all outshine him in one way or another, Ron could not be more unlikely to succeed in folktale terms. Giving Ron an opportunity to illustrate his inner hero sends a message to the reader seeking his or her own courage to face a difficult situation, whatever form it might take.[4]

Most often, of course, it is Harry who provides such inspiration. That Rowling gives Harry the position of "Seeker" on the Gryffindor Quidditch team is obviously not accidental. In fact, the title becomes a crucial feature of his identity in *Deathly Hallows* when he goes hunting Horcruxes hoping to put an end to Voldemort once and for all. In *Harry Potter and the Philosopher's Stone*, Harry enters the series as an infant with a scar marking him as a "chosen one," a phrase Rowling begins to use in *Half-Blood Prince*. Ironically the wizarding world erupts into "feasts and parties" just after the deaths of Harry's parents due to the mistaken belief in Voldemort's demise. Invariably Harry's quest for a sense of *personal* identity in the absence of parents, siblings, and close blood relatives becomes intertwined with his *public* role as hero. At its most basic level Harry's quest is deeply personal: he is an orphan whose parents die when he is too young to know them. Harry does not belong to anyone — yet he belongs to *everyone*. From the moment of his parents' deaths he becomes a symbol for the entire wizarding world, who toast him, as the narrator tells of "people meeting in secret all over the country ... holding up their glasses and saying in hushed voices: 'To Harry Potter — the boy who lived!'" (*Philosopher's Stone* 17).

Dumbledore explains Harry's position in *Order of the Phoenix* when he finally reveals the prophecy that "the person who has the only chance of conquering Lord Voldemort for good was born at the end of July, nearly sixteen years ago" (741). The prophecy goes on to utter words that remain unknown to the Dark Lord: "either must die at the hand of the other for neither can live while the other survives" (*Order* 741). Harry initially understands this to mean he is destined to be either "murderer or victim" (*Order* 749), so even before his infamous encounter with Voldemort, Harry is "marked," supposedly by fate but really by Voldemort, as the one who will either save or destroy the wizarding world. This becomes increasingly clear as the series goes on, but Rowling makes it explicit in the final book as he and members of the Order prepare to prematurely break the protection charm that ends on his seventeenth birthday. Even the Dursleys have some sense of what Harry faces, and one of their escorts Dedalus Diggle makes it plain when upon leaving he tells Harry: "The hopes of the wizarding world rest upon your shoulders" (*Deathly Hallows* 40).

In a series where the main character must repeatedly choose between good and evil, no one ever gives Harry the *option* of whether or not to take on the burden of saving the wizarding world. Even Frodo Baggins is given the opportunity to decide if he should step forward when the Council is debating who should take the One Ring to Mordor (Tolkien *LotR* 269–71). No council is called to see who might shoulder the burden of fighting Voldemort; the Order of the Phoenix does not even reconvene until thirteen years after Harry receives his famous scar, when he nearly dies (again) in his fourth go-round with Voldemort in *Goblet of Fire*. A possible exception occurs near the end of the last book when Harry faces the ultimate choice between life and death, but given what's at stake, he really has no choice even then, as I discuss in the last section of this chapter.

Of course, Harry makes myriad choices throughout his journey, but all of these are necessitated because of the two crucial moves made *on his behalf*: one by his mother, who sacrifices her life to save his, and the other by his greatest enemy, who according to Dumbledore's interpretation of Trelawney's prophecy "chose the boy he thought most likely to be a danger to him" (*Order* 742). Despite his lack of say in the matter early on, as Harry becomes more comfortable with himself and his losses to Voldemort grow in number and intensity, he incrementally accepts and embraces his role as "the Chosen One." This acceptance does not diminish but in fact intensifies his porter position, which becomes clearest in books six and seven as more details emerge about Dumbledore's past and conflict with Riddle/Voldemort. The final section of this chapter considers Harry's problematic relationship with Albus Dumbledore, which more than any other aspect of his own history and position in wizarding culture comes to define the boy wizard's status as the ultimate in-between.

Harry Potter Is a Horcrux

When Harry reaches the ethereal King's Cross Station in *Deathly Hallows*, Dumbledore says, "Can you forgive me for not trusting you?.... Harry, I only feared that you would fail as I had failed.... I have known, for some time now, that you are the better man" (571). The lines not only convey the flawed humanity of the "greatest wizard who ever lived," but also reveal the truth of Harry's position: he is and has always been a pawn in a battle that began long before his birth. Not until the seventh book, though, does his most powerful father figure finally provide Harry with the full story. Indeed throughout *Deathly Hallows*, Harry spends most of his time trying to second-guess Dumbledore and feeling as if the guide who meant so much to him has led him astray, perhaps to his own destruction and that of the entire wizarding world.

In *The Hidden Mysteries of Harry Potter* (Warner Bros. DVD 2007) actor Daniel Radcliffe hints at this idea in summarizing the headmaster's view of his character's connection to the Dark Lord, noting, "Dumbledore thinks Voldemort might be using Harry, with my eyes as *portals*, my mind as a way of seeing what I'm seeing" (emphasis added). Besides unknowingly using the term "portal" in the more expansive way this study proposes, Radcliffe acknowledges that Dumbledore is well aware of the danger of this connection. At the same time he insists Harry take Occlumency lessons with Snape in an effort to protect himself from Voldemort, Dumbeldore also uses the boy wizard in a similar albeit less diabolical way. At plot level, one can understand such withholding of information as a way to keep the reader guessing and interested through to the series' end, but the implications for Harry remain problematic. Dumbledore explaining his relationship with Grindelwald and his power struggle with Voldemort from the grave at a time when Harry must make the ultimate human decision between life or death only reinforces the naturalness of Harry's anger. For much of the series Harry (and his friends) face horrific dangers with very little aid, especially in the form of information. Rowling grants Harry numerous parental surrogates, both benign (the Weasleys) and malevolent (the Dursleys), but apart from his godfather, the headstrong and damaged Sirius Black, the adults go out of their way *not* to tell him anything that might aid in his ongoing battle.

Repeatedly throughout the series Voldemort seems to fight Dumbledore *through* Harry, begging the question, why do not the two most powerful wizards fight each other *directly*? Why would Voldemort rather fight a boy than a man? And why would Dumbledore not want to directly take down perhaps the only wizard as strong as he? For the Dark Lord's part, cowardice can be assumed, or his single-minded reliance upon the prophecy, or his burning need for vengeance against Harry, all of which are characteristic of evil as Rowling defines it. But what about Dumbledore?

Admittedly the headmaster does step in to directly confront Voldemort once in the series, but with dangerous consequences that plainly demonstrate Harry's porter position and foreshadow his status as a *Horcrux*, which is unveiled in the final book. In what the narrator of *Hidden Mysteries* calls a "battle for Harry's soul," Voldemort's connection to Harry vividly plays out in *Order of the Phoenix*, when after watching Sirius die and nearly killing Bellatrix Lestrange in a fit of revenge, Harry is pushed aside as Dumbledore finally confronts Voldemort for the first time in the series. The Order members identify Harry as a possible "weapon" early in this book, and he becomes exactly that near the end as Voldemort's most powerful tactic is to hit Dumbledore where he lives: his emotions, his fondness for Harry Potter. At a crucial moment, Dumbledore materializes on the plinth of the wizard fountain and throws himself "between Harry and Voldemort." Killing curses fly and Voldemort's last ditch effort is to inhabit Harry's body as the narrator describes: "He was locked in the coils of a creature with red eyes ... they were fused together, bound by pain, and there was no escape" (*Order* 719). Saying "*Kill me now, Dumbledore ... kill the boy,*" Voldemort's voice emanates from Harry's mouth; but when he thinks of Sirius, whose death he has just recently witnessed, Harry's emotions take over, releasing him from the Dark Lord's hold (*Order* 720, emphasis in original). The scene recalls the battle of wills between Gandalf and Saruman waged through the body and soul of Théoden in *Lord of the Rings*, as discussed here in Chapter Seven. In both cases, two powerful, opposing magical entities square off indirectly. As a result, the victims (Harry, Théoden) become vehicles to carry out a squabble that in Harry's case dates back centuries to the original school founders. The winning of the victim becomes the physical manifestation of the fight, objectifying him as a spoil of war.

Of course, this is not a war that Dumbledore began, and it is important to remember that his intervention in the above scene is what probably saves Harry's life in this particular battle. Even though the war has been ongoing since long before his birth, though, the series hinges on the moment offstage in the first book, which is recreated in Harry's mind in *Deathly Hallows* as he is nearly killed by the snake and channels Voldemort's reminiscence of killing the Potters and attacking Harry (279–82). Voldemort naturally targets Harry, given his failure to kill him the first time and also given his incomplete knowledge of the prophecy. Still, Dumbledore's repeated reticence to explain matters to Harry, and his typical lack of physical presence when things get violent, reinforce Harry's porter status, making the elder wizard slightly less admirable than the books want to acknowledge.

Supporting this idea, Dumbledore makes clear in his final scene with Harry at the phantom King's Cross Station that his primary reason for keeping Harry in the dark was because he "was scared that, if presented outright with the facts about those tempting objects, [Harry] might seize the Hallows as [Dumbledore] did, at the wrong time, for the wrong reasons" (*Deathly Hallows* 577). Here Rowling redeems Dumbledore to an extent, by having him own up to his mistakes. In doing so he proves his right to be the agent of Harry's final choice between life or death, a choice the headmaster himself makes in *Half-Blood Prince*. Dumbledore shows humility and grace in identifying Harry as "the worthy possessor of the Hallows." He asks Harry's forgiveness and places "the boy who lived" far above the "greatest wizard who ever lived," because Dumbledore's own fatal flaw—a love of power and "glory," he says—led him to make significant and costly mistakes (*Deathly Hallows* 571–7). The flaw remains intact, and Dumbledore's character somewhat tarnished, but on a greater scale his downfall becomes part of the series' engagement with the world outside the text. By making the larger-than-life wizard guide human, Rowling carefully demonstrates the seductiveness and corruptive nature of power as well as the large-scale destructive consequences of its pursuit.

In the story, Dumbledore's confession and repentance also reinforce Harry's status as a porter. Being the last Horcrux to contain a sliver of Voldemort's soul, Harry is probably the most definitive example of the living portal to date. Unlike the portkeys, which are "ordinary objects, easy to overlook," Horcruxes are "objects with a powerful magical history" (*Half-Blood Prince* 471), a phrase that also describes Harry. His psychic connection to Voldemort is not incidental, but the result of some of his characteristics and magical abilities being transferred to Harry in that first attack when he was a baby (*Deathly Hallows* 567–8). Like the locket with its beating heart, Harry carries deep inside of him the makings of another Voldemort, but like Dumbledore, he chooses to resist any way he can. Unlike his headmaster, though, Harry courageously confronts his own dark side and his archenemy head-on, because he understands and accepts what's at stake.

It is important to recognize that while Harry has good reasons for revenge, this is never his primary goal. Instead Harry is burning to prove himself worthy, to carry on what his parents, Sirius, Dumbledore, and other fallen Order of the Phoenix members began before his birth. As the Ring-bearer in *The LotR*, Frodo acts for identical reasons. Frodo increasingly comprehends the threat to the Shire and to the ascension of the rightful and worthy king of Gondor. Thus Frodo acts out of love for his culture, not out of revenge for a wrong already committed against him personally. More than Frodo, Harry has a specific, intimate motive for wanting revenge on Voldemort. Still, while this idea informs some of his actions (especially after Sirius's death and certainly in book seven), his overarching goal extends far beyond himself: to uphold the side of goodness in his world.

CHAPTER NINE

Portals Between Then and Now: Susan Cooper, Alan Garner, Diana Wynne Jones, Neil Gaiman, and Jonathan Stroud

If the doors of perception were cleansed, every thing would appear to man as it is: infinite.
— William Blake, *The Marriage of Heaven and Hell* [Plate 14]

It may seem unlikely to open this concluding chapter, which considers the portal as it has been further expanded since J.R.R. Tolkien's time, with a quotation from a work of the late eighteenth century. In truth, Blake's image of the "doors of perception" applies very well to literary fantasy and to the more expansive definition of the portal upon which this project is based, as a literal and/or figurative gateway through which transformation is made possible. Harold Bloom reminds us, "Blake lived, painted, wrote: to correct other men's visions, not into his own, but into forms that emphasized the autonomy of each imagination ... against any received notions that might seek to set limits to perception" (*Blake's Apocalypse* 70). With the imagination as a point of unification, David Sandner rightly aligns the Romantic sublime with the fantastic as "a kind of interpretation and presentation of the real" (62). Sandner also notes, "In both Romantic poetry and fantastic literature, the imagination reaches beyond its grasp in a movement towards transcendence" (Sandner 50). It is important to remember that Blake wrote *The Marriage of Heaven and Hell* in the 1790s, another *fin de siècle* epoch with a special need for "transcendence" for numerous reasons, not the least of which was the widespread revolution in Europe.

Blake's "interpretation and presentation of the real" in *Marriage* reiterates the power of fantasy as a political instrument, and unknowingly helps to establish the concept of the portal that underpins this project. His "doors of perception" symbolically refer to the need for a citizen — regardless of time period — to deliberately challenge the status quo. In *Marriage*, which has come to be viewed as a less orthodox brand of Christian fantasy (Manlove *Fantasy Literature* 29), Blake becomes the Angry Prophet and traces humankind's fall. The goal is "Paradise," which for Blake means a clearer understanding of human purpose and potential that can be implemented to improve the present and create a better future. Nearly a century and a half after Blake and the other Romantics helped make the fairy tale into an art form, Tolkien identified this process as "recovery ... re-gaining ... of a clear view" so that "the things seen clearly may be freed from the drab blur of familiarity — from possessiveness" ("On Fairy-Stories" 77). For Tolkien, only those stories that come closest to accomplishing this effect for the reader can be identified as the truest, most authentic kind of fantasy.

In various ways, *Portals of Power* has dealt with characters and societies caught up in this process. With their personal transformations entwined with myriad changes in the world around them, the magical agency they encounter, use, and embody becomes an instrument for understanding themselves. More importantly, these portals/porters influence things far *beyond* themselves, and while universal in their resonance, just like Blake's Angry Prophet, they also speak very specifically to and about the time and place of their invention. This phase of the journey concludes with a few of the most prominent authors of the twentieth and twenty-first centuries who construct new variations that build upon the achievements of Morris, Nesbit, Wharton, Wilde, Tolkien, and the other writers in this study, to further open up the portal concept. Susan Cooper, Alan Garner, Diana Wynne Jones, Neil Gaiman, and Jonathan Stroud acknowledge fantasy tradition while infusing magic into contemporary environments, thus linking past and present.

As John Stephens explains, "Many attributes of postmodernism are also attributes of *fin de siècle* mentality: a cultivation of radical interdeterminancy; a preference ... for surfaces-without-depth; the return of surrealism ... hostility toward 'high' culture; and so on" (15). At the same time Lance Olsen finds "the complex of concerns that we have come to call postmodernism may find expression at any time in history ... they have found pervasive expression in the culture existing in the second half of the twentieth century" (Olsen 279). In other words, virtually every "'culture' in crisis" — our own included — requires a "mode whose premise is a will to deconstruct" (Olsen 291). As an inherently symbolic and metaphorical mode, fantasy virtually demands to be deconstructed and yields different meanings with each attempt. What the authors in this final chapter do in these terms is to keep the past alive, influential, and interactive by making it a point of contrast to "explore the limits of civilizations" (Olsen 290); to articulate, humanize, and essentialize modern/postmodern experience.

While incorporating myth and folktale tropes is common in literary fantasy, this is not to say that *all* fantasy appropriates the past. Certainly much of it does; so the more important questions are *how* and *to what effect* does this appropriation operate. Further, how does the past engage with the present within a text and how does this engagement resonate beyond the text? This final section studies some of the ongoing uses of the portal in texts produced in the latter part of the twentieth into the twenty-first century, the millennial *fin de siècle.* As a pervasive vehicle for expressing the complexities of human power dynamics, the portal/porter unifies a fantasy tradition that stretches far and wide in both directions. If, as Catherine Madsen says, "All magic is linguistic in inspiration" (50), literary fantasy has been and will continue to be a formidable portal of power.

"Time Is Only a Mode of Thought"

E. Nesbit famously expresses this idea in *The Story of the Amulet* (210) and it has since become a helpful way to think of the uses of time in modern fantasy. In the several decades since Tolkien's *The Lord of the Rings* had people scribbling "Frodo Lives" in subway stations, many fantasists have followed him in drawing from the ancient myths, folklore, and traditions of the past to create their own mythologies. Even when the fantasist takes liberties with what has come before — especially with earlier fantastic tales — the past remains an inescapable presence for the writer and reader. For example, Maria Nikolajeva finds "the passage between ... worlds, is most tangible in time fantasy ... often connected with patterns such as the door, the magic object, and the magic helper (messenger), all of which are also manifest in Secondary world fantasy" (143). Although she does not identify it this way, the one-world fantasy also fits with Nikolajeva's line of thinking here. Given the overwhelming amount of "historical" detail in Tolkien's work, for instance, the past is accepted as having a crucial influence on every event in Frodo's present, and indeed in every decision made by him and the other inhabitants of Middle-earth. In all stories where past and present occur as concrete or even metaphorical spaces existing in tandem, the reader gains unique insight into the ways history real or invented shapes the here-and-now for an individual and a society.

As the last two chapters on Tolkien and Rowling illustrate, magical transition points arguably become more significant in one-world texts because the divisions between pockets of space are subtler, or even imperceptible. While I agree with Charles Butler's comment that "time slips and time travel" are largely meant to "satisfy [a] fundamental longing" to reach the past (61), I see time more often being expressed in works by Susan Cooper and Diana

Wynne Jones as co-existent rather than as "a linear progression from past to future" (Butler 63). For example, in her gothic/fantasy hybrid *The Time of the Ghost* (1981) Jones depicts a disembodied young woman whose past, present, and future converge after a schoolgirl enactment of an ancient ritual comes true. Butler makes a more compelling point in associating the time-travel trope with "an awareness of the inevitability of change" (60). Farah Mendlesohn adds that "magic is an effective metaphor for growth," which she defines as a "process of constant change, and negotiation with the change that is adolescence" (*Diana* 19).

Jones supports both of these arguments in *The Time of the Ghost* as Sally becomes disembodied as a result of a need to come to terms with two dysfunctional relationships and to define her own identity in light of them. Here "change" corresponds to growth occurring through transformation, a central theme of Sally's experience. She enters having already been transformed into a ghost-like presence and spends roughly the first half of the book floating about, wondering who she is and trying to get her sisters to notice her and understand what she wants. Chapter Seven ends with her struggling to resist "the Monigan force," a pagan spirit that becomes infused into an old doll, as she witnesses her past self and Julian Addiman performing the hen ritual. Toward the end of the chapter a "mist" emerges and the ghost focuses on a "thing" that springs up before her (Jones 136–40). Chapter Eight begins with her identifying the "thing" as "a foot and a leg encased in plaster," as she finds herself in a hospital bed, badly injured (Jones 141).

Between chapters seven and eight the ghost moves from one time to another, her past to her present. While this seems like a linear progression, in truth both times have been implicitly overlapping since the beginning of the novel, because "for Monigan all times ran side by side" (Jones *Time* 284). In *Diana Wynne Jones: Children's Literature and the Fantastic Tradition*, Mendlesohn maps a complex formula for deciphering Jones' notion of "block time," noting that, "it is only once Sally has accepted both that the past is not perfect and that she can change only her memory of it that she is able — as the ghost — to travel to moments she chooses" (*Diana* 55–6). Sally's ghost self equates an out-of-body experience as she lies near death, providing her with an opportunity to fight Monigan as the goddess tries to exercise her "right to claim a life seven years" in the future (Jones *Time* 256). This future is actually the book's present, the time when Sally realizes she is hospitalized because, as she finally recalls, "Julian Addiman threw me out of his car" (144), thus revealing one dysfunctional relationship that is fairly consistent from her past to her present.

Throughout the story Sally's ghost, or shadow self in Jungian terms, operates as a porter for her whole self. She and her sisters devise a plan for the ghost to return to the past and try offering Monigan something in exchange, which among other things turns out to be Imogen's dream of a "musical career," something that has defined her sense of identity throughout her childhood. Supporting Mendlesohn's theory by beginning to adjust her memory and feelings about the past, Sally notes, "She, like Imogen, had taken a wrong turn.... Both of them had wanted something to cling to, and they had both clung to something which was no good to them" (288). For Sally this "something" is Julian, who dies in a car crash in the present after she manages to "bargain" with Monigan in the past, leaving the sisters to believe the bloodthirsty spirit "had got her life after all" (291). The timing of these events confirms the connection between Sally's ghost haunting her own past and the cause of that haunting, her perceptions and choices in both childhood and adulthood.

Sally's other dysfunctional relationship similarly overlaps past and present. The "Plan" that separates Sally from her sisters in the past is meant to get their parents to pay attention to them: Sally goes to stay with a friend without telling her parents, whom the girls refer to as "Phyllis" and "Himself," hoping they will notice she is missing (Jones 95–6). That the ghost chooses this time to manifest has to do with the timing of the Monigan ritual, but also with the phase of life when she and her sisters probably feel the most vulnerable and abandoned. While she initially believes she may be Sally, for much of the story, the ghost cannot decide for certain who she is. Alternating between each of her sisters, she finds it difficult to believe she is not Imogen even late into the story (250). Jones gives Sally's journey decided gender-based implications since her parents run an all-boys school and leave the girls in a dirty house with ill-fitting, pieced-together clothing and whatever table scraps they can scrounge. When Fenella tells her mother she and her sisters are "neglected," Phyllis looks "wearily amused" and responds, "the boys are helpless and girls know very well how to look after themselves" (116).

Superficially this might be taken as an expression of female strength, but all of the other factors — the prank, Sally's relationship with Julian, and the girls' dabbling in witchcraft — combine to show that Phyllis is mistaken in her assessment of her daughters' needs and capabilities, at least as children. Their parents' absence significantly shapes their futures, but Jones paints female strength more positively in the end of the story as the girls begin to correct *their own* past mistakes. With Julian becoming "the supreme sacrifice" to Monigan, Jones suggests that while girls may need as much nurturing as boys, women can (eventually) take care of themselves. As Butler identifies, one "constant" in Jones's fantasy is her "commitment to stories about people's realization of their potential and their possibility of overcom-

ing adverse circumstances to achieve both self-belief and self-knowledge"
(233). To her sisters, Sally is known as the one who defends and actually
"loves her mother and father" (Jones *Time* 28). Like her ghost self, Sally's
deeply internalized responses to her parents' neglect and her own relationship with Julian illustrate her decided lack of "self-belief and self-knowledge," but by returning to the past in her mind she manages to overcome
both of these obstacles. In other words, she gives herself a second chance,
an opportunity to reset her life in the present. Unfortunately the catalyst for
her doing so is the trauma of a near-death experience, suggesting both the
power of the past and, more intimately, the far-reaching implications of
childhood experience as shaping influences on human development.

In a different way than Jones, Neil Gaiman also plays with the concept
of time in *American Gods* (and in the later *Anansi Boys*) by making it both
co-existent and linear. While the spiritual gods suggest a more linear progression in that they have changed over time — or that attitudes to them have
changed — they also retain their original glory; it's just that no one can see
it because people no longer believe in them. Being replaced by capitalism
and all its side-effects, the gods appear as humans. For example, the Norse
god Odin first approaches Shadow wearing a "pale suit" and a "black Rolex"
(21), calling himself "Wednesday," a play on his other name, *Woden*, for
which a mundane sort of weekday is named. The ancient Egyptian gods are
now morticians, Mr. Ibis and Mr. Jacquel (198–202), and the Queen of
Sheba, whose associations span biblical, Ethiopian, and Egyptian mythologies, becomes Bilquis, a man-eating prostitute (27–31). Exemplifying Gaiman's special brand of dark satire, the American gods seem to fit into
twentieth-century society, but always with an air of anachronism that continually interrogates the authority and rationality of the present.

Anchoring the gods is the human Shadow, Wednesday's "chosen one"
to carry out their designs on regaining their former glory. As in *The Time of
the Ghost* where Jones uses Sally's mind as a kind of portal and links her to
the possessed Monigan doll, Gaiman also devises a more tangible gateway
to unify time, one that becomes aligned with Shadow in important ways.
The carousel marks co-existent dimensions rather than literally enabling
travel to a Secondary world. Heading toward the big reveal when Shadow
gets a sense of what he is involved in, he and Wednesday "travel a spiral"
(123) in a magical ritual, passing the carousel rather than going straight to
it. When Shadow wonders about this, Wednesday explains the carousel is
"not there to be ridden, not by people.... It's there to *be*" (127, emphasis in
original). The gods in their earthly guises each choose a mount, and the narrator describes, "One moment Shadow was riding the World's Largest
Carousel ... and then the red and white lights stretched and shivered and

went out, and he was falling through an ocean of stars" (Gaiman 130). The "ocean of stars" suggests movement both through and outside of time, but instead of landing in another place entirely, Shadow stays in place and merely penetrates the illusion of the carousel.

In one "moment of double vision" he first sees Mama-ji as "an old woman, her dark face pinched with age and disapproval," then immediately notices "behind her ... something huge, a naked woman," carrying "knives, and swords, and severed heads" (Gaiman 138). The carousel provides the magical nexus point through which time and culture converge and collapse, allowing Shadow to see the gods simultaneously as they temporarily seem and as they eternally are. The effect points up the ephemeral nature of "now" and the thin threads of belief that offer little strength or inspiration in a society where people worship money and technology, where "God is a dream, a hope ... a house of many rooms" and "religions are places to stand and look and act, vantage points from which to view the world" (Gaiman *American Gods* 508). Going only in circles without really getting anywhere, the carousel embodies this idea and expresses the loss for that society as represented through and by the gods. Historically, gods have always been porters for belief. That the "American" gods are such a diverse group expresses the universality and perpetual nature of the human quest for meaning, further emphasizing the relationship of past to present and future in Gaiman's novel.

It remains unclear even at the end of *American Gods* exactly what the author wants to lament (if anything at all): lack of spiritual belief, lack of belief in general, or something else entirely. Leaving this undefined compels the reader to draw his or her own conclusions, which all the best books surely do. More importantly, I want to argue that belief is the story's central motif but only as a foundation for a more specific issue Gaiman says he wants to explore: "the immigrant experience ... what people believed in when they came to America" (Gaiman "How Dare"). Born in England and married to an American, Gaiman has a unique "vantage point from which to view the world" and the nation. He conceives the gods as "a metaphor for the way people arrived in America, treated America, and have or do not have beliefs in America" (Krewson). As the porter for a plan concocted by Odin and Loki, god of mischief, to try to get the world's attention, Shadow ponders how and what people believe. Ultimately he decides that regardless of specifics, "it is that belief, that rock-solid belief that makes things happen" (Gaiman *American* 536). Comments such as these throughout the novel suggest Shadow personally rejects the new order — technology — and values tradition, yet he has no faith in the old order — the gods. As a personification of the carousel, he goes in circles, coming to no conclusions. Through him, the past, present, and future spectacularly overlap; in other words, he is human; and as Gaiman says, "People carry worlds within them" ("Neil Gaiman").

Preceding Gaiman by several decades, Susan Cooper's *The Dark Is Rising* series is well known for its time-slips, and like Gaiman and Jones, she often favors co-existent time. The past does exist in discrete pockets for Cooper, but in certain moments throughout the series a character, usually Will Stanton, simultaneously experiences more than one of these pockets, or seamlessly transports from his own time to the past, without using any concrete conveyance. A particularly memorable scene in the last book of the series, *Silver on the Tree,* describes how, while fishing with his brothers, Will can see "through their phantom forms" to witness ancient Britons preparing for a siege (4). This particular slip ends with Will acknowledging that he is "no longer looking out of his own time into another" (5). He never actually departs his own time; because he and the other Old Ones exist "outside of time," his past and present *always* overlap. In a 2006 interview, Cooper, who was a student of Tolkien at Oxford, says, "Half of my head loves to write about real life, but nearly always, magic creeps in and my stories turn into metaphor" (Henneman). In this way her version of the one-world approach parallels that of J.K. Rowling, with both concrete and symbolic portals linking dimensions that exist concurrently within an approximation of our own world. As with the *Harry Potter* books, the "border between the human and the magical is ... a frequent site of tension" in *The Dark Is Rising* series, and a teenaged boy wizard embodies this "tension" (Butler 223). Given his task to carry out the last battle, Will is a porter who uses magic to access and provide a conduit for the past to help rescue, i.e., transform, the future.

Since Will's porter status is fairly straightforward, the more interesting porters in the series for my purposes are the two humans who are nearly as responsible as he for the victory of the Light. Their contributions are appropriate since, just as in *Lord of the Rings*, the fate of humankind is what's at stake in the final battle. While introduced into the series in different books, Jane Drew and Bran Davies are presented as parallel figures in *Silver on the Tree*; both previously drawn into the war between Light and Dark without really being given a choice. Shortly after she first meets Bran in *Silver*, a time-slip transports Jane to meet the Lady, who says, "It was intended from the beginning that you should carry the last message" (90). The Lady identifies Jane as "much the same" as herself and gives her the words she must repeat to Will. Upon the Lady's disappearance, the afanc rises up and confirms Jane's porter status: "tell me the instruction that only comes *through* you!" (90, 93, emphasis in original).

Bran steps in to vanquish the creature of the Dark, in the name of his father, King Arthur, the one who had initially sent away the afanc; and Will reveals Bran is "the Pendragon ... *Heir to the same responsibility in a different age*" (96–7, emphasis added). Paralleling the Lady's assessment of Jane's similarity to herself, Will adds that Bran "belongs to this age just as much as we do, yet at the same time he does not" (97). In other words, Bran stands at a meeting point where past and present, myth and modernity overlap. Further confirmation of Bran's porter role comes when he is the one to decipher the Lady's message through Jane as referring to another magical agent, "the Lost Land," which lies "between land and sea" (Cooper *Silver* 91). Through their adventures there, Bran and Will gain the last object of power; but again, it is Bran who is the sword's rightful heir and who breaks the "fifth barrier," releasing the sword *Eirias* to the Light (Cooper *Silver* 202–4). Like Jane but to a greater degree, Bran plays a crucial role in the final battle: with John Rowlands' help, he wields *Eirias* when the Dark finally comes "rising" (*Silver* 262–3). In strategizing for the Light, Merriman places Bran squarely in the middle: "If Bran can keep the sword safe, and if the Six and the Circle can keep Bran safe, then all will be well" (*Silver* 241). Rowlands echoes Bran's porter status when the Lady chooses him to judge in the Dark's argument that Bran should be left out of the battle (*Silver* 251), that "the old prophecies have been fulfilled only by [the Light's] manipulation of time" (*Silver* 253). As Arthur's son but with a close relationship to his adopted, human father in modern Wales, Bran's in-between position becomes multiplied here, and once again defined by time, specifically by his relationship to both past and present.

Rowlands determines Bran belongs to the present because he "attached himself to that time" and "such loving bonds are outside the control even of the High Magic" (Cooper *Silver* 254). After cutting the blossom from the tree, Bran validates Rowlands' belief by choosing not to "take [his] place outside of Time" with Arthur. When he wonders if this was "the right thing to do," Merriman affirms, "It was the right thing, for you and for the world," suggesting Bran will somehow as a mortal continue to influence events in the present, even though he "will remember nothing that has happened" (Cooper *Silver* 269). As a human hybrid of the mythical (Arthur, ancient Britain) and the real (Owen Davies, modern Wales), Bran also helps to support Butler's argument that Cooper's concern primarily lies with "the land itself and ... its history, rather than for the achievement of any of the individual races that have lived there" (Butler 145). While certainly paying tribute to British history and mythology, Cooper goes further to envision a place where "nothing is allowed to override the importance of shared humanity" (Butler 146).

More problematically, throughout the series Cooper's vision engages the issue of female power through Jane, who stands with Bran in the final battle as one of "the six [who] shall turn it back" (*Silver* 261–3). Her part becomes established earlier in book three, *Greenwich*, when Jane makes the wish that sways the title figure to give up her "secret" and help the Light to victory in this particular battle. Jane becomes closely connected with Greenwitch, a conglomeration of natural materials annually constructed in a Cornish spring ritual, which is "a mythic invention of Cooper's own" (Mikkelsen 41). Greenwitch is "a made creature," a female version of the Celtic Green Man, and in Cooper's mythology, a part of the Wild rather than the High Magic. She remains indifferent to the conflict between Light and Dark and outside their command. Thus she occupies an in-between space, not only of Light and Dark, but also of land and sea, mortal and immortal, mythic and real, past and present.

Greenwitch recognizes this, rejecting the possibility that she would not exist if it were not for "men" and telling Will and Merriman, "It is a game, a substitute. I am given real life only by the White Lady, who takes me down to the deeps" (103). The White Lady refers to her "mother" in the sea, but also implicates Jane, the one human who has shown any real concern for Greenwitch. Jane becomes a human stand-in for Greenwitch, and perhaps even for the White Lady, when a "terrible awe and a kind of pity" inspires her to "impulsively" utter, "I wish you could be happy" (30–1) before the figure is tossed into the sea to culminate the ritual. The wish creates a psychic bond between Jane and Greenwitch, so that they work together as porters for the Light to achieve its goals. On her own, Greenwitch refuses to aid either side and in so doing stands poised to help the Dark. In what Nina Mikkelsen reads as "a journey of the imagination that enables her to participate in the shaman shape-changing abilities of the Old Ones" (42), Jane communicates to Greenwitch that the "secret" is "important" to her. Hearing this, Greenwitch freely gives it to Jane, saying, "You made a wish that was for me, not for yourself. No one has ever done that. I give you my secret in return" (108–9). Jane awakes clutching the parchment that enables Merriman and Will to win this particular battle. While Will says, "Well done," Jane responds, "I didn't do anything," but he confirms the magnitude of her act in responding, "You made a wish" (Cooper *Greenwitch* 111). When he sees Jane carrying the parchment, Merriman behaves as if he has known all along what would happen, signifying that as with Bran and the Walker before him, Jane was pre-selected by the Light to perform a necessary service.

In Jane saying "I didn't do anything," Cooper risks undermining the girl's power, but reiterates her status as a porter through her association and ability to communicate with Greenwitch. Like Jane, Greenwitch is a vessel, but one with long-standing ties to the past and to folk culture. Even though

Greenwitch lives outside the limits of gender-based identification, she remains distinctly feminized for being "made" by only women according to Cooper's ritual. Being linked with her, Jane takes her place with Will, Bran, and Merriman in having the capacity to enable the very survival of the human race. A slight problem does exist in that Jane finds her power through stereotypically female means, through kindness and intuition rather than the exertion of masculine-esque force. Jane's role becomes strengthened when the Lady makes her the last messenger in *Silver*, but Cooper undermines her here, too, by having Bran step in to rescue her from the afanc. Still, Jane's warmer traits as described in *Greenwich* are counter-balanced by subtlety and intellect that reinforces her appearance of power. These are often the most important traits that Will, Merriman, and others of the Light have had at their disposal throughout time in their war against the Dark.

While starting his career slightly earlier than Cooper, like her Alan Garner similarly devises characters as conduits through which the past repeats or an ongoing struggle against evil continues. Rather than using the documented, historical past as a starting point, in *The Owl Service* (1967) Garner selects an alternate version, patterning his fantasy after the four ancient Welsh legends collectively known as the *Mabinogion*. Garner makes inheritance a central theme with Alison, Gwyn, and Roger as the most recent representatives of a triangle first created when Blodeuwedd fell for Gronw Pebyr. Being the shared love interest for descendant of Lleu Llaw Gyffes, Huw Halfbacon, and Alison's deceased relative, Bertram, Gwyn's mother Nancy experienced the "power" as a young woman in the role Alison now occupies. Halfbacon verifies this and defines cultural and familial inheritance as unavoidable when he reveals his relationship to Gwyn: "You are the lord in blood to this valley after me" (191).

The use of "lord" here may seem ironic given that the family and Gwyn see Huw as the "mad" groundskeeper, but Garner defines status as a function of tradition and a person's relation to the myths of the past. Money is only a superficial marker of status and power; for instance, Clive tells his son Roger, "You mustn't expect the Nancys of the world to have too much savvy" (106), but Nancy is clever enough to get money out of Clive every time she threatens to quit, making her seem like the more powerful one despite being of lower caste. Nevertheless both Nancy and the family repeatedly uphold the ritual of class-based segregation, especially when Gwyn shows an interest in Alison. Donna R. White sees *The Owl Service* as "represent[ing] the height of ... Garner's own conflict with his working-class heritage and his elite academic learning, between his intuitive non-rational self and his intellect" (77). I would add that Garner deals with these conflicts in *The Owl Service* by making the past an inescapable influence on the present, and always with a woman — Blodeuwedd, Nancy, Alison — caught in the middle.

In her investigation of *Memory, Heritage, and Childhood in Postwar Britain*, Valerie Krips reminds us that Garner's version of the magical "cycle is activated through an object: a set of plates with a design of owls upon them" (106). As such the "owl service" furnishes a concrete portal, linking past and present. However, the plates only house the magic; setting it free has always required human vessels, starting with the original lovers whose legend virtually defines the valley and all who live there. Woman occupies a precarious position in the mythology and also in Garner's interpretation of it. Perhaps even more than Cooper does with the Lady, Jane, and Greenwitch, Garner makes power a feminized construct, one that seems to be controlled by men but necessarily impacts everyone. Unlike Nancy who is traumatized by her experience as part of the triangle, and Alison who lies in Sleeping-Beauty fashion near the end of the story, Garner characterizes Blodeuwedd as a kind of Welsh Eve whose "actions determine the course of future events, not by controlling them but by setting loose uncontrollable passions" (White 83). Nancy and Alison similarly ignite such "passions" but succumb to their own emotions and become ineffectual compared to Blodeuwedd. Despite being conceived out of flowers, Blodeuwedd seems to be more like her namesake the owl, a hunter, with her husband and her lover killing each other over her and their descendants repeating the process.

As Blodeuwedd's double in the present, Alison provides a contrast when she submits to the status quo by going along with her mother's order that she not see Gwyn. In the end Alison lies unconscious in the grip of the "power," surrounded by feathers. Huw tells Gwyn "comfort her," and accuses both him and Roger: "she wants to be flowers and you make her owls" (218). By this Huw implies the men are responsible for turning the woman into a hunter, which diminishes her power by making it the result of *their* passion. The triangle always places the female in a precarious position, dating from the beginning when, as Garner tells it, Lleu Llaw Gyffes uses the "power" to make a woman out of flowers (55). Perhaps because they are human facsimiles, not magically conceived, Blodeuwedd's doubles lack her magnificence and formidability. Yet one might expect a modern re-enactment to take into account more progressive views on gender roles to allow the female more, not less, authority. The owls gain their freedom *through* Alison; she is the one who hears the "scratching" in the attic that leads to her and Gwyn discovering the plates in the opening chapter. Her illness confirms her sacrificial status as the main porter through which the myth perpetuates and the past survives. In the end, though, it is Roger who causes her transformation by saying, "Why didn't you cut the pattern into flowers, you silly girl?" while her other suitor Gwyn steps aside.

With this question, Roger effectively breaks the spell and the room fills with petals (216–19). Butler views this as an act of Roger transforming himself: by "mak[ing] a rational choice" he becomes "a person who is able to see flowers, and by seeing, make them real for his stepsister" (Butler 74–5). Indeed the story's ambiguous ending appears to correct the past, since Roger, in the role of Gronw, offers Gwyn/Lleu forgiveness just before this and finds a way to turn the owls to flowers, i.e., transforming Blodeuwedd/Alison to her original self. However, the ending also supports a conservative notion of power relations, both in terms of social status and gender roles. Order is only restored when the working-class Welsh boy loses to the upper-class English one and, as a result of the "proper" suitor's wish, the girl transforms from powerful (albeit tortured) hunter "owl" to stereotypical, fragile "flowers." Therefore the ending remains problematic in terms of female power, but upholds the idea of the past being deeply ingrained and bound to repeat regardless of the best "modern" efforts to resist.

Flowers figure even more prominently as a female symbol in *The Merlin Conspiracy*, but in contrast to Garner, Diana Wynne Jones links them with suffering and rage as well as with strength and resiliency — but not submission. After witnessing an act of dark magic, Roddy and her friend Grundo, who are offspring of Court magicians traveling with the King, visit her Welsh grandfather. When they blurt out what they know about the "plot" being perpetrated by Grundo's mother and her "manfriend" Sir James (87–8), her grandfather tells Roddy, "there is something *you* can do ... if you think you have the courage" (emph in original 88). He directs her to a "ruined village where people lived before History began" (121), and there she meets the flower-witch, arguably the most important character in the story and one of Jones's more compelling portrayals of feminine power across her vast body of work.

The meeting between Roddy and the flower-witch occurs in a timeslip similar to those used by Cooper in *The Dark Is Rising* series. Mendlesohn identifies "the plot in *The Merlin Conspiracy* [as] linear" but qualifies that the characters' "experience of the plot, and the structure of time ... [are] hologramatic," based on an "assumption that time is folded and that it is possible to move through the folds" (*Diana* 64). Bearing this out, as she approaches the witch's house Roddy encounters a "cloud of butterflies" not unlike the swarm of plume moths that appear after Will explains to his eldest brother Stephen about the Old Ones. Will understands the significance of the moths appearing at precisely this moment, recalling "an old saying that they carry memories away" (Cooper *Silver* 14). Rather than erasing a memory as the plume moths do for Stephen, Jones' butterflies transport Roddy *into* a memory that has become a myth, to "a place so much of the past that it has become somewhere of now" (Mendlesohn *Diana* 67), as if imprinted into the very earth of Britain. This move is almost imperceptible since according to Grundo, Roddy never leaves his sight in the present; she supports this by later describing how "many things seemed to happen at once" (125) after she followed the butterflies. Roddy also tells Grundo that the flower-witch "was lying in the place the butterflies were" (126), again linking the ancient woman to memory and confirming Jones's use of coexistent time. Positioning Roddy as the porter through which the past will rescue the present and future, Roddy's meeting with the flower-witch also bonds them together.

As the time-slip occurs, Roddy almost immediately feels the pain of the woman, who conveys the understanding that she had been "ritually injured when she was fifteen because she was a powerful witch" (126–7). Magical "law" holds that she has to "pass [her] knowledge down to someone," and after "search[ing] ... the millennia for the right person," as Roddy says, "she gave me her knowledge.... It was devastating" (126). Likening the knowledge to "files in a computer," Roddy notes that each one comes under the heading of a type of "dry and bitter" flower to match the woman's feelings (131). Besides her empathy for the woman, which physically manifests as pain in her own hip that flares up even after the "knowledge" transfer, Roddy admires the fact that the files contain no shred of "black magic." As a result, Roddy determines "to be worthy of her gift, to use it *properly* or not at all" (131, emphasis in original). The passing on of knowledge from an older to a younger woman is a common trope of the coming-of-age journey, and in the vein of most male heroes, the gift the flower-witch provides will enable Roddy to save the world, if she can learn how to control and implement it.

Roddy's porter status is plain in her carrying this stunning collection of magical knowledge from the past to the present, but more symbolically she becomes a connecting point between the folk rituals and beliefs that inform both magical practice and the very fabric of British life, even today. In truth, the spells the flower-witch bequeaths to Roddy equate the tales that have been repeatedly passed down through the ages, mostly by women. Jones confirms Roddy's position as a nexus point in time and culture by setting her on a path that leads to Stonehenge, the setting for the ceremony intended to move all the magical lines that keep order in *all* of the worlds from being "tipped entirely the wrong way" into "the realm of purest black magic" (*Merlin* 446). Much of Jones's work strays from the one-world approach that defines so much of modern fantasy. Even in books whose characters and plot lines bear no relation to one another, we are to understand that the setting is part of a multi-verse with thousands of galaxies, some magical and some not. In *The Merlin Conspiracy*, if Roddy fails, the result would not enshroud one world but the entire multi-verse in darkness. Understanding this, and wanting to rescue Nick, the teenage wizard-in-training she originally summoned for help, Roddy accesses the "hurt woman's files." She quickly discovers how to use them to "raise the land" before the "false Merlin" can do the same (445–6). Watching as "layers of magic" unravel, she wonders, "What *have* I done?" After the process finishes, she understands that she has wrought a major transformation: "magic [is] different, all over everywhere" (460).

While the difference is not negative, the disruption and rearrangement caused by her raising the land requires stabilization. Further reinforcing Roddy as a magical agent linking past and present, she receives help in this from "the white dragon of England" (460), who like the flower-witch up until this point has existed as part of the land itself, being initially mistaken by Nick as a "chalk cliff" (340). To understand the true significance of the act, it is important to recognize that Roddy's raising the land is *only made possible* by the transfer of the flower-witch's knowledge from out of the ancient past. Through Roddy, the flower-witch achieves justice; she spectacularly overrides the kind of evil that is also embodied by the chieftain who injured her. Enlarged, the flower-witch represents the power of story and storytelling as a perpetual influence and activity. Jones supports this toward the end of the book by revealing that *The Merlin Conspiracy* is actually a collection of journal entries. While Nick greatly contributes to the saving of Blest and to the account of how it happened, the book starts with Roddy and it is she who finally puts things right, rescuing him from becoming a "blood sacrifice" in the process. More than finding the courage and skill to decipher and use the flower-files, it is her role as the chosen vessel for the wise woman to enact a monumental, positive act of magic that defines Roddy as a porter of power.

Gateways to the Future: Jonathan Stroud

In her introduction to *Theorising the Fantastic*, Lucy Armitt cogently assesses the position of literary fantasy in relation to time: "Fantasy, even when projecting backwards into the past, foregrounds a trajectory into an unknown that, in textual terms, is always new and therefore always pointing forwards into the future" (2). Proceeding more or less chronologically, my interest in this book has been to expand the traditional portal concept by mapping this "trajectory" being interpreted in its most significant phases of development. Born of myth, folktale, and romance, literary fantasy comes of age as an art form in the nineteenth century and rises to rock-star status in the twentieth. Of course, Susan Cooper, Alan Garner, Diana Wynne Jones, and Neil Gaiman are merely representatives of all of those writing A.T. (After Tolkein) who have respected "the intricate web of Story" (Tolkien "On Fairy-Stories" 47). Numerous other contemporary fantasists such as Lloyd Alexander, Terry Pratchett, Ursula Le Guin, Phillip Pullman, and Garth Nix continue to appropriate myth and history today in works that provide fresh, innovative variations on the portal concept.

My favorite recent example is Jonathan Stroud. In *The Bartimaeus Trilogy* Stroud sets up an alternate version of late twentieth-century Britain in which the Empire has not yet fallen but stands on the brink with war breaking out across Europe and in the American "colonies." The first book introduces Nathaniel, a precocious pre-teen apprentice magician who summons Bartimaeus, a five-thousand-year-old djinni, to steal the Amulet of Samarkand in a revenge scheme targeting Nathaniel's master and Simon Lovelace, an unscrupulous Member of Parliament. More comparable to Gaiman than to the other writers discussed in this chapter, Stroud generally avoids Welsh, Celtic, and Norse legends in favor of ancient Egyptian mythology and much more proximate, albeit revisionary, British and European history. For example, the second book, *The Golem's Eye*, opens in 1868 with William Gladstone, "the most powerful magician ever to become Prime Minister" (*Amulet* 97), leading a successful British invasion of Prague armed with a supremely powerful walking staff (*Golem's Eye* 1–17). Like Tolkien, Stroud gives his version of enchanted Britain a history and around that history a mythology. In this way the purposeful inaccuracies not only increase the story's realism, but more significantly fuel his satire of power structures in the real world.

Being overtly political, *The Bartimaeus Trilogy* imagines a hierarchy with magicians at the top, running the government; however, their power comes from their enslavement of the spirits they call "demons," who can see across "seven planes, all coexistent" (*Amulet* 10). Stroud literally interprets the idea of magic being synonymous with power by placing at the bottom of the hierarchy the "commoners" who completely lack magical ability, and whose career options are limited to manual labor, basic administrative work, and service to the magicians. Like so many other examples in more recent fantasy, Stroud's universe includes magical objects, but his human characters never leave his approximation of an enchanted primary world that is modern yet temporally unspecified. That is, until Kitty devises her own plan of revenge. Only a shadowy figure of "the Resistance" in *The Amulet of Samarkand*, we find out in *The Golem's Eye* that Kitty's motivation stems from her miraculous escape of the magician's attack that permanently disfigures her best friend. Her level of magical resistance and sight seem to increase as the trilogy progresses so that she becomes a hero in her own right in *The Golem's Eye*.

The final book, *Ptolemy's Gate*, finds Kitty, after several years of planning and careful study, learning enough about magic to be able to summon Bartimaeus. In a classic case of gothic doubling, Kitty becomes a contemporary stand-in for the djinni's most revered master, Ptolemy, whom he calls "unique ... the exception" among mortals for believing it may be possible "to redress the balance" of power and "build trust" between humans and spirits (*Ptolemy's Gate* 169). Kitty shares this goal, but for a less scholarly benign reason, as a way to finally topple the magicians. In *Ptolemy's Gate*, Bartimaeus takes "to wearing the semblance of Kitty Jones, the Resistance girl Mandrake had persecuted years before" (40). Having told Nathaniel, now called by his magician's name of John Mandrake, that Kitty died in the confrontation with the golem, Bartimaeus uses her shape to annoy his master. Before this, the only other human shape Bartimaeus ever takes is that of Ptolemy, so his choice of Kitty marks her as a favorite. "Our encounter had been brief but stimulating," says Bartimaeus, "her passionate opposition to injustice reminded me of someone else I'd known a long time ago" (*Ptolemy's Gate* 41). Stroud's aligning of Kitty with Ptolemy reinforces her heroic status in the trilogy, while also connecting her to the ancient past and positioning her as a porter through which the wrongs perpetrated by the magicians may be corrected. Just as the flower-witch reaches through Roddy from the past to achieve justice, through Kitty, Ptolemy beings to realize his goal of uniting spirit and magician.

Ptolemy's Gate in itself offers a prime example of the traditional concrete portal, and Stroud's descriptions of Kitty's journey to the Other Place stand among the most captivating and useful in contemporary fantasy for pointing a direction toward which the portal concept may be heading in the twenty-first century. First, though, it is important to note that Kitty chooses to go because the situation in London spirals out of control when Makepeace puts into motion his plan to enable spirits to operate from within the body of a magician rather than as a dangerous extension. In other words, the magician would become a porter through which the spirits would operate, but the magician would supposedly retain control (*Ptolemy's Gate* 180–4). The flaw in Makepeace's plan, of course, stems from his magician's arrogance; he cannot see that the will and mind of the magician may not be strong enough to overpower the spirit living within. Neither does he take into account the possibility that the spirits might take advantage of this situation.

With Makepeace, whose name drips with irony, Stroud reiterates his use of the porter concept that starts in *The Golem's Eye*, this time expanding upon it by making the vessel human. In *Ptolemy's Gate*, Stroud also reverses the power dynamic inherent in the golem's operation by ultimately giving control to the spirit rather than to the magician. In real-world terms, Makepeace's power play vividly equates the political machinations of empire and their human consequences. As Robert Colls explains, "Nineteenth-century Liberalism represented English freedom as an ideal force ... [but] Liberal political culture which celebrated the disarming of one arbitrary power, the monarch, by the arming of another, Parliament, could be seen not as a myth of freedom at all but the sopping of one arbitrary power for another" (30, 32). Stroud satirizes precisely this process throughout the trilogy, playing upon the concept of the divine right of kings that forms the foundation for the British monarchy by having the magicians take into their bodies the spirits that give them power.

While Nathaniel/Mandrake initially views Ptolemy's Gate as "a fairy tale that all sensible magicians had long ignored" (363), Kitty determines to try to reach Bartimaeus, who takes an opportunity to return to the Other Place, refusing to join his fellow spirits when they start overpowering the magicians (346–7). Stroud's portrayal of Kitty's journey must be read in its entirety for full appreciation; for my purposes, the most crucial aspect of the scenes is Kitty's experience of drifting in a limitless chaos where all of the essences dwell as one. Their lack of individuation mirrors Ptolemy's hope to unify magicians and spirits. Enlarged, such unification symbolizes the breaking down of all of the material obstacles of class, gender, race, etc. which divide one person from another and cause strife in the real world. Idealistic, to be sure, but Stroud posits the power of human will as the instrument whereby such transformation of society might occur.

After Kitty "passe[s] through Ptolemy's Gate to the other side" she attempts to adjust to the "ceaseless swirl of movement" by "willing" a shape for her self (378–80). When Bartimaeus manifests, he explains that her sense of being unwanted in the Other Place comes from her efforts to "*impose order ... and order means limitations*" (400, emphasis in original). Bartimaeus, who appears in Ptolemy's form when Kitty requests that he take some kind of shape to talk to her, initially dismisses her plan to put down the spirits' rebellion. While she begins to find a way "to make her mannequin move about" (402), however, she also manages to knock down each of the djinni's objections. Her determination only intensifies in the chaotic setting, and Kitty finally convinces Bartimaeus by reminding him of his beloved master: "*If you come back, and help save London, you will be continuing Ptolemy's work. Humans and djinn working together. That's what he wanted, isn't it?*" (408, emphasis in original). As the only other person besides Ptolemy to travel to the Other Place and return alive, Kitty doubles her porter status. First, she completes Ptolemy's work, thus giving the past an extraordinary reach through 2,000 years to impact the present and future. Second, she recalls

Bartimaeus, whose aid becomes invaluable in helping Nathaniel/Mandrake to restore a semblance of order. Nathaniel also becomes a porter as Bartimaeus's sapped strength requires that he inhabit the magician's body, but the djinni makes plain Kitty's greater importance:

> I would never have done it had it not been for the girl ... it was a stupid idea and I didn't believe it.... But Ptolemy had believed it and ... the echo of his great faith was powerful enough to win me over when Kitty repeated his great gesture and came across to meet me" [425].

That Kitty, like Ptolemy before her, does not possess overt magical power only intensifies the importance of her act.

As the masculine-esque, conniving Jessica Whitwell and the ultra-feminine but deadly Jane Farrar exemplify, Stroud's portrayal of female power is not wholly positive. We must keep in mind, though, that Whitwell and Farrar are both magicians while Kitty, and Mrs. Lutyens, Nathaniel's childhood drawing teacher and the only other person who seems to emotionally reach him, are both commoners. Therefore, it is the lust for power, Stroud implies, that makes Whitwell and Farrar what they are. Traditionally fantasy centers on male heroes, but Kitty provides a good illustration of the female hero we also see in *The Merlin Conspiracy*'s Roddy, and that is becoming more prevalent in recent years in works by Neil Gaiman (*Coraline*), Garth Nix (*The Abhorsen Trilogy*), Phillip Pullman (*His Dark Materials* series), and Diane Duane (*The Young Wizards* series.) Perfectly satisfying the definition of the porter that grounds this study, Kitty provides the catalyst for an explosive (literally) transformation of the political, economic, and social structures of Stroud's enchanted Britain. This change comes at great cost, particularly for Kitty, Nathaniel, and Bartimaeus, and does not promise Utopia. For example, Kitty declines a position on the newly formed Council, believing that "anyone wishing to take part in a more open system of government would need qualities of supreme patience and endurance" (*Ptolemy's Gate* 493), qualities her journey to the Other Place has at least temporarily depleted. The faith and hope that drives her actions throughout the story remain intact, however, as Kitty exits the story telling Rebecca Piper, who is overseeing the rebuilding process, "It's possible. Not easy, but it's possible" (496).

Sealing the Portal (for now): Some Closing Thoughts

Regardless of how a fantasist sub-creates a Secondary space, he or she cannot help but be influenced by the politics and interpersonal power dynamics at work in the Primary world outside the text. If, as so many critics argue, fantasy is a literature of desire, the fact that numerous writers from William Blake to Alfred Tennyson, E. Nesbit to Edith Wharton, Diana Wynne Jones to J.K. Rowling, envision an "Other Place" in the way Jonathan Stroud does, as a vortex of magic where individuation vanishes, signifies both the state of contemporary society and the "movement toward transcendence" that aligns the romantic sublime with the literary fantastic (Sandner 50). The portal is undoubtedly a practical conveyance, a way to move a character from the Primary to the Secondary world. However, the breadth and depth of literary fantasy as it has evolved from Blake's time to today demands that the portal be viewed not merely as a concrete gateway, but as a symbolic nexus point where the rational and mythical/mystical interact. As Blake says, "Without contraries there is no progression. Attraction and Repulsion, Reason and Energy, / Love and Hate, are necessary to Human existence" (*Marriage* Plate 3). The moments, individuals, and experiences through which these contraries are made to come into contact with one another are inherent to literary fantasy, providing rare glimmers of insight, those "fleeting glimpse[s] of joy" (Tolkien "On Fairy-Stories" 86), for transforming the chaos of human life.

Their approaches to manifesting Faërie space differ, but in many ways Cooper, Garner Jones, Gaiman, Stroud, and numerous other modern fantasists follow Tolkien and his nineteenth-century predecessors in centralizing the side-effects that occur with shifting generations and in contemplating what happens when one way of life gives way to another and another. The past — whether within, between, or outside such texts — creates an unavoidable, haunting history. Going beyond the rational boundaries of realistic fiction, fantasists envision space psychologically, spiritually, politically, culturally — in terms of every imaginable realm of ideology. In her *Defense of Fantasy*, Anne Swinfen succinctly summarizes, "The writers of fantasy have provided the most satisfactory mode of expressing their ideas about the contemporary world and contemporary values. They have used it to explore new methods of expression and to expound a deep-felt sense of moral purpose" (230). Within this mode, as a device for bridging gaps and providing access to the seemingly inaccessible, the portal wields extraordinary power.

Chapter Notes

Introduction

1. Throughout this study I will use the word "real" with the understanding that reality is a wholly subjective concept. For the purposes of this book, real will be written without quotation marks but consistently refer to rational, scientifically explainable phenomena and experience.

2. For more on this topic, see my chapter, "J.R.R. Tolkien and the Child Reader: Images of Inheritance and Resistance in *The Lord of the Rings* and J.K. Rowling's *Harry Potter*," in *How We Became Middle-earth: A Collection of Essays on* The Lord of the Rings, ed. Adam Lam (Switzerland: Walking Tree, 2007).

Chapter 2

1. An earlier version of this chapter first appeared in *Mosaic: A Journal for the Interdisciplinary Study of Literature*, 3.2 (June 2001): 33–48.

2. Sir William Gladstone, British Liberal Party Statesman and four-time Prime Minister under Queen Victoria.

3. "Cecil" spelled backwards, another reference to British politics: Lord Robert Cecil, Prime Minister three times in Victoria's Reign, between 1885 and 1902; perhaps also Lord William Cecil, who was chief advisor to Elizabeth I for much of her reign.

Chapter 5

1. Based on the text we are to assume "Grief" was penned by the Old Man, but in truth it is a creation of Hodgson as the author, especially given that he devoted much of his time to writing poetry, starting from his childhood (Gullette). Likewise, Tennyson is presumed as the speaker of *In Memoriam* since his grief over Hallam's death is its inspiration.

Chapter 7

1. For example, recall that Walter finds the Wood by passing through the cleft in the cliff wall in *The Wood Beyond the World*, discussed in Chapter One.

2. Here and throughout the chapter I use the term "modern" to identify the postwar era, not in association with the modernist literary movement, which is an entirely different set of concepts outside the range of this project.

3. The name also appears in other tales: *Sir Gawain and the Green Knight*, one of Tolkien's medieval translations, places Camelot in such a realm. When describing the Green Knight's horse, the bard says, "Such a mount on *middle-earth*, or man to ride him / was never beheld in that hall with eyes ere that time" (30, emphasis added).

Chapter 8

1. Lending authenticity to the collection, Rowling published *The Tales of Beedle the Bard* (Children's High Level Group, December 2008) as a separate volume, "with a commentary on each of the tales by Professor Albus Dumbledore."

2. While the Arthurian legend is gathered from a range of sources, most of them French, the stories have become an acknowledged part of British history and mythos. For a history of the saga in these terms, see T.W. Rolleston, *Celtic Myths and Legends* (New York: Dover, 1990).

3. As the full scope of this argument lies somewhat outside my own argument for Harry's "in-between" status, I refer the reader to Daniel H. Nexon and Iver B. Neumann's excellent study, *Harry Potter and*

International Relations (Lanham, MD: Rowman & Littlefield, 2006), which examines the relationship between contemporary political structures and Rowling's portrayal of muggle/muggle-born/wizarding power struggles.

4. Rowling writes a similar scene for Neville Longbottom near the end of *Deathly Hallows,* as he also wields the sword and indeed commits one of the most important acts of heroism in the series.

Bibliography

Abrams, M.H. *Natural Supernaturalism*: *Tradition and Revolution in Romantic Literature*. New York: W.W. Norton, 1973.

Anatol, Giselle Liza. "The Fallen Empire: Exploring Ethnic Otherness in the World of Harry Potter." *Reading Harry Potter: Critical Essays*. Contributions to the Study of Popular Culture, Number 78. Westport, CT: Praeger, 2003. 163–78.

Anthony, Susan B. "Women's Rights to the Suffrage." *American Rhetoric*. 1873. http://www.nationalcenter.org/AnthonySuffrage.html.

Armitt, Lucy. *Contemporary Women's Fiction and the Fantastic*. New York: St. Martin's, 2000.

_____. *Theorizing the Fantastic*. New York: St. Martin's, 1996.

Arnold, Matthew. *The Works of Matthew Arnold*. New York: Wordsworth, 1999.

Attebery, Brian. *Strategies of Fantasy*. Bloomington: Indiana University Press, 1992.

Auchincloss, Louis. Introduction. *A Backward Glance*. By Edith Wharton. New York: Simon and Schuster, 1998.

Auden, W.H. "The Quest Hero." *Understanding the Lord of the Rings: The Best of Tolkien Criticism*. Rose A. Zimbardo and Neil D. Isaacs, eds. New York: Houghton Mifflin, 2004. 31–51.

Auerbach, Nina, and U.C. Knoepflmacher, eds. *Forbidden Journeys: Fairy Tales and Fantasies by Victorian Women Writers*. Chicago: University Chicago Press, 1992.

Barrie, J(ames) M(atthew). *Peter Pan*. New York: Penguin, 1986.

Bell, Anthea. *E. Nesbit*. New York: Henry Z. Walck, 1964.

Bettelheim, Bruno. *The Uses of Enchantment: The Meaning and Importance of Fairy Tales*. New York: Vintage, 1989.

Bixler, Phyllis. *The Secret Garden: Nature's Magic*. New York: Twayne, 1996.

Bland, Lucy. *Banishing the Beast: English Feminism and Sexual Morality, 1885–1914*. New York: Penguin, 1995.

Blieler, E.F., ed. "William Hope Hodgson: 1877–1918." *Supernatural Fiction Writers: Fantasy and Horror*. Vol. I. New York: Scribner, 1985. 421–28.

Bloom, Harold. *Blake's Apocalypse*. Ithaca, NY: Cornell University Press, 1963.

_____. *The Visionary Company: A Reading of English Romantic Poetry*. Ithaca, NY: Cornell University Press, 1971.

Boos, Florence S. "An (Almost) Egalitarian Sage: William Morris and Nineteenth Century Socialist-Feminism." *Victorian Sages and Cultural Discourse*. Thais E. Morgan, ed. New Brunswick: Rutgers University Press, 1990. 187–206.

_____. *History and Community: Essays in Victorian Medievalism*. New York: Garland, 1992.

Bottigheimer, Ruth B., ed. *Fairy Tales and Society: Illusion, Allusion, and Paradigm*. Philadelphia: University of Pennsylvania Press, 1986.

Bowles, Scott. "Harry Potter Leads Weekend Box Office Final Tally." *USA Today*, July 15, 2007. http://www.usatoday.com/life/movies/news/2007-07-15-weekendboxoffice_N.htm.

Braybrooke, Patrick. *J.M. Barrie: A Study in Fairies and Mortals*. New York: Haskell, 1971.

Briggs, Julia. *A Woman of Passion: The Life of E. Nesbit, 1858–1924*. New York: New Amsterdam, 1987.

Brothers Grimm. *The Complete Grimm's*

Fairy Tales. James Stern, ed. New York: Random House, 1972.

Burnett, Frances Hodgson. *The Secret Garden*. New York: Penguin. 1994.

Butler, Charles. *Four British Fantasists: Place and Culture in the Children's Fantasies of Penelope Lively, Alan Garner, Diana Wynne Jones, and Susan Cooper.* Lanham, MD: Children's Literature Association and Scarecrow Press, 2006.

Caine, Barbara. *English Feminism: 1780–1980.* New York: Oxford University Press, 1997.

Campbell, Joseph. *The Power of Myth.* New York: Doubleday, 1988.

Carlyle, Thomas. *Sartor Resartus.* New York: Oxford University Press, 2000.

Carpenter, Humphrey, ed. *The Letters of J.R.R. Tolkien.* New York: Houghton Mifflin, 2000.

Carpenter, Lynette, and Wendy K. Kolmar, eds. Introduction. *Haunting the House of Fiction: Feminist Perspectives on Ghost Stories by American Women.* Knoxville: University of Tennessee Press, 1991. 1–25.

Carroll, Lewis. "Alice's Adventures in Wonderland." *The Annotated Alice.* Martin Gardner, ed. New York: Random House, 1998.

Chance, Jane. *The Lord of the Rings: The Mythology of Power.* Revised Edition. Lexington: University Press of Kentucky, 2001.

Clark, Beverly Lyon. *Kiddie Lit: The Cultural Construction of Children's Literature in America.* Baltimore: Johns Hopkins University Press, 2003.

_____, and Margaret R. Higonnet. *Girls, Boys, Books, Toys: Gender in Children's Literature and Culture.* Baltimore: Johns Hopkins University Press, 1999.

Coats, Karen. *Looking Glasses and Neverlands: Lacan, Desire, and Subjectivity in Children's Literature.* Iowa City: University of Iowa Press, 2004.

Coleridge, Samuel T. *The Rime of the Ancient Mariner and Other Poems.* New York: Dover, 1992.

Colls, Robert. "Englishness and the Political Culture." *Englishness: Politics and Culture 1880–1920.* Robert Colls and Philip Dodd, eds. Dover, NH: Croom Helm, 1986. 29–61.

Cooper, Susan. *The Dark Is Rising.* New York: Simon and Schuster, 1973.

_____. *Greenwitch.* New York: Simon and Schuster, 1974.

_____. *Silver on the Tree.* New York: Simon and Schuster, 1977.

Damour, Lisa. "Harry Potter and the Magical Looking Glass: Reading the Secret Life of the Preadolescent." Giselle Lisa Anatol, ed. *Reading Harry Potter: Critical Essays.* Contributions to the Study of Popular Culture, Number 78. Westport, CT: Praeger, 2003. 15–24.

Davidoff, Leonore. *Worlds Between: Historical Perspectives in Gender and Class.* New York: Routledge, 1995.

Dickens, Charles. "The Magic Fishbone: Romance from the Pen of Miss Alice Rainbird." *Holiday Romance and Other Writings for Children.* J.M. Dent, ed. Rutland, VT: Charles E. Tuttle, 1995. 408–18.

Dickerson, Matthew T., and David O'Hara. *From Homer to Harry Potter: A Handbook on Myth and Fantasy.* Grand Rapids: Brazos Press, 2006.

Dusinberre, Juliet. *Alice to the Lighthouse: Children's Books and Radical Experiments in Art.* New York: St. Martin's, 1987.

Dyman, Jenni. *Lurking Feminism: The Ghost Stories of Edith Wharton.* New York: Peter Lang, 1996.

Eager, Edward. *The Time Garden.* New York: Harcourt Brace, 1999.

Eby, Cecil Degrotte. "Peter Pan's England." *The Road to Armageddon: The Martial Spirit in English Popular Literature, 1870–1914.* Durham: Duke University Press, 1987. 128–48.

Fedorko, Kathy A. *Gender and the Gothic in the Fiction of Edith Wharton.* Tuscaloosa: University of Alabama Press, 1995.

The Fellowship of the Ring. Dir. Peter Jackson. Special Extended DVD Edition. New Line Entertainment, 2002.

Filmer, Kath, ed. *Twentieth-Century Fantasists: Essays on Culture, Society and Belief in Twentieth-Century Mythopoeic Literature.* New York: St. Martin's, 1992.

_____. *The Victorian Fantasists: Essays on*

Culture, Society, and Belief in the Mytho-poeic Fiction of the Victorian Age. New York: St. Martin's, 1991.

Fisher, Sheila. "Taken Men and Token Women in Sir Gawain and the Green Knight." Seeking the Woman in Late Medieval and Renaissance Writings: Essays in Feminist Contextual Criticism. Sheila Fisher and Janet E. Halley, eds. Knoxville: University of Tennessee Press, 1989. 71–105.

Ford, Ford Madox. "The Brown Owl." The Victorian Fairy Tale Book. Michael Patrick Hearn, ed. New York: Pantheon, 1988. 261–316.

_____. The Feather. New York: George Braziller, 1965.

_____. The Queen Who Flew. New York: George Braziller, 1965.

Fracasso, Evelyn E. Edith Wharton's Prisoners of Consciousness: A Study of Theme and Technique in the Tales. Westport, CT: Greenwood Press, 1994.

Friedman, Lester D. "Hooked on Pan: Barrie's Immortal Pirate in Fiction and Film." Second Star to the Right: Peter Pan in the Popular Imagination. Allison B. Kavey and Lester D. Friedman, eds. New Brunswick, NJ: Rutgers University Press, 2009. 188–217.

Gaiman, Neil. American Gods. New York: Perennial/HarperCollins, 2001.

_____. "How Dare You?" Neil Gaiman Official Web Site. http://neilgaiman.com June 11, 2009.

_____. Neverwhere. New York: HarperCollins, 1997.

Garner, Alan. The Owl Service. New York: Harcourt Brace, 1999.

Geduld, Harry M. Sir James Barrie. New York: Twayne, 1971.

Greenburg, Reva Pollack. Fabian Couples, Feminist Issues. New York: Garland, 1987.

Grenier, Richard. "Society and Edith Wharton." Commentary 96.6 (1993): 48–52.

Gullette, Alan. William Hope Hodgson: Reporter from the Borderland. October 20, 2004. http://alangullette.com/lit/hodgson/whhbio.htm.

Hall, Donald E. Fixing Patriarchy: Femi-nism and Mid-Victorian Male Novelists. New York: New York University Press, 1996.

Haystock, Jennifer. Edith Wharton and the Conversations of Literary Modernism. New York: Palgrave MacMillan, 2008.

Hearn, Michael Patrick. Introduction. The Victorian Fairy Tale Book. New York: Pantheon, 1988. xv–xxvii.

Henneman, Heidi. "Just Like Magic: Susan Cooper Casts Another Captivating Spell." Rev. of Victory by Susan Cooper. First Person Book Page. 2006. ProMotion, Inc. June 8, 2009.

Hodgson, Amanda. The Romances of William Morris. Cambridge: Cambridge University Press, 1990.

Hodgson, William Hope. The House on the Borderland. New York: Carroll and Graff, 1996.

Holmes, Martha Stoddard. "Peter Pan and the Possibilities of Child Literature." Allison B. Kavey and Lester D. Friedman, eds. Second Star to the Right: Peter Pan in the Popular Imagination. New Brunswick, NJ: Rutgers University Press, 2009. 132–50.

Honeyman, Susan. Elusive Childhood: Impossible Representations in Modern Fiction. Athens: Ohio University Press, 2005.

Honig, Edith Lazaros. Breaking the Angelic Image: Woman Power in Victorian Children's Fantasy. Westport, CT: Greenwood Press, 1988.

Horan, Patrick M. The Importance of Being Paradoxical: Maternal Presence in the Works of Oscar Wilde. Cranbury, NJ: Associated University Press, 1997.

Houghton, Walter E. The Victorian Frame of Mind 1830–70. New Haven: Yale University Press, 1957.

Houston, Gail Turley. Royalties: The Queen and Victorian Writers. Charlottesville: University Press of Virginia, 1999.

Italie, Hillel. "Potter Magic: Book Breaks Sales Records." ABC News/Associated Press. July 23, 2007. http://abcnews.go.com/Entertainment/wireStory?id=3402498.

"J.K. Rowling Outs Dumbledore as Gay." BBC News. October 20, 2007. http://

news.bbc.co.uk/1/hi/entertainment/705
3982.stm.
"J.K. Rowling Press Conference." CBBC
NewsRound. BBC Online. July 18,
2005. http://news.bbc.co.uk/cbbcnews/
hi/newsid_4690000/newsid_4690800/4
690885.stm.
Jack, R D S. *The Road to the Never Land: A
Reassessment of J M Barrie's Dramatic Art.*
Aberdeen: Aberdeen University Press,
1991.
Jones, Diana Wynne. *The Merlin Conspiracy.* New York: Greenwillow, 2003.
_____. *The Time of the Ghost.* New York:
HarperTrophy, 1981.
Kavey, Allison B. "'I do believe in fairies, I
do, I do': The History and Epistemology
of Peter Pan." *Second Star to the Right:
Peter Pan in the Popular Imagination.* Al-
lison B. Kavey and Lester D. Friedman,
eds. New Brunswick, NJ: Rutgers Uni-
versity Press, 2009. 75–104.
Kegler, Adelheid. *The Victorian Fantasists:
Essays on Culture, Society, and Belief in
the Mythopoeic Fiction of the Victorian
Age.* New York: St. Martin's, 1991.
Killinger, John. *God, the Devil, and Harry
Potter: A Christian Minister's Defense of
the Beloved Novels.* New York: Thomas
Dunne/St. Martin's, 2002.
Kirchoff, Frederick. *William Morris: The
Construction of Male Self, 1856–1872.*
Athens: Ohio University Press, 1990.
Koppes, Phyllis Bixler. "Tradition and the
Talent of Frances Hodgson Burnett: *Lit-
tle Lord Fauntleroy, A Little Princess* and
The Secret Garden." *Reflections on Chil-
dren's Literature.* Francelia Butler and
Richard Rotert, eds. Hamden, CT: Li-
brary Professional, 1984. 201–14.
Krewson, John. "An Interview with Neil
Gaiman." *Neil Gaiman Official Web Site.*
HarperCollins Publishers. June 11, 2009.
http://www.neilgaiman.com.
Krips, Valerie. *The Presence of the Past:
Memory, Heritage, and Childhood in Post-
war Britain.* New York: Garland, 2000.
Kutzer, M. Daphne. *Empire's Children:
Empire and Imperialism in Classic British
Children's Books. Children's Literature and
Culture.* Volume 16. New York: Garland,
2000.

Laybourn, Keith. *The Rise of Socialism in Bri-
tain, c. 1881–1951.* Stroud: Sutton, 1997.
Ledger, Sally. *The New Woman: Fiction and
Feminism at the* fin de siècle. New York:
Manchester University Press, 1997.
_____, and Roger Luckhurst. *The* Fin de
Siècle: *A Reader in Cultural History, c.
1880–1900.* Oxford: Oxford University
Press, 2000. xiii–xxiii.
Lobdel, Jared. *The Rise of Tolkienian Fan-
tasy.* Chicago: Open Court, 2005.
Lundin, Ann. *Constructing the Canon of
Children's Literature: Beyond Library
Walls and Ivory Towers.* New York: Rout-
ledge, 2004.
Lurie, Alison. *Don't Tell the Grown-ups: The
Subversive Power of Children's Literature.*
New York: Little Brown, 1990.
_____. "Ford Madox Ford's Fairy Tales for
Children." *The Presence of Ford Madox
Ford.* Sondra J. Stang, ed. Philadelphia:
University of Pennsylvania Press, 1981.
130–44.
MacAndrew, Elizabeth. *The Gothic Tradi-
tion in Fiction.* New York: Columbia
University Press, 1979.
MacDonald, George. *Lilith: A Romance.*
Grand Rapids: Wm. B. Eerdmans, 1998.
_____. *Phantastes: A Faerie Romance.* Grand
Rapids: Wm. B. Eerdmans, 2000.
Madsen, Catherine. "'Light from an Invis-
ible Lamp': Natural Religion in The Lord
of the Rings." *Tolkien and the Invention
of Myth: A Reader.* Jane Chance, ed. Lex-
ington: University Press of Kentucky,
2004. 35–47.
Manlove, Colin N. "Fantasy as Witty Con-
ceit: E. Nesbit." *Mosaic: A Journal for the
Comparative Study of Literature and Ideas*
10.2 (1977): 109–30.
_____. *The Fantasy Literature of England.*
New York: St. Martin's, 1999.
_____. "Victorian and Modern Fantasy:
Some Contrasts." *The Celebration of the
Fantastic.* Donald E. Morse, Marshall B.
Tymn, and Csilla Bertha, eds. Westport,
CT: Greenwood Press, 1989. 9–22.
Mathews, Richard. *Fantasy: The Liberation
of Imagination.* New York: Twayne, 1997.
_____. *Worlds Beyond the World: The Fan-
tastic Vision of William Morris.* San Ber-
nardino, CA: Borgo, 1978.

Mellor, Anne. *Romanticism and Gender.* New York: Routledge, 1993.

Mendlesohn, Farah. "Crowning the King: Harry Potter and the Construction of Authority." *The Ivory Tower and Harry Potter: Perspectives on a Literary Phenomenon.* Lana A. Whited, ed. Columbia: University of Missouri Press, 2002. 159–181.

_____. *Diana Wynne Jones: Children's Literature and the Fantastic Tradition.* New York: Routledge, 2005.

_____. *Rhetorics of Fantasy.* Middletown, CT: Wesleyan University Press, 2008.

Mikkelsen, Nina. *Susan Cooper.* New York: Twayne, 1998.

Morris, William. "News From Nowhere." *Stories in Prose.* G.D.H. Cole, ed. New York: Random House, 1934. 3–197.

_____. *The Story of the Glittering Plain* and *Child Christopher.* Bristol, England: Thoemmes Press, 1996.

_____. "A Theory of Life." *News from Nowhere and Selected Writings and Designs.* Asa Briggs, ed. New York: Penguin, 1986. 151–3.

_____. *The Water of the Wondrous Isles.* Bristol, England: Thoemmes Press, 1994.

_____. *The Wood Beyond the World.* New York: Dover, 1972.

Moser, Thomas C. *The Life in the Fiction of Ford Madox Ford.* Princeton, NJ: Princeton University Press, 1980.

Moskowitz, Sam, ed. *Out of the Storm: Uncollected Fantasies by William Hope Hodgson.* West Kingston, RI: Donald M. Grant, 1975.

_____. Preface. *Science Fiction by Gaslight: A History and Anthology of Science Fiction in the Popular Magazines, 1891–1911.* Westport, CT: Hyperion, 1968. 11–14.

Murphy, Patricia. *Time Is of the Essence: Temporality, Gender, and the New Woman.* Albany: State University of New York Press, 2001.

Nassaar, Christopher S. *Into the Demon Universe: A Literary Exploration of Oscar Wilde.* New Haven: Yale University Press, 1974.

Natov, Roni. "Harry Potter and the Extraordinariness of the Ordinary." *The Ivory Tower and Harry Potter: Perspectives on a Literary Phenomenon.* Lana A. Whited, ed. Columbia: University of Columbia Press, 2002. 125–39.

"Neil Gaiman on American Gods." *Author Interview.* HarperCollins Official Web Site. http://www.harpercollins.com/author/authorExtra.aspx?authorID=3417&isbn13=9780380973651&displayType=bookinterview.

Nel, Philip. *JK Rowling's Harry Potter Novels: A Reader's Guide.* New York: Continuum, 2001.

Nelson, Carolyn Christensen. "Women Writers of the *fin de siècle.*" *British Women Writers of the 1890s.* New York: Twayne, 1997. 1–7.

Nelson, Claudia. "The 'It' Girl (and Boy): Ideologies of Gender in the Psammead Trilogy." *E. Nesbit's Psammead Trilogy: A Children's Classic at 100.* Raymond E. Jones, ed. Lanham, MD: Children's Literature Association and The Scarecrow Press, 2006. 1–15.

Nexon, Daniel H., and Iver B. Neumann, Eds. *Harry Potter and International Relations.* Lanham, MD: Rowman & Littlefield, 2006.

Nikolajeva, Maria. "Fairy Tale and Fantasy: From Archaic to Postmodern." *Marvels and Tales* 17.1 (2003): 138–56.

O'Keefe, Deborah. *Readers in Wonderland: The Liberating Worlds of Fantasy Fiction.* New York: Continuum, 2003.

Olsen, Lance. "Nameless Things and Thingless Names." *Fantastic Literature: A Critical Reader.* David Sandner, ed. Westport, CT: Greenwood Press, 2004. 274–92.

Page, Edwin. *Gothic Fantasy. The Films of Tim Burton.* London: Marion Boyars, 2007.

Pease, Edward R. *The History of the Fabian Society.* Second Edition. London: George Allen & Unwin, 1925.

Peel, Robin. "Ford and the Simple Life: Gender, Subjectivity, and Class in a Satirized Utopia." *Ford Madox Ford's Modernity.* Robert Hampson and Max Saunders, eds. New York: Rodopi, 2003. 59–70.

Petty, Anne C. *Tolkien in the Land of Heroes: Discovering the Human Spirit.* Cold Spring Harbor, NY: Cold Spring Press, 2003.

Pharr, Mary. "*In Media Res*: Harry Potter as Hero in Progress." *The Ivory Tower and Harry Potter: Perspectives on a Literary Phenomenon*. Lana A. Whited, ed. Columbia: University of Missouri Press. 53–66.

Propp, Vladmir. *The Morphology of the Folktale*. Austin: University of Texas Press, 1998.

Pugh, Patricia. *Educate, Agitate, Organize: 100 Years of Fabian Socialism*. New York: Methuen, 1984.

Reid, Siân. "As I Do Will, So Mote It Be: Magic as Metaphor in Neo-Pagan Witchcraft." *Magical Religion and Modern Witchcraft*. James R. Lewis, ed. Albany: State University of New York Press, 1996. 141–67.

Reimer, Mavis. "The Beginning of the End: Writing Empire in E. Nesbit's Psammead Books." E. *Nesbit's Psammead Trilogy: A Children's Classic at 100*. Raymond E. Jones, ed. Lanham, MD: Children's Literature Association and The Scarecrow Press, 2006. 39–62.

The Return of the King. Dir. Peter Jackson. Special Extended DVD Edition. New Line Entertainment, 2004.

Richey, Esther Gilman. "Only Half Magic: Edward Eager's Revision of Nesbit's Psammead Trilogy." *Nesbit's Psammead Trilogy: A Children's Classic at 100*. Raymond E. Jones, ed. Lanham, MD: Children's Literature Association and The Scarecrow Press, 2006. 255–69.

Robbins, Keith. *The Present and the Past: Great Britain: Identities, Institutions and the Idea of Britishness*. New York: Longman, 1998.

Robson, Catherine. *Men in Wonderland: The Lost Girlhood of the Victorian Gentleman*. Princeton: Oxford University Press, 2001.

Rolleston, T.W. *Celtic Myths and Legends*. New York: Dover, 1990.

Rose, Jonathan. *The Edwardian Temperament: 1895–1919*. Athens: Ohio University Press, 1986.

Rowling, J.K. *Harry Potter and the Chamber of Secrets*. London: Bloomsbury, 1998.

_____. *Harry Potter and the Deathly Hallows*. London: Bloomsbury, 2007.

_____. *Harry Potter and the Goblet of Fire*. London: Bloomsbury, 2000.

_____. *Harry Potter and the Half-Blood Prince*. London: Bloomsbury, 2005.

_____. *Harry Potter and the Order of the Phoenix*. London: Bloomsbury, 2003.

_____. *Harry Potter and the Philosopher's Stone*. London: Bloomsbury, 1997.

_____. *Harry Potter and the Prisoner of Azkaban*. London: Bloomsbury, 1999.

Rubinstein, David. *Before the Suffragettes: Women's Emancipation in the 1890s*. Brighton: Harvester, 1986.

Sandner, David. *The Fantastic Sublime*. Westport, CT: Greenwood Press, 1996.

Schacker, Jennifer. *National Dreams: The Remaking of Fairy Tales in Nineteenth-Century England*. Philadelphia: University of Pennsylvania Press, 2003.

Shelley, Mary. *Frankenstein*. New York: Bedford/St. Martin's, 2000.

Shippey, T.A. *J.R.R. Tolkien: Author of the Century*. New York: Houghton Mifflin, 2001.

Silver, Carole. "Socialism Internalized: The Last Romances of William Morris." *Socialism and the Literary Artistry of William Morris*. Florence S. Boos and Carole G. Silver, eds. Columbia: University of Missouri Press, 1990. 117–26

_____. *Strange and Secret Peoples: Fairies and Victorian Consciousness*. New York: Oxford University Press, 1999.

Sir Gawain and the Green Knight, Pearl, and Sir Orfeo. 2d ed. Translated by J.R.R. Tolkien. New York: Ballantine, 1975.

Smith, Elton E. "Winged Ghosts: Alfred, Lord Tennyson and the Return to the Mystical." *The Haunted Mind: The Supernatural in Victorian Literature*. Elton E. and Robert Haas, eds. Lanham, MD: Scarecrow, 1999. 1–9.

Snitow, Ann Barr. *Ford Madox Ford and the Voice of Uncertainty*. Baton Rouge: Louisiana State University Press, 1984.

Stanton, Michael N. *Hobbits, Elves, and Wizards: Exploring the Wonders and Worlds of J.R.R. Tolkien's* The Lord of the Rings. New York: Palgrave Macmillan, 2001.

Stephens, John. "'Is This the Promised End...?': *Fin de Siècle* Mentality and Children's Literature" *Reflections of Change:*

Children's Literature Since 1945. Sandra L. Beckett, ed. Westport, CT: Greenwood, 1997. 15–22.

Sterling-Folker, Jennifer and Brian Folker. "Conflict and the Nation State: Magical Mirrors of Muggles and Refracted Images." *Harry Potter and International Relations.* Daniel H. Nexon and Iver B. Neumann, eds. New York: Rowman and Littlefield, 2006. 103–125.

Stewart, Clare. "'Weird Fascination': The Response to Victorian Women's Ghost Stories." *Feminist Readings of Victorian Popular Texts.* Emma Liggins and Daniel Duffy, eds. Burlington, VT: Ashgate, 2001. 108–25.

Stoker, Bram. *Dracula.* New York: Bedford/St. Martin's, 2002.

Stolzenbach, Mary M. "Braid Yorkshire: The Language of Myth? An Appreciation of *The Secret Garden* by Frances Hodgson Burnett." *Mythlore* 78 (Winter 1995): 25–9.

Stroud, Jonathan. *The Bartimaeus Trilogy, Book One: The Amulet of Samarkand.* New York: Hyperion, 2003.

_____. *The Bartimaeus Trilogy, Book Two: The Golem's Eye.* New York: Hyperion, 2004.

_____. *The Bartimaeus Trilogy, Book Three: Ptolemy's Gate.* New York: Yperion, 2006.

Sweeney, Michelle. *Magic in Medieval Romance from Chretien de Troyes to Geoffrey Chaucer.* Portland: Four Courts, 2000.

Swinfen, Ann. *In Defence of Fantasy: A Study of the Genre in English and American Literature Since 1945.* Boston: Routledge, 1984.

Talbot, Norman. Introduction. *The Water of the Wondrous Isles.* By William Morris. Bristol, England: Thoemmes Press, 1994.

Tennyson, Alfred, Lord. "In Memoriam: A.H.H." *Poems of Tennyson.* Jerome Hamilton Buckley, ed. Boston: Houghton Mifflin, 1958. 178–259.

Thacker, Deborah. "Playful Subversion." *Introducing Children's Literature: From Romanticism to Postmodernism.* Deborah Cogan Thacker and Jean Webb, eds. New York: Routledge, 2002. 139–50.

Thomas, Joyce. *Inside the Wolf's Belly: Aspects of the Fairy Tale.* Sheffield, England: Sheffield Academic Press, 1989.

Thompson, E.P. *William Morris: Romantic to Revolutionary.* London: Lawrence and Wishart, 1955.

Thurschwell, Pamela. *Literature, Technology, and Magical Thinking, 1880–1920.* New York: Cambridge University Press, 2001.

Tim Burton's Corpse Bride. Dir. Tim Burton and Mike Johnson. DVD. Warner Home Video. 2006.

Tolkien, J.R.R. *The Lord of the Rings.* Fiftieth Anniversary One-Volume Edition. New York: Houghton Mifflin. 2004.

_____. "On Fairy Stories." *The Tolkien Reader.* New York: Ballantine, 1966. 33–99.

The Two Towers. Dir. Peter Jackson. Special Extended DVD Edition. New Line Entertainment. 2003.

Viera, Meredith. "Harry Potter: The Final Chapter." *Dateline NBC.* NBC News Online. July 30, 2007. http://www.msnbc.msn.com/id/20001720/.

Waelti-Walters, Jennifer. *Fairy Tales and the Female Imagination.* St. Albans, VT: Eden, 1982.

Waldrop, Shelton. *The Aesthetics of Self-Invention: Oscar Wilde to David Bowie.* Minneapolis: University of Minnesota Press, 2004.

Warwick, Alexandra. *Oscar Wilde: Writers and Their Work.* Devon, UK: Tavistock, 2007.

Weinstock, Jeffrey Andrew. *Scare Tactics: Supernatural Fiction by American Women.* New York: Fordham University Press, 2008.

Weiss, Timothy. *Fairy Tale and Romance in Works of Ford Madox Ford.* New York: Lanham, 1984.

Westman, Karin E. "Specters of Thatcherism: Contemporary British Culture in J.K. Rowling's Harry Potter Series." *The Ivory Tower and Harry Potter: Perspectives on a Literary Phenonemon.* Lana A. Whited, ed. Columbia: University of Missouri Press, 2002. 305–28.

Wharton, Edith. "After Holbein." *Roman Fever and Other Stories.* New York: Scribner, 1997. 201–34.

_____. *A Backward Glance.* New York: Simon & Schuster, 1998.

_____. "The Lady's Maid's Bell." *The Ghost Stories of Edith Wharton.* New York: Scribner, 1997. 12–35

_____. "The Looking Glass." *The Ghost Stories of Edith Wharton.* New York: Scribner, 1997. 254–73.

White, Barbara A. *Edith Wharton: A Study of the Short Fiction.* New York: Twayne, 1991.

Wilde, Lady Esperanza. Preface. *Legends, Charms, and Superstitions of Ireland.* 1887. Mineola, NY: Dover, 2006.

Wilde, Oscar. *The Canterville Ghost and Other Stories.* Mineola, NY: Dover, 2001.

_____. *Complete Fairy Tales of Oscar Wilde.* New York: Signet, 1990.

_____. *The Picture of Dorian Gray.* New York: Oxford University Press, 1981.

Wilson, A.N. *The Victorians.* New York: W.W. Norton, 2003.

Wilson, John R. "The Eve and the Madonna in Morris's *The Wood Beyond the World.*" *Journal of Pre-Raphaelite Studies* 4, no. 1 (1983): 52–55.

Womack, Kenneth. "'Withered, Wrinkled, and Loathsome Visage': Reading the Ethics of the Soul and the Late-Victorian Gothic in *The Picture of Dorian Gray.*" *Victorian Gothic: Literary and Cultural Manifestations in the Nineteenth Century.* Ruth Robbins and Julian Wolfreys, eds. New York: Palgrave, 2000. 168–81.

Wordsworth, William. "Ode: Intimations of Immortality." *The Norton Anthology of English Literature. Fifth Edition.* Vol. 2. M.H. Abrams, ed. New York: W.W. Norton, 1986. 207–14.

_____. *The Prelude: 1799, 1805, 1850.* Jonathan Wordsworth, M.H. Abrams, and Stephen Gill, eds. New York: W.W. Norton, 1979. 153–85.

Zahorski, Kenneth J., and Robert H. Boyer. "The Secondary Worlds of High Fantasy." *The Aesthetics of Fantasy Literature and Art.* Roger C. Schlobin, ed. Notre Dame: University of Notre Dame Press, 1982. 56–81.

Zipes, Jack. Afterword. *Complete Fairy Tales of Oscar Wilde.* By Oscar Wilde. New York: Penguin, 1990. 205–13.

_____. Introduction. *Victorian Fairy Tales: Revolt of the Fairies and Elves.* New York: Routledge, 1987. xiii–xxix.

Index

213